MW01273554

'Fiat currency central banks claim to fight the inflation they cause, and likewise to offset the financial instability and systemic risk they create. The depreciation of the currencies they issue at will often cause falls in foreign exchange value, goods and services inflation, or asset price inflations. Of these, asset price inflations are the most insidious, for while they last they are highly popular, leading people to think they are growing rich and to run up their debt. When the asset inflations collapse, the central banks can come as the fire department to the fire they stoked. Nobody is better at diagnosing and dissecting these central bank games than Brendan Brown, whether it is the Federal Reserve (*The Global Curse of the Federal Reserve*) or the European Central Bank – this book, *Euro Crash*. It will give you a healthy boost in your scepticism about those who pretend to be the Platonic guardians of the financial system.'

—**Alex J. Pollock**, *Resident Fellow, American Enterprise Institute, Washington, DC; former president and chief executive officer, Federal Home Loan Bank of Chicago.*

Also by Brendan Brown

BUBBLES IN CREDIT AND CURRENCY

WHAT DRIVES GLOBAL CAPITAL FLOWS

EURO ON TRIAL

THE YO-YO YEN

THE FLIGHT OF INTERNATIONAL CAPITAL

MONETARY CHAOS IN EUROPE

THE GLOBAL CURSE OF THE FEDERAL RESERVE

Euro Crash

How Asset Price Inflation Destroys the Wealth of Nations

Third Edition

Brendan Brown

First published 2010
Second edition published 2012
Third edition published 2014 by
PALGRAVE MACMILLAN

Palgrave Macmillan in the UK is an imprint of Macmillan Publishers Limited,
registered in England, company number 785998, of Houndmills, Basingstoke,
Hampshire RG21 6XS.

Palgrave Macmillan in the US is a division of St Martin's Press LLC,
175 Fifth Avenue, New York, NY 10010.

Palgrave Macmillan is the global academic imprint of the above companies
and has companies and representatives throughout the world.

Palgrave® and Macmillan® are registered trademarks in the United States,
the United Kingdom, Europe and other countries.

ISBN 978–1–137–37148–5

This book is printed on paper suitable for recycling and made from fully
managed and sustained forest sources. Logging, pulping and manufacturing
processes are expected to conform to the environmental regulations of the
country of origin.

A catalogue record for this book is available from the British Library.

A catalog record for this book is available from the Library of Congress

Typeset by MPS Limited, Chennai, India.

To the memory of Irene Brown

Contents

Foreword

Brendan Brown is a *rara avis* – a practising financial economist and shrewd observer of financial markets, players, and policies, whose prolific writings are informed by profound theoretical insight. Dr Brown writes in plain English yet can also turn a phrase with the best. 'Monetary terror' vividly and succinctly characterizes the policy of the Fed and the ECB to deliberately create inflationary expectations in markets for goods and services as a cure for economic contraction; the 'virus attack' of asset price inflation well describes the unforeseeable suddenness, timing, and point of origin of asset price increases caused by central bank manipulation of long-term interest rates and the unpredictable and erratic path the inflation takes through the various asset markets both domestically and abroad.

Indeed Dr Brown's prose is reminiscent of some of the best writers in economics and economic journalism such as Lionel (Lord) Robbins and Henry Hazlitt. And like these eminent predecessors, Brown is generous to a fault in carefully evaluating the views of those he criticizes, while rigorously arguing his own position without waffling or compromise. Best of all, Brown is fearless in naming names and ascribing blame to those among the political elites and the upper echelons of financial policymakers whose decisions have been responsible for the chaotic state of the contemporary global monetary system.

In this book, Brown deploys his formidable expository skills to argue the thesis that the current crisis and the spectre of EMU collapse are attributable to profound flaws in the original monetary foundations of the euro. These flaws rendered the EMU particularly vulnerable to the asset price inflation virus which was originally unleashed on an unsuspecting world by the Federal Reserve shortly after the euro saw the light of day in 1999.

In the course of presenting his case, Brown courageously stakes out and defends several core theoretical positions that are in radical opposition to the prevailing orthodoxy. For example, Brown strongly dissents from the conventional view of what constitutes monetary equilibrium. He explicitly rejects the position associated with Milton Friedman and Anna Schwartz that is now deeply entrenched in mainstream macroeconomics and central bank policymaking. This superficial doctrine arbitrarily and narrowly construes monetary equilibrium as 'price stability' in markets for consumer goods and services, while completely ignoring asset markets. In contrast, Brown formulates a much richer and more profound concept of monetary equilibrium that draws on the ideas of Austrian monetary and business cycle theorists, namely Ludwig von Mises, Friedrich Hayek, Lionel Robbins, and Murray Rothbard.

In Brown's view, a tendency toward monetary equilibrium obtains when monetary policy refrains from systematically driving market interest rates out of line with their corresponding 'natural' rates. Interest rates determined on unhampered financial markets are 'natural' in the sense that they bring about spontaneous coordination between voluntary household decisions about how much to save and what profile of risk to incur and business decisions about how much and in what projects to invest. Such coordination ensures accumulation of capital and increasing labour productivity and a sustainable growth process that maintains dynamic equilibrium across all goods and labour markets in the economy. The main thing that is required to maintain monetary equilibrium in this sense is strict control of the monetary base as was the case, for example, under the classical gold standard regime. In the context of existing institutions, which is Brown's focus, monetary equilibrium requires a rule strictly mandating the Fed to completely abstain from manipulating market interest rates and, instead, to exercise tight control over growth in the monetary base.

Brown's concept of monetary equilibrium therefore countenances – indeed, requires – price deflation over the medium run in response to natural growth in the supplies of goods and services. This was the experience during the heyday of the classical gold standard in the latter part of the nineteenth century when declining prices went hand-in-hand with rapid industrialization and unprecedented increases in living standards. For Brown, it is precisely the attempt to stifle this benign and necessary price trend by a policy of inflation targeting on the part of 'deflation phobic' central banks that inevitably distorts market interest rates and creates monetary disequilibrium.

Brown explains that such monetary disequilibrium is not necessarily manifested in consumer price inflation in the short run. In fact, it is generally the case that the symptoms first appear as rising temperatures on assets markets. Indeed some episodes of severe monetary disequilibrium, such as those that occurred in the U.S. during the 1920s, the 1990s, and the years leading up to the financial crisis of 2007–8, may well transpire without any discernible perturbations in goods and services markets. Yet overheated asset markets are completely ignored in the Friedmanite view of monetary equilibrium that underlies the Bernanke–Draghi policy of inflation targeting. Brown perceptively argues that one reason for the wholesale neglect of asset price inflation is the positivist approach that is still dominant in academic economics. Speculative fever in asset markets is nearly impossible to quantify or measure and thus does not fit neatly into the kinds of hypotheses that are required for empirical testing.

Having laid out his theoretical approach, Brown uses it as a foundation to construct a compelling interpretive narrative dealing with the origins, development, and dire prospects for the euro. In the process, he pinpoints and details the flawed decisions and policies of the ECB and the Federal Reserve that account for the current condition of the euro. But *Euro Crash* tells more than the story of the currency of its title; it unravels and makes sense of the complex tangle of events and policies that have marked the parlous evolution of the global monetary system since the 1990s.

This book is a radical challenge to the prevalent, but deeply flawed, doctrines that have defined monetary policy since the 1980s. Be forewarned: reading it is a bracing intellectual experience. Like a headlong dive into a cold pool, it will refresh your mind and awaken it to a wealth of new ideas.

Joseph T. Salerno
Academic Director, von Mises Institute

Acknowledgements

Elizabeth V. Smith, who recently obtained a Master's in Economics from University College London, provided invaluable help in research, and in toiling through the manuscript at its various stages of preparation.

I appreciate the opportunity given to me by the European Mises Circle to give a lecture on the topic of this new edition at the same time as discussing my previous book *The Global Curse of the Federal Reserve*.

In developing my ideas about asset price inflation I have benefited immensely from my discussions with Alex J. Pollock, Scholar at the American Enterprise Institute, and he has given me the great opportunity to present my views to meetings there.

1
Asset Price Inflation: What Do We Know about this Virus?

Why did European Monetary Union (EMU) enter existential crisis so soon after its creation? According to the 'Berlin view' everything would have been fine if it had not been for a number of governments contriving to circumvent the strict fiscal discipline stipulated in the budget stability pact that accompanied the launch of the euro. The 'Paris and Brussels' view by contrast traces the crisis to a failure of the founding Treaty to provide for a fiscal, debt and banking union.

The leading hypothesis in this book puts the blame for the crisis and for the highly probable eventual break-up of EMU on the failure of its architects to build a structure which would withstand strong forces driving monetary instability whether from inside or outside. These flaws could have gone undetected for a long time. In practice though, very early in the life of the new union, the structure was so badly shaken as to leave EMU in a deeply ailing condition.

A severe economic disease, called 'the asset price inflation virus', attacked EMU. The original source of the virus can be traced to the Federal Reserve, but the policies of the European Central Bank (ECB) added hugely to the danger of the attack. Serious inadequacies in Europe's new monetary framework meant that EMU had no immunity.

When the disease of asset price inflation 'progressed' into the phase of asset price deflation, the political elites in Brussels, Paris, Berlin, Frankfurt and Rome could not deny (though they could struggle to downplay the extent of) the damage to their union. Yet they remained united in their refusal to hear monetary explanations of the catastrophe. This unwillingness to listen continued amid the new wave of asset price inflation fever that started to spread around the global economy from 2010 onwards as the Federal Reserve chief, Professor Bernanke, pursued his Grand Experiment. (The hypothesis tested: 'well-designed' non-conventional monetary tools 'applied skilfully' can accelerate the pace of economic expansion in the 'difficult aftermath' of financial panic and great recession when the self-recovery forces of the capitalist economy 'are feeble'.)

At first this new strain of disease largely passed EMU by but not altogether. As the US monetary experimentation intensified, however, with the launching of 'QE infinity' (summer 2012) and a new version of the Fed's 'long-term interest rate manipulator' (2011–12), symptoms of speculative fever became apparent in the form of yield-hungry global investors buying recently distressed European sovereign and bank debt.

The speculative fever helped bring some transitory respite for EMU from its existential crisis. The eventual agreement of Berlin to a series of bail-out programmes for weak sovereigns in Europe reflected the contemporary German export machine's particular success in selling to those countries around the globe (China, Brazil, Russia, Turkey, Middle East oil exporters) whose economies were 'enjoying' (during 2010–11/12) the temporary stimulus of speculative fever originating in the Bernanke Fed's new asset price inflation virus. The tolerance of German taxpayers for such bail-outs – essential to Chancellor Merkel's political calculation – could break if and when asset price deflation follows asset price inflation.

Disease denial and then acceptance

Asset price inflation is a disease about which still much is unknown. Indeed early leading monetarist economists were in a state of denial about the phenomenon. A reader of *A Monetary History of the US* by Milton Friedman and Anna Schwartz (1963) does not find one mention of this virus (asset price inflation) and the same is true for Allan Meltzer's epic *A History of the Federal Reserve* (2004). Why were those economists so determined not to even entertain the idea that monetary disequilibrium could be the source of a virus which would cause speculative fever to build and spread in the asset markets, choosing instead to focus entirely on the potential consequences of goods and services inflation? The question is particularly pertinent to Milton Friedman, given that for many years he walked the paths of the same campus at the University of Chicago as Friedrich von Hayek who, in the 1920s, had written about the creation of asset price inflation by the Federal Reserve Bank of New York (then the centre of power within the Federal Reserve) under Benjamin Strong and who had warned about the likely denouement of bust and depression (see Hayek, 2008).

One answer lies in Milton Friedman's emphasis on positive economics. Almost by definition the concept of asset price inflation is difficult to fit into positive economics. Measurement of speculative fever is notoriously challenging – so how can the positive economist design neat empirical tests of various theoretical hypotheses concerning the disease? Moreover, for Milton Friedman 'asset price inflation' would have meant the original Austrian concept built around distortions in the relative price of capital and consumer goods. The 'Austrian' hypothesis was that that monetary disequilibrium (with interest rates manipulated say, far below their 'natural' level) would cause the relative price of capital goods (in terms of consumer goods) to be artificially high. The result would be over-production of capital relative to consumer goods. That is a distinct and less widely appealing concept than asset price inflation as now widely understood albeit that the two ideas overlap.

According to this popular modern definition, monetary disequilibrium causes a wide range of asset markets to display (not all simultaneously but rather in a process of rotation – see below) excessively high prices (relative to fundamentals) due to a build-up of speculative fever (sometimes described as 'irrational exuberance'). The ill-results include mal-investment and a long-run erosion of the risk-appetite essential to the free market capitalist economy delivering prosperity. Mal-investment means capital spending that would not have occurred if price-signalling had been undistorted by the monetary virus and which eventually proves to be economically obsolescent.

The writers of the Maastricht Treaty had no knowledge about the disease of asset price inflation let alone any prophetic vision of its potential threat to the survival of their cherished monetary union. The monetary constitution in the Treaty was put together by a committee of central bankers who made low inflation (euphemistically described as 'price stability'), as measured exclusively in the goods and services markets, the key objective. The famed monetarist Bundesbankers of the 1970s (subsequently described in this volume as 'the Old Bundesbankers') had departed the scene to be replaced by politicos and econometricians.

The Old Bundesbankers, in fairness to their successors, also had no clear understanding of asset price inflation. But they did instinctively realize that strict monetary base control (MBC) in which interest rates were free of manipulation was essential to overall monetary stability in a wide sense (which transcended the near-term path of goods and services prices). Instinctively they applied a doctrine of pre-emption.

According to this the pursuance of strict monetary control would mean less danger of various forms of hard-to-diagnose economic disease (possibly as yet unclassified), including those characterized by excessive financial speculation, with their origin in monetary disequilibrium.

The intuition of the monetarist Bundesbankers took them one stage further than Milton Friedman's famous pronouncement that 'inflation [goods and services] is always and everywhere a monetary phenomenon'. Indeed, we should say the same about asset price inflation. Goods (and services) price inflation and asset price inflation are the two forms of monetary disease that plague the modern economy. They have their joint source in money 'getting out of control'.

J.S. Mill famously wrote (see Friedman, 2006) that: '*Most of the time the machinery of money is unimportant. But when it gets out of control it becomes the monkey wrench in all the other machinery in the economy*'. In modern idiom we would say that 'most of the time the software of money does not matter but when it mutates it spreads a virus which attacks all the other software behind price signals (in both the goods and capital markets) that guide the invisible hands of the capitalist economy'. An economy afflicted by monetary disequilibrium will eventually display symptoms of one or both types of virus attack – goods and services inflation and asset price inflation.

These two forms of economic disease of common origin (monetary disorder) have many similarities and also some dissimilarity. Moreover, if the virus of goods and services inflation is rigorously specified in monetary rather than crude statistical terms, then it would be rare not to find this present albeit in a weak form alongside the virus of asset price inflation (see next section, p. 7).

The exact path and strength of each monetary virus (asset price inflation, goods inflation) varies considerably between different business cycles. Just as Balzac wrote that the author's skill is to typify individuals and to individualize types so it is with business cycle analysis. The analyst realizes that the key dynamic in each and every business cycle is the path taken by the two monetary viruses and how these paths interact. Yet each cycle is unique in that the paths are never identical.

Sometimes the cycle is dominated by the virus of asset price inflation without clear symptoms of the goods inflation virus ever emerging. Sometimes the virus of goods and services inflation plays a disproportionately large role. Sometimes this large role is anticipatory – long-term interest rates spike due to fears of building goods inflation; this spike in turn causes asset price inflation to turn to asset price deflation.

Similarities and dissimilarities between the spread of asset and goods inflation

How the disease forms and spreads is somewhat different in the case of asset price inflation from that of goods and services inflation. In the spread of the latter disease (goods and services inflation) key catalysts can be the exchange rate (which often plunges at an early stage), inflamed expectations regarding future prices, and strong demand in several important commodity, product, service, rental, or labour markets (there are many markets for highly differentiated types of labour). In the spread of the former disease (asset price inflation), catalysts include positive feedback loops (price gains apparently justifying a tentative speculative hypothesis), the emergence of popular new stories (for example technological innovations), and central banks of countries subject to hot money inflows (many of these economies are regarded widely as dynamic and so provide fertile ground for exciting speculative stories) deciding to inflate rather than allow their currencies to appreciate sharply (see below).

As the disease of asset price inflation attacks the economic system, various forms of irrational exuberance emerge (see Shiller, 2005 and Brown, 2013). We can think of irrational exuberance as a state where many investors are wearing rose-coloured spectacles that exaggerate the size of expected returns and filter out the risks (the dangerous possible future scenarios). More technically, it is a state where investors tend to put too low a probability (relative to actual level) on bad possible future scenarios and too high a probability on one or more good possible future scenarios. How does monetary disequilibrium encourage them to do this? There are three possible connections (see Brown, 2013).

First, monetary disequilibrium characterized by medium-term and long-term interest rates manipulated far below neutral level creates some froth in capital markets. In those asset classes where there is an appealing speculative hypothesis (illustrations include Spain as the Florida of Germany; EMU financial integration causing yields in the various government bond markets – Greece, Portugal, Germany, etc – to converge and providing European banks with great new opportunities to expand; the Draghi–Merkel coup against the Maastricht Treaty ending the crisis of EMU; Abe economics bringing long-run prosperity to Japan), asset market froth is seen as evidence by investors that the hypothesis is true (positive feed-back loops as described by Robert Shiller).

Second, a long period of low interest rates, even if in line with neutral, may stimulate 'yield desperation' by investors if there are no periods during which monetary assets deliver a real bonus (as would occur under a regime of monetary stability where the prices of goods and services would sometimes fall and sometimes rise – consistent with stable prices in the long run – and where market interest rates fluctuate freely).

Third, monetary disequilibrium and distortion, by generating terror about an outbreak of high inflation at some distant point in the future, can stimulate a scramble into real assets in the present, where this scramble is characterized by some degree of irrationality.

Both viruses – asset price inflation and goods inflation – are hard to detect at an early stage. This difficulty is particularly great with respect to asset price inflation as there are no statistical yardsticks which could even half-reliably suggest the presence or severity of the suspected virus infection.

A senior Federal Reserve official, Professor Janet Yellen, once remarked that if price-earnings (P/E) ratios in the US equity market are below 15 and rental yields on housing above 4% there can be no irrational exuberance, but this totally misses the point that sometimes there are one or more potential future states of the world of significant probability of becoming reality which are highly menacing. At such times a failure of the earnings yield (inverse of P/E ratio) or rental yield to rise well above normal level could be evidence of irrational exuberance. Famously, in early summer 1937, on the eve of one of the greatest stock market crashes in US history, a sober-rational P/E ratio taking account of then huge political, geo-political and monetary uncertainty, might have been nearer 10 than the actual 15.

By contrast, for goods and services inflation, a diagnosis *sometimes* can be made with the help of direct statistical evidence. Even this is easier said than done! The confirmation of a rising trend in goods and services prices can take considerable time given the extent of white noise in the data. And even once reasonably sure of the trend, the analyst should then consider whether the rising trend is monetary in origin.

Moreover, there are occasions when monetary goods and services inflation is present even without any statistical finding of general price level rise being possible. This would be the case where equilibrium prices in some key labour and commodity markets have fallen. A driving force behind the fall could be strong productivity gain or severely increased competition from abroad.

As illustration, computerization and digitalization plausibly led to the substitution of capital or cheap foreign labour for domestic US labour in many routine 'white collar' jobs during recent years, with much of this substitution occurring suddenly in the wake of the Great Panic (2008). Simultaneously many one-time skilled workers suddenly found their human capital worthless as the mal-investment of the boom was laid bare. In consequence the equilibrium price in important segments of the labour market (and related service or product markets) has fallen.

The efforts of the Federal Reserve to 'fight deflation' meant that those falls were moderated in nominal terms, or even did not occur. Some fall happened in real terms due to a cumulative 'moderate' rise in prices on average. Hence monetary goods and services inflation could have been strong even though statistical measures stayed weak.

An additional complication in the statistical recognition of monetary goods and services price inflation is the possibility that a rising price trend could be consistent with monetary equilibrium (no monetary inflation) as during a period of famine or wartime shortages or falling productivity or during a recovery phase of the business cycle following a recession phase when prices fell to a below normal level. And when it comes to assessing whether money is in excess supply, thereby driving a process of goods and services monetary inflation, the equilibrium demand for money cannot usually be assessed with a high degree of confidence within a narrow range. (The emergence of asset price inflation is less closely tied to excess money growth and more influenced by central bank manipulation of short-term and ultimately long-term interest rates, albeit that this manipulation is likely to be accompanied by high-powered money growing 'too fast'; this last concept though is hard to empirically test, particularly over short periods of time).

Hence by the time asset price inflation or goods inflation can be detected with any high degree of likelihood, each virus is likely to have been around for a considerable time – with that time (between creation and detection) probably, but not always, longer in the case of asset price inflation than goods inflation. Virus creation does not have to be a simultaneous process – the asset price inflation virus might come into being sooner than the goods and services inflation virus. In real time (if instant diagnosis were hypothetically possible) the lag between monetary disequilibrium forming and the emergence of significant inflation might well be shorter in the case of assets than goods and services.

Asset price inflation turns eventually into asset price deflation (endogenously and without policy action – see p. 11) and this process is accompanied by economic downturn. Depending on the characteristics of the given business cycle and in particular the path of monetary disequilibrium this metamorphosis can occur before any incipient inflationary virus in goods and services markets has gained strength. And so there can be a complete business cycle with no recognizable outbreak of goods and services inflation.

Both forms of inflation can emerge early in a business cycle expansion. Virulence at this stage, though, is more likely in the case of asset price inflation than goods and services inflation. An outbreak of early cycle asset price inflation is possible where the central bank ramps up the monetary base as part of a program of long-term interest rate manipulation and deliberately inflaming far-out inflation fears. Consistently the central bank may be holding short-term rates at very low levels while seeking to influence long-term interest rate determination by promising that low rates will persist for a long time given the seriousness of a 'deflation threat' (ECB and Federal Reserve policy of 2003–5).

This 'fight against deflation' is likely to create also a virus of monetary goods and services inflation. This may well not reveal itself at first as a rise in 'the general price level' but rather as a (hard to recognize) counterfactual benign fall which did not take place. Sometimes there is a rise of the 'general price level' even at an early stage, as when the monetary disequilibrium triggers a big fall in the national currency coupled with, say, rampant real estate speculation and thereby puts upward pressure on key items in the goods and services basket (including residential rents). In consequence inflation expectations rise generally and affect wage-setting behaviour despite weak labour market conditions.

The germs of asset price inflation and goods and services inflation can cross-fertilize each other crucially via the markets in foreign exchange, commodities and real estate. In the regime of manipulated (down) interest rates and monetary terror local investors reach for safer foreign monies and they may indeed exaggerate the potential returns from these (especially in the carry trade). The cheap national money puts upward pressure on traded goods prices (in terms of the local currency) and inflames inflation expectations. In turn fear of goods and services inflation ahead can add to the strength of asset price inflation. If global commodity markets (especially oil) become infected by an asset price inflation virus this can in turn stimulate expectations of goods and services inflation. And in the residential real estate markets asset price inflation tends to go along with a hoarding of space, which means upward pressure on rents, again inflaming expectations of higher prices for a spectrum of goods and services (including residential rents).

The virus of asset price inflation, unlike that of goods and services inflation, attacks in a rotational fashion. Symptomatic of asset price inflation are rises and falls (sometimes violent) in speculative fever across a series of asset classes. In some episodes of asset price inflation, investors desperate for yield chase one speculative story after another or several at the same time. As the early ones fade in plausibility, new ones emerge. When the virus is at the peak stage of generating speculative fever sometimes a more general story (featuring often the "wonders" of a new monetary regime, tool, or "maestro") emerges across a wide-range of asset classes – examples include the "Great Moderation Hypothesis". Mania (speculative temperatures extremely high) often grips one or more small asset classes at this stage (examples include the Florida land mania 1926–7). And even when the virus infection has started to move on to its next stage, asset price deflation, this transition might be camouflaged by the late arrival of a speculative story in one or more asset classes which attracts a big following.

No wonder that central bank officials fall into the trap of becoming eventually convinced that asset price inflation is present by observing yet a further case of suspected speculative fever in an important asset class when in fact the virus at the level of the economy as a whole has already moved on to its deflationary phase. The moon of asset price deflation rises before the sun of asset price inflation has yet fallen into the sea and the glow can yet light up one or more asset classes.

The asymmetric power of the United States to spread asset price inflation

The asymmetry of power which central banks of large countries or currency areas possess (vis-à-vis small central banks) to unleash asset price inflation on their neighbours is greater than any similar asymmetry with respect to goods and services inflation. For example, the Federal Reserve in manipulating long-term rates downwards and spreading monetary terror (by dislocating the monetary base as anchor and thereby creating huge uncertainty about its political will and technical ability to prevent high inflation far into the future) stimulates investors throughout the dollar zone to adopt various forms of irrational behaviour (the 'search for yield').

Similarly affected is a wide range of investors outside the dollar zone who use the dollar as their base currency. And so important is the global weight of these investors that their yield chasing fuels asset price inflation across a range of asset classes also outside the dollar area. (For example investors might chase emerging market currencies or real estate in London or recovery stocks in Madrid or an Abe-boom in the Tokyo equity market – in all cases putting an unrealistically high probability on a popular speculative hypothesis proving true). Even if each national central bank outside the dollar area religiously avoided easing their monetary policies in response to Federal Reserve "stimulus" (the aim of easing would be to moderate the rise of their currencies against the dollar) some of their asset markets – those where there were a good speculative story to chase – would become subject to asset price inflation.

Central banks of small countries outside the dollar zone can reduce their economic vulnerability to an attack of US-origin asset price inflation by zealously aiming to eliminate domestic sources of monetary stability in the context of a freely floating exchange rate. A violently fluctuating and possibly violently appreciating national currency under the circumstances of US monetary instability should mean any asset class in that small country (other than the national currency itself) is less than otherwise appealing to the desperate-for-yield dollar-based investors. In particular those small-country central bankers by vigorously seeking to eliminate domestic sources of monetary instability (at the expense of great exchange rate turbulence) can hope to prevent their local real estate markets becoming infected by asset price inflation.

The willingness of central bankers in the small countries to act defensively in this way against a possible virus attack of asset price inflation from the dollar area will be greater where considerable wage and price flexibility exists in their economy – specifically where wages in the export sector readily adjust downwards in nominal terms so as to sustain an albeit lowered level of profitability there and where prices across a wide range of goods and services also can fall (coupled with expectations that these price and wage falls would be reversed when the present bout of US monetary instability eventually becomes less intense). Indeed a transitorily very strong currency may be a great opportunity for local investors and enterprises to buy up cheap (in terms of the national currency) foreign assets. Entrepreneurs may see opportunities to bring forward capital spending (in the small country) to take advantage of temporarily cheap import prices and indeed also of many domestic prices which have fallen but are likely to recover subsequently.

Small country central banks can potentially insulate their economies against goods and services inflation in the US even though this insulation has costs. Sticking to the aim of no domestic source of monetary instability (in the small country) when the Federal Reserve for example is trying to 'breathe inflation back into the US economy' could bring a very big short-term real appreciation of the domestic (small) money. Moreover 'no monetary instability of domestic source' for a small country becomes a more difficult task technically in the context of huge US monetary instability.

As illustration, keeping to an x% expansion for the domestic monetary base might be inconsistent with the aim of no monetary instability of domestic source if demand for the local money grows sharply in consequence of the US money having become unstable. But how much temporary over-ride of the normal rule should the guardians of monetary stability in the small country allow to take place in these circumstances? They have no crystal ball or clear insight into a possibly big shift in money demand.

How asset price inflations burn out

The ending of goods and services inflation is different from that of asset price inflation and the long-term consequences diverge. The defeat of goods and services inflation depends on a reversal of monetary policies – the abandonment of monetary excess. In turn the post inflation economy should not be held back by the earlier experience of inflation. Indeed the end of goods and services inflation should be positive for economic prosperity even in the near-term. By contrast, the end of asset price inflation usually means economic dislocation for a considerable period of time. And the end would come about without monetary action. Historically central banks confront the disease so late that an endogenous asset price deflation is already pre-programmed.

We have seen already how the rotational form in which asset price inflation attacks the economy adds to the likelihood of the central bank diagnosing the virus as present when it has already 'progressed' to its next phase of asset price deflation. Hence the inevitable economic downturn becomes a severe recession. That was the story of Federal Reserve policy in 1928–9 with the rising speculative fever in Wall Street prompting a late and savage tightness, even though the US real estate markets and German capital markets were already cooling (Florida land crash 1927, German stock market crash 1928). Unknown to the Federal Reserve, the virus of asset price inflation was already shifting into its next phase of asset price deflation. It was a similar story in reverse in 1989 (speculative fever in the US equity market had already peaked in late 1987 but had then emerged in various real estate markets) and in 2008 (when the ECB and Federal Reserve kept policy tight out concern about the emergence of high speculative temperature in the oil market even though the giant quakes in the global credit markets the previous summer might have suggested that asset price inflation had already progressed to its next deflationary phase). There are other examples, including the Bank of Japan's late tightening in 1989/90.

(It is too early to tell whether the buying frenzy in European equity markets during summer and autumn 2013 on the speculative hypothesis of 'European recovery from the EMU crisis recession of 2011–12' fits with the stereotype late appearance of speculative fever in a new market when the asset price inflation virus has already passed its peak phase this time under the influence of higher long-maturity US interest rates triggered by widespread anticipation of the Federal Reserve 'tapering' its quantitative easing policies. One observation in favour was the plunge in speculative temperatures across emerging market currencies. The US economy, however, was beating expectations.)

How do asset price inflations burn themselves out and evolve into a subsequent period of asset price deflation? Over-investment and mal-investment stemming from the distortion of capital market prices by the monetary virus bring about a fall in profits. Even before that point, bouts of ugly reality may well splinter the rose-coloured spectacles which investors have been wearing during the asset price inflation and which have filtered out the dangers (when today's ugly reality was still just potential rather than actual) and magnified expected returns.

Occasionally, though, the kaleidoscope of future possible scenarios improves markedly, so that yesterday's distorted capital market prices even underestimate the new improved economic environment. An economic miracle may occur (see below, p. 15). In general, though, leaving the rare exception aside, the sequence of asset price inflation and deflation leaves in its wake a shrunken appetite for equity risk and it can take many years of monetary stability before this appetite again becomes healthy. In the very long run, though, a successful eradication of the monetary viruses – asset price inflation and goods (and services inflation) – would contribute greatly to enduring economic prosperity.

The disease of asset price inflation has a very different political impact from the disease of goods and services inflation. In general, high goods and services inflation or the spectre of much higher goods and services inflation ahead is dis-liked by electorates, giving advantage to the party or candidate who promises to take credible actions towards lowering the level of threat. In the case of goods and services inflation, much of the voting public can be convinced that the central bankers and perhaps a flawed monetary regime have been responsible for their misery.

By contrast, asset price inflation enjoys some popularity (especially amongst those sections of the population which hold the assets gaining in value) so long as it lasts, albeit that the rising residential rent and gasoline prices which might accompany the phenomenon are disliked by important segments of the electorate (higher house prices are mixed in their impact – winners are the owners who were in at the start, losers are the renters, future renters, and possibly late owners). The asset price deflation phase, associated with recession and possibly financial crisis, is hugely unpopular but typically public wrath does not identify the central bankers and the monetary regime as the culprits. Instead the target for public anger becomes the investment bankers, the real estate industry, and loan sharks.

Perhaps with the passage of time, public opinion will come to realize that violent cycles of asset price inflation and deflation are indeed a disease of monetary source with serious long-run negative consequences for their economic prosperity. But as of now the monetary origin of the goods and services inflation disease is much more widely known and recognized than that of asset price inflation.

Perfectly anticipated asset price inflation cannot 'stimulate' an economy

Beyond understanding the political implications of asset price inflation compared to those of goods and services inflation it is useful to make a distinction between anticipated and non-anticipated inflation. The early monetarist revolutionaries taught a half-century ago that the so-called stimulus effect of goods and services inflation depends on it being unanticipated and unrecognized. Specifically, a central bank by effecting an un-announced acceleration of monetary growth might cause individual businesses to believe that they face a real sustainable increase in demand for their products. As prices advance their profits rise without labour at first realizing that its real living standards are lagging.

This stimulus effect fails to operate once households and businesses become wise to the danger of inflation and adjust their expectations almost as soon as monetary disequilibrium is suspected. A similar (though not identical point) can be made in the case of asset price inflation. A policy of inducing economic stimulus via asset price inflation is less successful the more widely it is anticipated.

What do we mean by anticipated asset price inflation? This is where every investor and their dog realize that the Federal Reserve, say, is deliberately trying to engineer a rise in asset prices, especially equities, with the intention of accelerating the pace of economic recovery. The method by which the Federal Reserve does this involves the deliberate downward manipulation of medium-term and long-term interest rates (by promising to keep short-term rates very low for a long time to come and also possibly absorbing large amounts of long-term interest rate risk on its own balance sheet) and sometimes alongside creating monetary terror (fear of a surge in goods and services inflation) with respect to the long-run future (for example creating massive amounts of excess reserves and effectively dislodging the monetary base from the pivot of the monetary system, meaning there are serious grounds to doubt whether the Federal Reserve even with the best of intentions could steer a stable monetary path further ahead).

Desperation for yield and fear of long-run inflation mean that many investors do become prone to some forms of irrational behaviour. In this condition, they are unusually gullible listeners to absorbing speculative stories. Also they bid up the price of near-term expected earnings on stocks while under-rating the risks. The prices of actual or potential earnings streams from those fairly safe projects not highly sensitive to the course of the business cycle also rise. A premium builds on equities that have high dividend pay-out ratios and where the dividend streams are reliable. But the 'exit problem' or possible earlier asset market collapse looms large over other earnings flows (for example from projects whose earnings are highly dependent on the business cycle and on economic growth and which extend well into the future).

The 'exit problem' refers to that uncertain time in the future when the Federal Reserve will pull back from its unconventional policies, meaning that monetary base would be reined back towards a normal relationship with overall money supply. In tandem with that reining back, the Federal Reserve would raise money rates via the use of novel policy instruments (in that usual instruments do not work when there are large excess reserves). There are grounds to fear that the exit might bring at some stage a sharp fall in equity markets and also a severe economic slowdown or actual recession. (Indeed speculative temperatures might plummet without an actual exit). And so investors when they look at potential earnings flows from new projects perhaps several years into the future calculate an expected value (the mean of the probability distribution for each period from which earnings are drawn) which is weighed down by the exit problem.

The desperation for yield means that investors might not weigh down expected earnings (over the uncertain period of the exit) fully in line with likely reality, but nonetheless their discounting of the exit does act as a depressant on present stock market values and on the amount of business investment taking place (for which the criterion is positive net present value of the expected cash flows using the appropriate equity cost of capital). Hence equity market froth (market prices above fundamental value) does not translate into economic strength though it might impart some modest stimulus in the sense of higher business spending than if monetary uncertainty were discounted fully in equity prices. Owner-managers of medium-sized or small-sized companies are not motivated by today's equity market prices but where they think these will be several years from now when they might be selling their equity (either in an initial public offering (IPO) or in a take-over). They would not expect any present speculative fever to persist that long. And as regards large public companies in many cases the key decision-makers own long-dated options on their shares that cannot be exercised any time soon, so again they would be more concerned with likely equity values after the speculative fever has died down.

It is conceptually possible though, that if there are particularly exciting speculative stories across several key asset classes (including, say, US and foreign advanced economy equities, emerging market assets, high yield bonds, and real estate) that this gets magnified enough (through the wearing of rose-coloured spectacles) to generate short-run stimulus even though there is a general awareness of the future exit problem. Moreover, amid the optimism regarding those key asset classes there may develop an expectation that an economic miracle will occur, meaning that an exit problem would not materialize.

Taking off their rose-coloured spectacles, though, investors would realize the high likelihood that the present cycle of asset price inflation will be followed by asset price deflation and that this violent sequence will diminish long-run economic prosperity. (Diminution stems from large-scale 'mal-investment' and also a sickness of equity risk appetite – see Brown, 2013). Yes many commentators talk about the unconventional monetary policy buoying equity prices which may have risen far from the lows reached during the asset price deflation low-point following the previous wave of asset price inflation, but the key question in counterfactual history is whether the level of equity prices and economic prosperity would have been much higher by now under a permanent regime of monetary stability.

By contrast to known and expected asset price inflation as in the years of Bernanke 'stimulus' following the Great Recession of 2008–9, we can compare unknown and unexpected asset price inflation. (It is plausible that some passing 'stimulus' did in fact emerge at various points in the 'Grand Experiment': this would be the case if 'excess' optimism on the various speculative stories reached such a pitch as to outweigh the drag of expectations concerning the eventual exit problem – where these speculative stories included first the growing economic pre-eminence of China and emerging market economies and then the potential of the shale gas revolution for US economic prosperity.)

For example in the early and mid-1920s few practical investors even thought about the possibility of asset price inflation. The Benjamin Strong Federal Reserve in steering money rates along a low nominal level, which it viewed as appropriate to a situation of a stable price level, and thereby bringing downward influence on medium and long-maturity interest rates (which under the pre-1914 gold regime had been free of such manipulation given that short-term money rates had been so volatile) did not even think about the danger that this could be inconsistent with monetary stability in an era of rapid technological progress.

Yes, Hayek (see 2008) and Robbins (2007) may have been warning about credit or asset price inflation and lecturing why the 'natural rhythm' of goods and services prices was now downwards (consistent with a surge in productivity stemming from the 'Second Industrial Revolution') meaning that stable prices corresponded to monetary inflation. But no one at the Federal Reserve and apparently very few in the marketplace were listening or had any comprehension of their arguments. By 1927 some officials and market participants were worried about excess speculation, but they did not make the link to already long-running monetary disorder. There was little fear at large about 'exit problems' (when rates would return to neutral) or subsequent asset price deflation.

In the 1920s monetary disequilibrium was more powerful in producing asset price inflation and a business spending boom than could have been the case had these phenomena and their potential problems been widely known. And even if there had been greater knowledge, the speculative story that investors were chasing was particularly powerful (including a once in a century technological revolution) and could have encouraged the view that economic miracle would cancel out any monetary mistakes so that they would not detract from prosperity.

A similar case (with respect to the power of unrecognized and undiagnosed asset price inflation to stimulate economic and market boom) can be made with respect to the information technology (IT) boom in the late 1990s (when the Greenspan Fed was steering rates at a low level due its perception that goods and services inflation was low), even though Greenspan's 'irrational exuberance' speech (December 1996) in principle might have stimulated some concerns amongst a wider public. Greenspan himself quickly dismissed those concerns from his own consciousness.

The credit and price inflation on both sides of the Atlantic in the 2000s may partly meet the definition of 'widely known and recognized' but not entirely. At the ECB the word was that this time really was different. There was no credit bubble but a new efficient allocation of capital within Europe, the catalyst for this being the launch of EMU. And the ECB did not view dollar weakness as an indicator of US monetary disequilibrium but as a result of an unsustainable US current account deficit in large part due to manipulated exchange rates and an arcane dollar bloc in East Asia. In the marketplace those views were widely shared.

In principle a leading central bank could surreptitiously seek to create asset price inflation with the aim of stimulating the economy in the short run, (without concern for the long run as we are all dead then!), keeping quiet about its program so as not to decrease its effectiveness. (As once everyone and their dog realize what the central bank is doing, then it becomes ineffective, as discussed above). Perhaps that is a good description of the Greenspan Federal Reserve's policy of 'breathing back inflation into the US economy' during 2003–5. And perhaps such thoughts even circulated amongst ECB officials when they were combating the 'spectre of deflation' and as Germany struggled with near-recessionary conditions in 2001–3. Several economic commentators close to Federal Reserve decision-makers were talking about creating a housing bubble so as to stimulate the economy out of its malaise in the wake of the bursting IT bubble but such thinking never made its way into official pronouncements or minutes.

Some central bankers seeking to stimulate their economy by infecting it with asset price inflation might believe that they or an economic miracle or both in combination can cure the infection before it enters its harmful stage. Others might be the loyal functionary of a wise Prince who is not troubled by far-out ill consequences which he will blame according to the principles of Machiavelli on others. The pay-back for asset price inflation and its short-run stimulus benefits is the pain and waste of the subsequent asset price deflation plus long-run economic enfeeblement (caused by sick equity risk appetite in particular). That can come about even without any subsequent big tightening of monetary conditions if much mal-investment and over-capacity builds up or if reality diverges sufficiently from what investors were viewing through their rose-coloured spectacles. If asset price deflation is long delayed, the central bank would find itself meanwhile caught up in growing market speculation about a serious tightening of monetary policies in response to obvious bubble dangers or goods and services inflation.

Even if the central bank long postpones taking any such action and promises everyone who listens that there will be no early rise in money interest rates, bond yields could spike. Higher bond yields, with or without simultaneous monetary tightening, could cause asset price inflation to turn into asset price deflation, albeit that it would be difficult to attribute the transformation with certainty to monetary influences if other adverse factors were materializing at the same time. And note that within the context of a steeply rising yield curve – say from rates close to zero up until 2-year maturities – followed by say a climb to 3.0% at 10-year maturities, the implied forward long-term rates are well above the actual spot rates. In this example, the 2-year forward 10-year rate would be around 4.25%. And so investors in the present would ask themselves whether froth in certain asset markets created by desperation for yield would survive at this higher level of yields. Such doubts could cause asset price deflation to arrive early.

Folklore of 1937 still distorts treatment of asset price inflation

It is possible that, if all the facts were known, 1937 would fit the above description of surreptitiously produced asset price inflation. From 1934 to 1936 huge gold inflows to the US, following the mega devaluation of the dollar by the Roosevelt Administration, were monetized by the Federal Reserve and Treasury. In consequences short-term interest rates remained pinned at zero while long-maturity Treasury bond yields stuck at a then super-low level of 2% per annum. In 1936 US equity markets and commodity markets boomed, ignoring the sharp rise of the dollar in the second half of that year (as the European gold bloc collapsed), rising geo-political risks (Nazi Germany, Imperial Japan), and the landslide victory for Roosevelt and the Democrats in November 1936. Speculative stories that investors were chasing included a new wave of technological change (airplanes, television) and the magic of Keynesian economic policies. There was growing buzz of what we could describe today as 'Fed speak' – Federal Reserve officials and outside commentators talking about the need for some monetary restraint to counter excess speculation and commodity price rises. And indeed from late 1936 the Federal Reserve started to raise reserve requirements. Long-maturity bond yields rose moderately in the first quarter of 1937 (from 2.00 to 2.40%).

Milton Friedman and Anna Schwartz (1963) argue that this 'premature' tightening of monetary policy was the key factor behind the severe Roosevelt recession which the National Bureau of Economic Research (NBER) dates as running from May 1937 to June 1938. Yet an alternative narrative (see Brown, 2012) attributes the severity of the recession to the sudden end of asset price inflation and the succession of asset price deflation – a destructive sequence that stemmed from monetary disequilibrium in the preceding years. In particular there was a 40% collapse of the US equity market in the four months from August 1937. The gap between reality (US economic slowdown, Supreme Court ruling in favour of Roosevelt's trade union legislation in May, Japan's war with China (Marco Polo bridge incident, July), continuing European currency depreciation) and what investors had been viewing through their rose-coloured spectacles had become so great as to splinter their lenses.

Yes, the modest rise in bond yields and shift in monetary stance could have played some catalytic role in the timing of asset price deflation. But the idea that the Fed in 1937 could have piloted an alternative course along which the Roosevelt recession would not have taken place is implausible. A reversion in monetary stance was built in as a high probability event right from the start of the period of extraordinary monetary base expansion. When markets began to anticipate the change (one direct measure of this anticipation was the rise in long-term interest rates) then there was a raised chance that asset price inflation would be transformed into asset price deflation in the short-run future.

Chasing of speculative stories and the carry trade

In general, asset price inflation, whether recognized or unrecognized, tends to attack virulently a tight range of markets while leaving many largely unaffected. This is in contrast to goods and services inflation, which tends to show up in a wide range of markets. For example, the asset price inflation virus could attack a new economy sector of the equity market, which is then set alight. This could represent a real technological leap, or in the case of financial equities a market innovation (including, as an example, European integration) or a real estate market in a particular metropolis or region (where the story could include the new availability of finance to households, perhaps due to innovation in financial product-making or to European integration).

The essence of asset price inflation is the chasing of speculative stories and these can only be found in selected asset classes or sub-classes. The disease of asset price inflation often emits a symptom in the form of a hyperactive carry trade whether in currencies, high-yield (high-risk) bonds, or long-maturity (default-free) bonds (see p. 20). What do we mean by carry trade?

The below neutral level of medium-term and long-term 'riskless' rates as produced by monetary disequilibrium mean that rates less directly subject to manipulation, or in fact in dynamic economies outside the country or currency area where the manipulation is taking place, become an attractive destination for speculative flows. Positive feedback loops or other forms of irrationality associated with artificially low rates in the US (or other large money centre) spur the speculation. As an illustration of the positive feed back loop, large present returns on the carry trade may encourage the view based on a presently popular speculative hypothesis that, in fact, there will be a permanent high rate spread in line with economic fundamentals and no subsequent capital loss which would eradicate any income advantage.

Hence as US investors in the mid-1920s made handsome carry trade gains from buying bonds in Germany where high yields (compared to the artificially low yields in the US held down by the Benjamin Strong Fed) could be seen as reflecting an economic miracle in the Weimar Republic following the mark's stabilization and the end of hyperinflation. Hence they considered the risks of default or of exchange rate depreciation as very small compared to the income gains. They came to believe more and more in the reality of the miracle, despite counterwarnings from a few pessimistic commentators. And so these investors became less scared of subsequent loss.

In the early 1990s as the Greenspan Federal Reserve was manipulating interest rates downwards the carry trade of US funds going into high yielding Mexico bonds boomed. Many of the speculators came to believe the story, endorsed by the International Monetary Fund (IMF), that an investment miracle was indeed taking place in that country.

Fast forward to the European credit bubble of the 2000s and the gains which the carry traders made from getting out of German government bonds and ploughing funds into Greek and Spanish bonds produced a positive feedback loop where investors could persuade themselves that perhaps M. Trichet, Professor Issing, and Professor Bernanke were all correct when they extolled the dawning of a unified and integrated European market! Their credulity was likely enhanced beyond the limits of rationality by investors desperate to get yields in a context where the ECB and Federal Reserve were steering rates at an artificially low level out of concern about a 'deflation threat' and with the aim of 'breathing back in a low rate of inflation'. Long-term rates in core European bond markets were correspondingly depressed.

We can identify in fact carry trades in three main forms. First, there is the currency carry trade, characterized by risk arbitrage out of a low interest rate currency into a high interest rate currency, where the arbitrager takes the view that the interest rate differential compensates handsomely for any underlying exchange risk. Second, there is the credit currency trade, marked by arbitrage out of debt paper of low credit risk on which yields are feeble into debt paper (in the same currency denomination) of high credit risk offering much higher yields, where the arbitrager speculates that the risk of default is much less than the income gain. Third, there is the yield curve carry trade, in which the risk arbitrager moves out of low yielding short-maturity debt paper into higher yielding long-maturity debt paper (of the same near zero default risk and in the same currency), speculating that the risk of loss from adverse rate moves (unanticipated steepening of the yield curve) is less than the income gain.

Market critics sometimes describe the carry trade and other popular forms of speculation that characterize episodes of asset price inflation as ponzi-like. By definition this means that many of the participants suspect they are likely playing in a negative sum game. They hope to get out, however, before the others, perhaps greedier and less knowing. These others would suffer the loss that is the counterpart to their profit.

Ponzi-like activity

Ponzi-like activity does not describe those markets under conditions of asset price inflation where all the players are wearing rose-coloured spectacles and actually believe what they see through them. In a market where there are some players wearing rose-coloured spectacles and some who are not, the latter are intending to profit from the arrival of more spectacled players at which point they will make their exit. If the non-spectacled players all calculate correctly, then when midnight strikes, only spectacled players are at the table. That is when the ponzi scheme collapses. In reality many of the non-spectacled players may miscalculate and find themselves amongst the victims.

It is in the essence of monetary disequilibrium as described (manipulated interest rates and monetary terror) to produce ponzi-like behaviour where sober-rational players hope to take advantage of those displaying various forms of irrationality (as induced by the monetary distortions). Some of the infected markets will display ponzi characteristics, others will not. And sticking to definitions no market is a pure ponzi scheme (where outsiders in aggregate are bound to make substantial loss). It is always possible that an economic miracle or lesser order good surprise will inject new value into the asset in question meaning that when the wearers of the rose-coloured spectacles eventually take these off they will not be disappointed with what they see. Even a miracle or good surprise may not be needed – just a string of good luck with reality turning out significantly better than a sober-rational calculation of probability weighted scenarios would have suggested.

In the case of the virulent asset price inflation that attacked various asset classes in EMU during the first decade of the twenty-first century perhaps Greek, Portuguese and Spanish government bonds, European financial equities and bank bonds, and Spanish real estate mortgage-backed bonds could be considered as the most ponzi-like games. Some players, especially those who concentrated on the short maturities, hit lucky. Governments in the core EMU countries ploughed huge amount of funds into the schemes, some via newly created support agencies such as the European Financial Stability Facility (EFSF), some through the back door of the ECB, so as to allow the players to bail out, in many cases still with considerable cumulative profit. The reader will discover how that was possible in the course of the narrative through the remaining chapters of this book.

2
The Franco–German Dollar Union that Did Not Take Place

In that wonderful cartoon of Jacques Faizant depicting the historic ceremony in January 1963 at which the Franco–German friendship treaty was signed, President De Gaulle says to Chancellor Adenauer (in their 70s and 80s respectively) 'hurry up Conrad, you are not immortal'. Adenauer's hesitation stemmed from concern that de Gaulle was trying to wean Germany away from its close alliance with the US. The real pity of that moment emerges now, almost a half-century later. If only the two heads of state had agreed then on a monetary union between France and Germany. And it would have been so simple given that both countries were on the dollar standard within the context of the Bretton Woods international monetary agreement. The Deutsche mark and French franc would have become fully convertible into each other at the par exchange rate between them (all margins of fluctuation extinguished), while a Franco–German authority would have steered the growth of the monetary base (for the union) so as to keep the common currency within its permitted range of fluctuation against the US dollar.

Those photos of President Mitterrand and Chancellor Kohl clasping hands in the First World War cemetery of Verdun (September 22, 1984) stir the same sense of historical regret. If only the two heads of state in their desire to make war impossible again between France and Germany had resolved on a quick Franco–German monetary union. (As a matter of historical counterfactual it is unconvincing that the First World War would not have taken place if Germany along with France, Switzerland, Belgium, Italy, Romania, Bulgaria, Serbia and Greece, had been a member of the Latin Monetary Union (LMU).)

The contours of such a deal would have included a Franco–German monetary institute, with an equal number of board members from each country, operating under a constitution designed to safeguard monetary stability. This could no longer be achieved via pegging the common currency to the US dollar given the breakdown of the Bretton Woods system in 1971 and the surrounding history of huge US monetary instability. (Indeed in counterfactual history, if de Gaulle and Adenauer had formed a dollar union in 1963 this would have had required radical reform by 1984.) The franc and mark would have survived as legal entities and there would have been no element of fiscal or transfer union between the two countries.

Instead a generation of French politicians (spanning say 1973–98) strove to end German monetary hegemony in Europe and to advance multi-polarism (replacing US geo-political dominance with multi-poles including China, Russia, the US and of course "Europe" – a concept which to the French political elite meant "France in Europe" and "Europe in France" illustrating the extent of influence which Paris hoped to have in the evolving European Union) by driving forward the project of EMU. Mitterrand seized the moment of the Berlin Wall coming down (November 1989) and Germany's Second Re-Unification (1990) to negotiate a Grand Bargain. In exchange for France fully supporting German political union and the extension of the EU to include the central European countries, Germany would take a place in the drivers' cabin on a rapid train journey towards EMU, accepting the eventual loss of monetary power by the Bundesbank.

Mitterrand had already famously realized that the way to push the EMU project forward at the EU level was to exclude the EU Finance Ministers. In 1988 he had got Kohl's agreement to the blueprint for EMU being drafted by a committee of central bankers headed by Jacques Delors, his close political ally and by then EU Commission President. The central bankers would rule over the new union with virtually complete independence from political authorities and with a vast amount of discretionary power.

Milton Friedman and Friedrich von Hayek would have been aghast at the idea of basing a new monetary 'order' on an absolutist central bank, answerable virtually to no one, and with no set of constitutional rules (determining crucially a pivotal role for a monetary base and how this would be expanded over time) established in advance of its birth so as to keep it on the rails of pursuing monetary stability. Friedman in his writings had been steadfastly critical of the Federal Reserve and by extension of central bankers. At every significant stage as analysed in his *Monetary History of the US* (jointly authored with Anna Schwartz) the Federal Reserve had added to the extent of monetary instability compared to what would have occurred without its meddling. Friedman argued that monetary stability depended on the observance of strict monetary rules. If political necessity or accident of history meant that there had to be a central bank, then strict rules in place should limit the scope for discretionary decision-making, which almost inevitably would turn out badly. Hayek would have despaired in advance of any government institution, including a central bank, being able to achieve monetary stability.

Friedman might have favoured an EMU in which the central bank was constitutionally mandated to follow a fixed rate of monetary expansion, leaving all interest rates to be market determined, while eschewing any price level or inflation target. Hayek might well have argued for a version of the gold standard to be implemented within the context of a wider international return to gold. Both Friedman and Hayek would have been horrified at the vision of an authoritarian central bank setting its own monetary framework and not even constructing a 'monetary pillar' as it had promised in its architectural designs, instead adopting a form of quasi-inflation targeting.

Hayek's understanding of monetary stability turned out to be much more insightful than Friedman's as the first decade of EMU unfolded. Hayek, in the tradition of J. S. Mill, viewed the concept of monetary stability in broad terms realizing that monetary disorder distorted a whole range of market prices (including capital market prices) leading to economic loss. Hayek cautioned against defining monetary stability as short- or medium-term stability of the 'price level'. For Hayek fluctuations of prices both upwards and downwards over the short or medium term were fully consistent with long-term monetary stability and indeed were essential to the capitalist economy continually re-finding balance along a long-run path of progress. Friedman's concept of monetary stability belonged to the time-warp of contemporary macro-economics with its emphasis on tame business cycles and continuously low or even zero inflation as the twin aims of sound monetary policy. In reality it was a wild rise of speculative temperatures in asset and credit markets (otherwise described as virulent asset price inflation) occurring in the context of apparent macro-economic stability and low inflation (through the years 2002–7) which proved to be so lethal for EMU.

The monetary instability that emerged through the first decade of EMU ultimately caused intense pressure to build up inside the whole edifice, threatening a fatal explosion. The pressure was exacerbated by the uneven way in which the disease of asset price inflation attacked the member economies of the monetary union. (This uneven pattern is intrinsic to the nature of asset price inflation – see Chapter 1.)

A group of periphery zone members where speculative temperatures in key asset markets had been particularly hot during the boom found their anchoring to EMU severely weakened by the intensity of temperature downswings suffered into the bust phase. In particular, the gathering clouds of insolvency over the banking systems and government debt markets in those periphery zone countries triggered episodes of capital flight as depositors moved their funds into the EMU core countries. Such capital flight had the potential to force one or more of the periphery zone countries out of the union unless it was checked by a massive offsetting flow of funds from the ECB or by a big injection of bail-out funds from governments in the euro-core. In fact, both means of resisting the forces of disintegration involved aid transfers from the financially stronger countries to the weaker.

The ECB in making massive loans against dodgy collateral to likely insolvent banks in the periphery (sometimes the national central banks as in Greece and Ireland acted as intermediary by extending 'emergency liquidity assistance' against the full nominal amount of collateral offered by their member banks, in effect obtaining ECB permission to print euros for this purpose) or in accumulating weak sovereign debt as part of its 'securities market programme' and financing these operations by issuing deposits or money market securities has been drawing on the implicit guarantee (or actual revenues) of governments in the financially strong core member countries. And so the bizarre situation has developed in which the central bankers in Frankfurt issued more and more contingent or actual claims on taxpayers in the strong countries (in that they potentially – albeit not unreservedly or inevitably – stand in as guarantors of ECB liabilities) towards sustaining the continuing membership of the troubled periphery. No democratic authority in those strong countries vetoed or even attempted seriously to block such transfers.

Professor Axel Weber, President of the Bundesbank, fought from Spring 2010 a rearguard action to block or slow the flow, but without the strong backing of the German government and evidently without shining success. His successor as Bundesbank President, Jens Weidmann, had no backing either (from the German government) when he dissented in late Summer 2011 from an ECB Board decision to accumulate further periphery government debt (this time aimed at conducting a bear squeeze operation against short-sellers of Italian and Spanish government debt). Neither did Berlin back Jens Weidman a year later when he opposed the ECB's plan to monetize weak government debt under certain circumstances (see Chapter 7).

At first, the ECB argued that its bad bank operations were only transitory in nature, undertaken so as to 'normalize the monetary transmission mechanism' (utterly meaningless!) and on the assumption that its loans would be taken over by the governments in the financially strong countries (most plausibly via the EFSF (European Financial Stability Facility), the new EMU bail-out fund which, according to a July 2011 Summit decision, was due to gain considerably enhanced powers). But the ECB received no government undertakings to take over the loans in advance of its interventions.

The transfers of aid within EMU as determined by EU decisions (as against 'emergency' actions via the ECB) occurred on an intergovernmental basis, at first via makeshift agreements (as in the case of Greece) and then via decisions regarding the newly created EFSF. The German government took the lead in restraining the extent of such direct transfers by insisting on IMF involvement and on case-by-case consideration under conditions of unanimity amongst the government shareholders (in the EFSF). IMF involvement, though, could add to the ultimate burden of the EU bail-out on taxpayers in the financial strong EMU member countries, in that the Washington institution's claims would be senior to all other outstanding debts.

If German or French citizens had been told back in the early 1990s that the formation of EMU could leave them liable for huge transfers of aid to weaker members or to investors and banks who had gambled and lost on lending to these it is all but certain that they would have rejected (with an overwhelming majority) the whole project. In Germany, citizens were never in any case given an opportunity to vote in a referendum on monetary union, and in France the referendum (in September 1992) on the Maastricht Treaty (of which monetary union was a key chapter) only came down in favour by a tiny margin. The question of huge potential bail-outs just did not surface at all in the French referendum campaign. The Treaty itself, if any voter had read it, seemed to rule out transfers from taxpayers in one member country to another. Under a more enlightened debate than that which occurred, the possibility of transfers (given the unclear wording in some treaty clauses) should surely have come to the forefront of public awareness. And it is even possible that to counter public concerns during the campaign the French government would have pressed for a commitment from its EMU partners to the Maastricht Treaty being amended so as to strengthen no bail-out clauses and to correspondingly set out a clear legal exit route for any member which could not otherwise (without bail-out) survive inside the union.

In retrospect if German negotiators (in the EMU process) had been seriously competent in making sure that monetary union remained a union of sovereigns with no fiscal transfers or other related burdens on their fellow (German) citizens, they would have insisted on much more stringent conditions under which the ECB could undertake loan operations. There should have been no question of the ECB at its own discretion setting eligibility criteria for collateral against which it would lend and this collateral should not have included government bonds of any description. And any so-called lender of last resort function should have been strictly curtailed or non-existent. Emergency liquidity assistance (ELA) in the form of national central banks obtaining permission from the ECB to print a certain amount of money for lending to their member banks under stress would have been out of the question. If financial crisis erupted then the ECB would have been able to increase the supply of base money (bank reserves and cash) in line with increased demand as is typical at such a time. But any loans made to stricken financial institutions, whether to tide over liquidity problems or threatened insolvency (and in the crisis moment it is notoriously hard if not impossible to distinguish the two) should have been possible only on a direct basis by the relevant member government (and any other government that wished to help). Each national finance ministry would have at its disposal an instant reaction force to deal with such situations.

If such rules had been in place, then the ECB could not have turned itself into Europe's Bad Bank and then sought a partial metamorphosis back into a good bank by imploring governments to take over its bailout operations. If a member country found itself at the storm centre of financial crisis with its banks in a funding emergency (unable to replace fleeing deposits), its government unable to issue bonds under its own name to overcome this, and governments of stronger countries unwilling to help out, there would have been no alternative but to withdraw from EMU. A resuscitated money printing press in the exiting country would have created a burst of high inflation in the process of re-establishing (via a levy on creditors equal to the erosion in the real value of their claims, whether bank deposits or bonds) bank solvency along with other aims (including fiscal crisis resolution). As a group of sovereign countries joined in monetary union with no transfer union, the constitution of EMU should surely have included a section dealing with how an exit and reincarnation of the national money should take place in such an emergency including some provision for transitional loans from the remaining EMU.

These rules prohibiting the ECB from changing itself into a bad bank and EMU becoming a transfer union were one big omission from the Maastricht Treaty and were incredibly overlooked even by those German politicians most concerned at the possibility of free rides by the fiscally profligate countries at the expense of the German taxpayer. The second big omission was a monetary constitution which would restrain the ECB from going down the path of creating monetary instability. If the founding governments of EMU had drawn up a set of constitutionally enshrined rules so as to safeguard the pursuance of monetary stability (interpreted to mean ideally the elimination of monetary disease whether goods and services inflation or asset price inflation) rather than stipulating a dangerously fuzzy aim of stable prices, then the whole history of massive credit boom (including such aspects as investor appetite for periphery government debt at tiny margins over core government debt and for bonds issued by rapidly expanding banks in the periphery backed by exploding issuance of mortgage paper stemming from hot real estate markets) and bust would surely have been less wild. The founders would also have had to make clear that monetary stability for the union as a whole could mean some episodes of 'good deflation' (a fall in prices not due to monetary shortage but such factors as productivity surge or cyclical downturns) even at the level of the union as a whole and more frequently in some member countries, including the largest (Germany). The founders would also have admitted that total elimination of monetary disease – whether asset price inflation or goods inflation – would be impossible in the context of huge US monetary instability.

For such a large economic area as the EMU, monetary stability always should have taken precedence over any exchange rate stabilization aims. Indeed the attempt of the ECB in the period of currency warfare initiated by the Bernanke/Greenspan Federal Reserve in the early to mid 2000s (2003–5) to keep a lid on the euro at the cost of allowing the proverbial monetary monkey wrench to get inside the euro area economic machinery should have been illegal under a well-written founding monetary constitution. After all a main objective stated by the lead advocates of EMU was that this should be a zone of monetary stability insulated as much as possible from the repeated pattern of US monetary turbulence. But for that ambition to be realized the dollar–euro exchange rate could not be a significant factor determining how the ECB set monetary policy. If the ECB sought to prevent the euro soaring at times when the Federal Reserve lurched into monetary instability (with its symptom eventually appearing, most likely after a considerable period of time, in the form of either asset or goods price inflation or both) then it would simply import this instability.

The reader might have imagined that when the immensity of the bubble-bursting process and its costs became evident to all, public opinion in the countries where taxpayers were called upon to bear the brunt of 'burden-sharing' (albeit in some cases to salvage the domestic banking system which had recklessly lent to the periphery zone countries) would have swung behind politicians (and political parties) pressing an agenda of reform to make good the defects listed above in the initial design. In general, though, no such agenda has emerged in mainstream political debate. There have been particular controversies about specific bailouts, but no calls for a thorough revision of the monetary treaty (backed up by the potential bargaining power of one or more lenders to the bail-out funds). And the ECB itself has escaped mainstream criticism. There has been no Senator Bunning yelling at ECB President Trichet or Draghi 'you are the systemic risk', or a Representative Paul unafraid to call monetary incompetence to account, and no public opinion poll showing that the ECB has become even more unpopular than the tax collectors (as is the case for the Federal Reserve).

Instead of putting forward a comprehensive agenda for reform including a monetary constitution, no Bad Bank expansion by the ECB, and provisions for EMU exits, the demands of the German government have been lodged in terms of long-run strict rules for budget balances in each member state together with toughened up sanctions for their disregard and wider economic reforms (in terms of no indexation of wages for example). Evidently the policymakers in Germany have not determined a viable programme for undoing the initial mistakes in the construction of monetary union which in any case they have still failed to identify fully. Berlin has composed no blueprint for turning EMU fully into a monetary union of sovereign states without transfers and of which the fundamental aim is monetary stability. Those deficiencies could be explained in part by a lack of vision, but also no doubt by the perceived limits of what was 'politically feasible' or 'politically correct' in terms of the euro-zone as a whole.

There is also the dilemma of the starting point – a version of the Irish joke about the man who asked the way to Dublin, to be told that 'you should not be starting from here'. In the situation of 2014 it may well be that the first task should be to decide which countries are indeed fit to 'start from here'. Indeed that should have been the first task in early 2010 when the Greek sovereign debt crisis erupted. Instead the nonsense 'euro contagion' hypothesis gripped euro-officialdom (defined to include key policymakers in France and Germany, at the ECB, and more broadly) – if Greece were forced out of EMU or into default (or both), a tsunami of capital flight would quickly break the defences of other less weak EMU members. But was it not more plausible that if Greece were denied aid (except on the basis of traditional IMF funding in the aftermath of a mega devaluation having first exited EMU) then the semi-core member country of Italy would be in a more secure position. If German taxpayers had not been called upon to pay for huge transfers related to the threatened Greek insolvency then they might have willingly accepted the justification for a Franco–German solidarity loan to Italy at a later date. 'Solidarity' could take the form of a German equity participation in the ailing Italian banking system.

When it comes to defending a monetary union the same law might well apply as in military science – strength comes from a limited retreat first. The process of retreat would include re-incarnating sovereign monies in the periphery (a procedure which would involve re-denominating loans and liabilities of those countries exiting EMU, official support from the IMF and EU for the transition so that there would be confidence in the new devalued or floating monies) and governments in the financially strong countries dealing with banks (within their political jurisdiction) unable to re-capitalize themselves in the private markets in the wake of losses on their loans to the now exited periphery.

But how could the financially strong countries start the journey of limited retreat for EMU? One conceivable way would be for a Franco–German secret summit to take place. An historic opportunity came and went on that weekend in early May 2010 when Chancellor Merkel was dragging her feet about joining in a bail-out for Greece (or more exactly for lenders to Greece) and President Sarkozy threatened that France would withdraw from EMU in the absence of an immediate agreement. If Chancellor Merkel had said, 'OK leave!' it is surely likely that President Sarkozy would have crawled back within 24 hours and begged for Germany's terms for holding monetary union together. The terms which Chancellor Merkel could have offered then would have included a secret undertaking that both countries would come to the support of Italy, but before that line in the sand had been reached there would be no bail-outs except in the context of conventional IMF post-devaluation arrangements (for members which had exited EMU). And Chancellor Merkel could have insisted on a joint Franco–German commission to recommend treaty amendments for monetary union in line with the agenda of reform discussed above.

In reality, however, 'Frau Maus' (as German Chancellor Merkel was described by one tabloid) would have had no menu of terms ready to hand and nor were any of her advisers at all minded to put one together. In fact she came round to agreeing to the bail-out for Greece before that fateful Saturday evening in early May 2010 was out.

The most likely future of EMU is one of no monetary reform but of continuing rancorous negotiations between the financially strong and weak members about the terms and conditions for limited transfers through the front door (intergovernmental arrangements as through the EFSF) while the ECB continues to make huge 'temporary' transfers through the back door (without any explicit political agreement but nods from Berlin and Paris) as required to deal with any funding crisis in the periphery or indeed potentially within the core. There will be a lot of continuing pressure from Berlin in particular towards tighter rules with respect to members' budgetary policies and penalties for ignoring these.

This focus on creating a better and tighter fiscal straightjacket is in contradiction to the historical record. The debt crises in the periphery zone were fundamentally monetary in origin. Without the giant monetary disequilibrium created by the ECB and Federal Reserve there would not have been those armies of irrational investors (banks and their shareholders or long-term debt holders were prominent amongst these) ready to buy Greek bonds or Spanish mortgage backed securities or a whole range of other dubious securities (including Spanish government bonds given the likelihood of government revenues collapsing once the construction boom turned to bust) at such tiny margins above the yields on prime quality bonds (including German government bonds).

The purpose of rancour over bail-outs from the viewpoint of, say, the German government will not be to expose historical truths but to demonstrate to German taxpayers (and also to taxpayers of other financially strong countries) that they will not be funding open-ended transfers. Cynically EMU officialdom will continue to turn a blind eye to liquidity loans through the ECB back door (the expansion of its Bad Bank operations) keeping Humpty Dumpty together. A big question is whether markets also will continue to ignore the floods at the back door or at some stage begin to weigh the prospect that the financially strong members of EMU, if they decide in favour of continuing membership, could be saddled with large extra debts (relative to their economic size) towards an eventual re-capitalization of an insolvent ECB. (This re-capitalization will be hidden most likely from public view.)

Humpty Dumpty's future is likely to be short-lived. Bank insolvency in the periphery zone is set to get worse ultimately even though the asset price inflation virus emanating from the Federal Reserve's QE policies has provided some temporary relief (in particular by stimulating a demand from investors suffering under conditions of interest income famine for high-yielding bonds, including periphery European sovereigns and weak European bank debt). Many banks there (in the periphery) hold portfolios of loans whose quality is still deteriorating. And these banks have investment portfolios which are highly concentrated in government debt issued by the local sovereign. Why would depositors continue to lend to weak banks in the periphery holding such portfolios (stuffed with periphery government bonds alongside dubious private sector loans including mortgage-backed securities) except at rates that are well above those in the core countries of EMU? Yet how could banks pass on higher costs to borrowers in an already enfeebled economic and financial environment? It is dubious that the weak banks could raise equity capital in the markets on viable terms and meanwhile the overall economic climate would be burdened by the lending squeeze. Add to this combustible mixture an element of political instability (in a periphery zone country) and an episode of capital flight could force one or more of the periphery zone countries to exit EMU. The route to that exit featuring occasional giant transfusions of further aid is likely to be much more costly for taxpayers in the financially strong countries than the alternative routes of a quick slimming down (of EMU) to an inner core or a lightning consummation of a Franco–German union.

3
How the Virus of Asset Price Inflation Infected EMU

The global credit bubble in the early and mid 2000s and its sequel of great financial panic and great recession have set off a long search for the culprits. The investigation has been fundamentally historical rather than criminal. The actions and flaws of institutions and individuals have come under scrutiny. The investigators have also turned to wider social and economic forces which in combination might have been responsible for the disaster.

A search for the causes of economic and financial breakdown has some similarity with the pursuit of blame for the eruption of war. The analogy is only partial because investigations into the breakdown of peace can lead to indictments of war guilt. The identified person or organization could be due for punishment (sometimes posthumously in a purely hypothetical court process) for crimes against humanity or lesser charges. Crime and punishment is not usually at issue in the investigation of economic debacle albeit that alongside the economists the prosecutors of financial fraud might well be unusually busy.

In general, blundering central bankers and finance ministers, unlike ministers of war, did not deliberately or knowingly stoke up the possibility of eventual calamity in a wager which could bring alternatively national, political, and personal gains at least in the short run. Perhaps some of the economic policymakers at a rare moment during the phase of stimulus might have had a fleeting insight as to how things could all go very wrong. Maybe they should have acted on those insights by the exercise of greater caution. Perhaps they were influenced by personal financial and political greed. Even so, unlike the war minister, there was no target for their recklessness – no designated victim to pay for the potential gains, no enemy to be vanquished.

The main purpose of the investigation into economic calamity – and this is also an important purpose in war investigations – is the exposure of frailties and fault lines which allowed the catastrophe to occur. The hope of many investigators is that a better understanding of what went wrong can lead on to a set of remedies which will prevent anything similar happening in the future.

Historical investigations are decentralized. There is no chief prosecuting counsel. Rather, experts, politicians and commentators, undertake their own research and analysis, sometimes alone, sometimes in organized groups. In the example of such investigations into the global credit bubble of the mid-2000s and its subsequent bust, the areas of suspicion have included implementation of half-baked or downright false monetary doctrines, regulatory regimes with no safeguards against the regulators falling asleep and which inadvertently overrode and distorted automatic disciplinary mechanisms operating in the marketplace (the so-called invisible hands), financial intermediation based on systemic underestimation of risk and perverse standards of remuneration, severe inefficiencies in capital market pricing – embracing the crucial topic of how to value bank equities, Confucian tradition in East Asia and many others.

In reflective mood, investigators have raised important concerns about inherent flaws in the functioning of market forces – in particular those guiding the production and dissemination of reliable and insightful financial information, whether by stock market analysts or investigative business journalists.

Many of the eventually identified culprits and their defenders have responded by attempting to demonstrate that others were to blame.

A sampling of the literature and media on the subject of blame would reveal that 'indictments' handed out so far by the decentralized investigation are far-reaching. In some 'trials' or pre-trials, the targets (of the indictment process) have been prominent central bank officials, all the way down from Alan Greenspan and Ben Bernanke (where the charge list starts with inducing severe monetary disequilibrium).

In other trial processes, it is collective entities or groups that stand accused – the government of China (for its exchange rate policy), East Asian households and businesses for saving too much, regulators – including prominently the Securities and Exchange Commission (SEC), Bank for International Settlements (BIS) and central banks in Europe and the US – for being blithely unaware of what was occurring in the areas they were regulating, innovators for producing flawed financial products, business managers or clients who failed to spot the problems, analysts or journalists who failed to discover or uncover what was really going on (especially in terms of leverage and broader risk-taking) within

the financial sector, investors who did not look at, or were in a state of
delusion concerning, the risks of leverage and who put an extraordinarily high probability on one particularly favourable scenario (without
rationally making appropriately high estimates of probability weights
for less favourable scenarios, or even thinking about these clearly).

A big omission in the list of potential suspect areas has been the
new monetary regime in Europe which, at the end of 1998, replaced
the previous regime headed by the Deutsche mark and the Deutsche
Bundesbank. Correspondingly there has been no indictment either
against EMU or against the ECB, or any leading euro officials. Also
remarkable has been the complete silence of governments and mainstream oppositions in EMU member countries with respect to monetary
failure (whether in monetary framework or ECB policy actions) and
its contribution to the European debt crises that in reality were a part
of the global credit bust following the preceding bubble. The Japanese
publisher of this book's second edition noted that the apparent political
consensus to shield the ECB from criticism put it in a position compa-
rable to the Emperor of Japan.

The central theme of this book is that the launch of the euro
unleashed forces which played a critical role together with the originating force of US monetary chaos in generating the global credit bubble.
The burst was unnecessarily painful and wasteful, most of all in Europe.
A succession of bad policy choices by the ECB and flaws in EMU design
are an integral part of that case.

As we shall discover in the course of the narrative, structural flaws
in the new monetary union – some of which might have been less
severe if the founders of the union had not handed responsibility for
designing the framework of monetary policy to the just-created ECB
(within which the secret committee in charge of the design project,
headed by Professor Otmar Issing, newly appointed Board Member and
Chief Economist, was given only a few weeks to complete the task) – and
policy mistakes by its operatives (including crucially those at the
ECB) combined to make the outcome so much worse. The distinction
between structural flaw and operating error cannot be hard and fast in
that there are grey areas where the two are inseparable.

In this chapter a set of accusations is levelled at EMU and specifically
its central bank (the ECB) as the prime culprits. This forms the indictment. In subsequent chapters the evidence to support the indictment is
presented in full and so are the claims in defence of the accused (much
of which takes the form of diverting blame to other targets). A balancing
of accusation and counter-claims leads to a hypothetical judgement as

to the best way forward for monetary union in Europe. This judgement includes an outline of remedies to contain the dangers posed by EMU both during the painful continuing bust of the great bubble and far into the distance beyond.

Let us start with the summary indictment.

Summary indictment

The launch of EMU in 1998 set off a *sequence of monetary and capital market developments* in Europe that seriously contributed to the global credit bubble and subsequent bust through its first decade and beyond. The European dimension of the crash was perhaps less obvious at first than the US dimension. Whereas mainstream opinion in the global marketplaces had already adopted a plausibly harsh analysis about the extent of US damage from the bust by early 2009, the reckoning was delayed in Europe. Realistic estimates of the European fall-out from the period of virulent asset price inflation (2003–7) – the disease attacked markets in real estate, sovereign debt, financial equities and credit generally – emerged in stages well into 2010, 2011 and 2012 as the sovereign debt crises erupted amid a continuous process of market discovery. Eventually it came to light just how rampant irrational exuberance had become regarding a wide range of European asset markets during the bubble period.

Though the ECB undoubtedly faced big challenges and was handicapped by essential flaws in the architecture of monetary union, its poor design of monetary framework (even recognizing constraints due to public scepticism regarding its mission of achieving price level stability) had played a key role in fermenting the bubble and burst. The bad mistakes in its policymaking, which magnified greatly the economic damage, were avoidable.

We proceed to the charges in detail.

Faulty instrument board

The *sequence of developments* from the launch of the euro to the credit bubble-and-burst started with an almost total unreliability of the instrument board to be used by the pilots of monetary policy (the central bankers) in the newly created union.

A key problem with the instrument board was the lack of basis for confidence that any chosen definition of money supply in the new union as constructed would be a reliable guide for policymakers seeking to achieve the aim of price level stability as mandated by the founding Treaty of Maastricht let alone aspiring to pursue the aim of monetary stability in its wider sense (to include asset price inflation) non-mandated by the Treaty.

This absence of confidence stemmed from the fact that little was known about either the extent of demand (in equilibrium) for the new money (in the form of banknotes and bank deposits) or the dynamics behind its supply (how vigorously the overall stock of bank deposits would expand for any given path of monetary base).

Even the best monetary engineers under skilful instruction could not have fully fixed that problem. We shall see later (Chapter 8), though, how enhanced monetary base control together with modestly high reserve requirements might have partially fixed it especially if this had gone along with strict free market determination of interest rates (both short and long) without any manipulation (sometimes described as 'guidance') by the central bank.

With the passage of time the problem might have been expected to become less severe as learning took place both inside the central bank and in the market-place. And it was possible to hope, not with any great confidence given overwhelming historical evidence concerning discretionary judgement of monetary officials, that policymakers would devise extra checks and balances to contain the extent of monetary instability caused by the unreliability of the instrument board and thereby the ultimate damage which might result. Such faint hopes were dashed.

Flawed monetary framework and incomplete mandate

Right at the start of the monetary union, and indeed even in the half-year before its formal start (from mid- to end-1998), the founder members of the ECB Council took a series of ill-fated decisions regarding the design of the monetary policy framework.

In seeking to understand how these mistakes occurred, we should not underestimate the difficulty of the task that confronted the founding policymakers of the ECB, especially in view of the defective instrument board.

The ECB Council, in the short time from the EU Summit of May 1998 (where the heads of state took the formal decision to proceed to the final stage of EMU) until the last date possible to have worked out a fully operational plan (autumn 1998) ahead of the euro's launch (1 January 1999), had to decide how to interpret and implement the key Article 105 of the Maastricht Treaty with respect to the new monetary union.

Article 105 states:

> The primary objective of the European System of Central Banks (ESCB) shall be to maintain price stability. Without prejudice to the objective of price stability, the ESCB shall support the general economic policies in the Community with a view to contributing to the achievement of the objectives of the Community as laid down [in article 2].

The treaty left it to the ECB to interpret carefully what price stability should mean and how it could be achieved. As it turned out, the feasible time for deliberations stretched only over a few weeks. All of this was unfortunate.

The treaty writers should have composed a clear set of guiding monetary principles. The guiding principles in the Treaty (the monetary clauses) should have included the goal of *monetary stability* alongside the aim of *price level stability in the long run*.

Monetary stability means that money does not become a source of serious disequilibrium in the economy (the proverbial monkey wrench in the complex machinery of the economy – or in modern idiom the source of a virus which attacks the software determining the key price signals in the capitalist economy – see p. 4).

One key aspect of money becoming a source of disequilibrium is the driving of market interest rates (as quoted for that range of short and medium maturities most relevant for business and household decision-making) far out of line with the neutral or natural rate level (distinct for each given maturity). The neutral level refers to a span of market rates (across the different maturities) which would be consistent with the economy following that path in which all markets (for goods, labour, money, capital etc.) would be in equilibrium through time (allowing for frictional costs of adjustment).

Monetary instability can form without the early emergence of any symptom suggesting the possible presence of monetary inflation in goods and services markets. Instead the symptom that first appears (and this may be with a considerable lag behind the initial emergence of monetary instability) might be suggestive of the other type of monetary virus – asset price inflation. The trained and talented analyst might detect a rise of speculative temperature in some asset and credit markets (high temperatures mean a lot of irrational exuberance and very high temperatures can bring about bubbles). As illustration, a temperature rise might be driven in considerable part by the central bank first creating monetary conditions (including 'forward rate guidance') so as to steer market interest rates (across a wide range of maturities) far below neutral in a period of time when the economy is recovering (after a recession-shock) and later in similar fashion weighing down market interest rates with the intention of force-feeding the pace of economic expansion. (The *neutral* level of interest rate is the *natural* rate plus the average annual rate of price increase expected over the very long run; in the gold standard world, that rate of increase was zero, and so economists originally made no distinction between the two terms.) The tools which the modern central bank typically uses for influencing market rates (predominantly for short and medium maturities) are an official peg to short-maturity money market rates and strong hints as to how the peg is likely to be adjusted over the short and medium term.

Monetary stability and *price level stability in the very long run* are partly overlapping concepts and are sometimes not mutually achievable. The goal of monetary stability has to be missed (to a moderate degree) over some medium-term periods so as to achieve the aim of long-run price stability.

The element of trade-off between the two aims here – monetary stability and price stability in the very long-run – shares some superficial (but misleading) appearances with the trade-off in the much discussed dual mandate of the Federal Reserve, which is charged by Congress to pursue price stability and full employment. But that dual mandate is in main part phoney, based on a Keynesian notion of higher employment rates being attainable via the engineering of inflation. As we see below, the dual mandate of monetary stability and price stability in the long-run, though harder to grasp, is not phoney at all.

The friction between the requirements of monetary stability and long-run price stability is an essential and perennial source of disturbance in the modern economy. The friction arises from the fact that the aim of *price level stability over the very long run* might require the deliberate creation of some limited monetary instability. Moreover the pursuit of monetary stability is fully consistent with short and medium-term periods during which prices of goods and services are on average rising or falling significantly even though this might induce some concerns about the likely attainment of price level stability in the very long run. In a stable monetary order these concerns would not be validated.

For example, during a spurt of productivity growth or terms of trade improvement, the price level should be allowed to fall. If by contrast the central bank tries to resist the forces driving down prices it would likely fuel asset price inflation

Similarly if the central bank resists price level rises driven by real sources, such as sudden energy shortage, an abrupt fall in productivity or in the terms of trade, it would create monetary disequilibrium which would spawn a process of asset price deflation.

Moreover some price level fluctuation up and down with the business cycle coupled with expectations of price level stability in the long run is intrinsic to the benign process by which the capitalist economy pulls itself out of recession or resists being drawn into unsustainable boom. Such fluctuations should not be fought by a central bank mistakenly zealous about achieving price level stability over too short a time period. Alternatively, it may be that the price level has drifted through time well above or below the guidelines consistent with long-run stability, even though there has been no serious episode of monetary instability. For example, most of the real shocks (such as spurts of productivity growth or terms of trade improvement) may have been in the direction of driving the price level downwards.

In that case there has to be some injection of controlled monetary disequilibrium (supply of money base growing in excess of demand, interest rates below neutral) towards achieving the long-run price level target. This can be done in a context of decades rather than years – as indeed occurred under the gold standard (see Brown, 1940) where automatic mechanisms regulated the extent of controlled monetary disequilibrium. As illustration, during years when the prices of goods were depressed relative to their long-run average, profits in the gold mining industry would rise and spur production (of the yellow metal). The slowness of the monetary injection meant less danger of serious asset price inflation as a periodic side effect of pursuing price level stability in the long run.

No attempt to construct automatic money control mechanism

In our monetary world outside the golden Garden of Eden (a romanticization of a complex reality!) from which we were expelled in 1914, we have to construct a replacement stabilizing mechanism (for fine-tuning the extent of monetary disequilibrium to be created towards attaining price stability in the very long run), and one which functions as automatically as possible. The likely delicate mechanism has to be capable of allowing a limited degree of monetary instability to emerge sometimes in the form of a rise in speculative temperatures in several important asset markets so as to achieve price stability in the very long run.

The drafters of the Maastricht Treaty did not mention at all the fundamental juxtaposition of monetary stability with the aim of long-run price level stability. They did not specify how the best automatic mechanism should be designed for limiting the possible extent of monetary instability required for long-run price level stability. This big omission left the way clear for fatal errors in design of the monetary framework and in subsequent policymaking.

The Treaty should have provided for a much more comprehensive review surrounding the design of monetary framework and for this to take place in an open, not secret, forum. There should have been ample time (perhaps one year between the EU Summit deciding to proceed with EMU and on which countries would be founder members to the actual start, rather than just six months) for the design process and even longer to allow for needed institutional modifications (especially as regards reserve requirements) to occur towards creating the best possible money control system.

There was a wide range of suggestions available from the well-known literature of monetary economics for the ECB framework-design committee (under ex Bundesbanker Professor Issing) to take on board in the course of their work. The literature is of course heterogeneous in terms of its driving political philosophy and economic principles – a reason why optimally the writers of the Maastricht Treaty should have drafted a rule-based monetary constitution rather than delegating the drafting of a framework to ECB officials.

Botched output from the secret 'Issing Committee'

No available evidence indicates that the ECB at the start undertook an appropriate review of alternative ways in which the Treaty's albeit imperfect specification of price level stability as the ultimate aim should be made operational, even if an impossibly short time-framework for final decisions on monetary framework was amply to blame.

One possibility – choice 1 – would have been the targeting of a trajectory for money supply growth over time at a low average rate (deemed to be consistent with the price level being 'broadly stable' over the very long run, albeit with considerable swings possible up or down over multi-year periods and also with considerable short-term volatility). The 'central path of the price level' (abstracting from white noise and transitory disequilibrium) would be determined by equilibrating forces which would balance supply and demand for money as for all other goods in general equilibrium. The price level at any time would be one variable among many to be solved in the process of achieving general equilibrium.

This monetary targeting might have been coupled with the setting of a quantifiable guideline for price level stability in the very long run (say a ten-year average price level – calculated for the present and previous nine years – which is 0–10% higher than the previous ten-year average for the period 10–20 years ago) so as to monitor that this ultimate aim is indeed likely to be achieved. (Perhaps the broadest of all price indices, thoroughly revised on the basis of new evidence about the past, the GDP or private consumption deflator, would have been used in this calculation). Signs that the price level path might be going astray relative to the aim of stability in the very long run would lead to a twigging of the monetary targeting – meaning a revision in particular to the rule specifying the expansion rate.

Monitoring signs of potential difficulties in meeting the aim of price level stability in the very long run while achieving monetary stability in the present was bound to be challenging in the new monetary union given the lack of knowledge about the nature of the demand for money (technically the money demand function). The accumulation of evidence that the aim (of long-run price level stability) might well be in danger or that monetary instability was forming would feed back to a review of the rule used to determine the targeted path for the chosen monetary aggregate. There would be the key issue of what particular definition of money to select, with the possibilities ranging from narrow to wide.

Later in this book the argument is presented that the narrowest of definitions would be best, subject to a revamp of reserve requirements (so as to foster a more stable demand for reserves which would be non-interest bearing – see Chapter 8).

In effect the target would be set for high-powered money (reserves plus cash in circulation) – alternatively described as 'monetary base' – and not for any wider aggregate. The revamp of reserve requirements, however, which would be essential towards the success of a monetary base targeting system, was not feasible, even if deemed as optimal, in the rushed circumstances of summer 1998. (The UK, so long as it kept open the option of being a founder member of EMU, had blocked all discussions of this issue. But in May 1998 the UK had made the final decision against becoming a founder member.)

Choice 1 (of method to make the Treaty's ultimate aim of price stability operational) would have been consistent with the propositions of Milton Friedman (even though he did not recommend that his famous

x% p.a. expansion rule should apply to monetary base but to a wider – yet still narrow – aggregate and he would have been cool to the suggested variation of including a guideline for the price level in the long run), who in his famous collection of essays under the title of *The Optimum Quantity of Money* (Friedman, 2006) had rejected the setting of a price level target in favour of a money supply target. In technical jargon the money supply would be the intermediate target selected so as to achieve the long-run aim of price level stability.

Choice 1 might also have found favour with the Austrian School economists, even though in principle they would be opposed to any discretionary power vested in a monetary authority.

The 'Austrians' (see, for example, Hayek and Salerno, 2008) argue that the price level consistent with monetary stability (including money performing its function of reliable long-run store of value) can vary up or down by significant amounts over the short or medium run as for example in the situation of big shifts in productivity growth or the terms of trade. Also the price level should fluctuate in accordance with the business cycle, with a wide span of prices (most of all in the cyclically sensitive industries) falling to a low point during the recession phase and picking up into the recovery phase.

This pro-cyclical movement of prices is indeed in principle a key automatic stabilizer – inducing consumption and investment spending by the financially fit households and businesses during the recession (as they take advantage of transitorily low prices) and in encouraging some households and businesses to postpone spending in the boom phase of the cycle (in the expectation that prices will be lower during the cooler next phase). These cyclically induced changes in the price level should not be interpreted as signifying monetary disequilibrium. These key insights of the Austrian School were referred to earlier in this indictment (see pp. 40–1).

According to the Austrian School (see Hayek and Salerno, 2008 and von Mises, 1971) the overriding principle of monetary management should be that money does not become the 'monkey-wrench' in the economic machinery (the phrase attributed to J. S. Mill and famously re-quoted by Milton Friedman – see Friedman, 2006). This means (as highlighted in an earlier indictment above – see p. 40) in particular that monetary conditions should not shift in a way such as to cause market rates (illustratively for those maturities which are key to household and business decision-making) to get far out of line with neutral or natural levels (which in turn fluctuate through time according to such influences as range of investment opportunity or propensities to save).

Monetary stability is defined by money not becoming the source of virus attack on all the software determining the price-signals to which the invisible hands of the capitalist economy respond (see Chapter 1, p. 4).

A big question for the Austrian School is how practical policymakers should implement this prescription in a world where the automatic mechanisms of the gold standard are broken and the demand for money is unknown within wide limits. The span of neutral or natural rates (across a range of maturities) varies considerably over time and is hard for even the most gifted of policy-makers to estimate with any precision. In any case what meaning should be given to 'far out of line'? When an economy is in severe recession, ideally the normal self-recuperative forces in a capitalist economy should produce a path for interest rates which for some time would (with long-run money supply growth firmly anchored) be well below the neutral or natural level which would prevail in long-run equilibrium. The solution is to give markets as big a role as possible in the estimation of the neutral interest rate (as specified for varying maturities) and where this lies relative to long-run norm during a period marked by considerable economic disturbance. The authorities should not engage in such practices as rate pegging in the short-term money markets which might get in the way of this process.

By contrast, the well-known 'Taylor rule' stems from an attempt to discover the optimal path for a central bank in its pegging of short-term money rates. In the world of the Taylor rule there is no notion of market revelation. Instead there is the all powerful black box of econometrics (built on Keyensian principles including a trade-off between unemployment and inflation) and optimal control theory (applied to targeting inflation over the medium-term). Application of the rule requires that the monetary authority knows the normal neutral rate of interest (which fits long-run equilibrium) and the exact degree of slack in the economy. The econometrics assumes stability of the underlying relationships estimated.

Some 'Austrians' could concur with those monetary economists from other schools who argue that the most practical way forward would be to target high-powered money while allowing as much scope as feasible for markets to determine even short-term interest rates (which would be very volatile).

ECB architects destroy pivot role for monetary base

A key argument for targeting high-powered money (the monetary base) is grounded on the belief that, given a firm monetary anchor (in this case a target for high-powered money growth), the market would do a better job of steering interest rates close to the ideal equilibrium path (and in discovery of the natural or neutral interest rate level – a crucial element in the auto-piloting process) than the monetary bureaucracies (central banks).

Very short-term money rates would be highly volatile as was the case under the gold standard regime. The volatility would stem from passing shortages and excesses in the market for bank reserves. The average level of these rates, though, over several months, should be fairly stable. Anyhow it is the rates for medium-term and long-term maturities which would have the greatest information content and would be most relevant to business and household decision-making.

Austrians and monetarists would be united in concern about possible abuse of discretionary power to twig the monetary expansion rule to take account of new information regarding the likely profile through time of the real demand for money (especially high-powered money) consistent with overall equilibrium. Yet both would be fully aware that non-flexibility has economic costs. And some deliberate controlled overshoots or undershoots of the rule could be required to attain long-run price level stability even though that means some monetary instability.

Essential to the operation of monetary base (high-powered money) targeting is first, unrestricted scope for the differential between the zero rate of return on excess reserves (beyond the legal minimum) and on other risk-free assets to fluctuate so as to balance supply and demand in the market for bank reserves. Second, an institutional structure must have been designed in which demand for monetary base is likely to be a stable function of a few key identifiable variables, including in particular real incomes.

The first requirement is achieved where the rate of interest on reserves (and excess reserves) at the central bank is fixed at zero throughout. The second requirement is satisfied by a high level of reserve requirements on the public's transaction deposits with the banks.

The ECB in its design of monetary framework jettisoned both requirements for the operation of monetary base targeting or for any fulcrum or pivot role for monetary base in policymaking. Moreover its scheme for paying interest on reserves had the potential to become an infernal destabilizing force during a severe financial crisis, as in fact was to occur in 2007–8 (see p. 131).

High reserve requirements were rejected in part to meet UK objections (see p. 43) but also in line with current fashionable views of not cramping banking industry competitiveness by imposing a tax on transaction deposits sold by resident banks as against other near-alternative assets including offshore deposits.

In the mid-1990s the Bundesbank had reduced reserve requirements substantially already towards countering competitive pressures for German banks from Luxembourg in particular. Professor Issing has recounted how the old Bundesbankers (not including himself!) had fought a rearguard action against this reduction. Even so the Bundesbank continued with payment of zero interest on reserves right up to the end of its sovereign existence.

Such concerns about competitiveness were doubtless a factor in why the architects of EMU's operating system decided in favour of paying interest on deposits with the ECB at only a modest margin below official repo rates, albeit mitigated by Luxembourg becoming a part of EMU and thereby subject to any reserve requirements. But another factor was the concern (among members of the Issing Committee) to reinforce the new central bank's power to control short-term interest rates within tight limits of the chosen official peg (adjusted, typically by micro-amounts at a time, in line with monetary micro-policy decisions).

Professor Issing rejects advice from Vienna and Chicago

There is no evidence from any published material or from any other source that Professor Issing's secret committee designing the monetary policy framework (in summer 1998) gave weight to the Austrian School's arguments.

'Giving weight to' does not mean comprehensive endorsement. The committee could have raised important practical reservations. In particular, in view of the newness of EMU and public scepticism about the ECB's likely success in avoiding inflation, there had to be an easily understandable target to measure the ECB's success. Austrian 'poetic' concepts of monetary stability might have jarred with that purpose.

It can well be doubted whether a sceptical public would have had patience with the sophisticated argument that monetary inflation need not show itself up as rising prices for goods and services but as rising asset prices, or that a rising price level for goods and services might not be symptomatic of monetary inflation.

It would have been possible in principle for Professor Issing's Committee to include the concept of monetary stability (defined to include absence of asset price inflation) alongside a goal of long-run price level stability even though this concept had not been specified in the founding treaty.

In so far as public scepticism meant that such a dual mandate (stable price level in the very long-run plus monetary stability) was impractical, then creation of a new monetary union was likely to incur a considerable cost in terms of potential monetary instability.

The omission of an overriding concept of monetary stability along Austrian School lines played a key role in the global credit bubble-and-bust which was to follow.

Under its self-imposed code of secrecy, the ECB has never released transcripts or other documentary evidence of key discussions between its policymakers – including their chosen external advisers – in the critical months before the euro's launch. Perhaps if these officials had known that all evidence, including the transcript of the discussions, would be published, the deliberations on this key issue would have been fuller and more efficient.

The ECB's first chief economist and founding board member Professor Otmar Issing writes (see Issing, 2008) that he did discuss within his research team the concern that severe monetary disequilibrium capable of eventually producing credit and asset bubbles could coexist with observed price level stability (as defined by a target average inflation rate over say a two-year period set at a low level).

And there is also some autobiographical evidence (from Professor Issing) to suggest that there was a passing informal review of something similar to the Friedman proposal for money supply targeting without an explicit short- or medium-term numerically expressed aim for the price level.

None of these deliberations, however, which occurred in a necessarily very short period of time during summer and early autumn 1998, translated into any impressive design features of the monetary framework. Yes, there was the sketch of what was subsequently described as the 'monetary pillar', but this remained little more than a blurred section of the original architectural drawing. The main and clearest section of the architectural drawings was filled with what most economists would recognize as a system of inflation targeting even though Professor Issing repudiated that description.

Indeed, the second possible way in which to make the Treaty's specification of price level stability operational – policy choice 2 – (for outline of policy choice 1, see pp. 43–4), was for the ECB to reject definition of the ultimate aim in terms of a very long-run price parameter (as in choice 1). Instead the ECB would stipulate a medium-term (say, two years) desired path for, the overall consumer price index (CPI), expressed as an average annual rate of change. A practical problem here, amid the many theoretical problems already discussed on the basis of Chicago and Vienna critiques, would be that the so-called harmonized index of consumer prices (HICP) hammered out in committee by the EU Statistics Office excluded altogether house prices or rents and once estimated remained unchangeable even if subsequent re-estimation revealed past error.

In seeking to achieve this two-year path for the price level, the central bank could set a target for growth in a selected money supply aggregate – choice 2a – adjusting the target on the basis of any serious new evidence concerning the relationship between money and inflation. Its tool for achieving the money target could be either strict but adjustable pegging of a key money interest rate (for example, overnight) or the setting of a subsidiary target for so-called high-powered money growth (reserves and cash) while allowing even the overnight and other short-term rates to fluctuate within a wide margin as determined by conditions in the money market.

Or alternatively the central bank (in its pursuance of the two-year path for the price level) could set no target for money supply – choice 2b – and instead rely on forecasts for goods and services inflation based on an array of econometric tools to be applied to a whole range of variables to be monitored, one of which could be money supply. In this case the central bank would repeatedly adjust the peg for very short-term rates so as to forge a path for these and for longer-term rates (in so far as these could be manipulated) that would hopefully achieve the ultimate objective for the price level (over a two-year period).

Rate-pegging is a 'fair-weather' operational policy. If continued during a financial crisis it becomes a catalyst to a vicious cycle of instability (see pp. 132–3).

A variation of choice 2b – let us call this 2ba – would be to give money supply a special place amid these monitored variables and set an alarm to ring if ever money supply growth estimated over a given stipulated interval strayed outside its specified range. In principle, the alarm would not be turned off even if the monitors determined that no danger existed in the form of the price level target being missed over the 'medium-term' (meaning in practice two years) unless they were also satisfied that there were no other dangers present (for example, inflation in the long run or a bubble in the credit market).

Response to the alarm would include a change in the official interest rate (normally specified with respect to a very short maturity in the money market), which under all versions of policy 2b is set on an entirely discretionary basis in line with policymakers' views about how changes in short-term money market rates influence the actual inflation outcome.

The fantasy of the monetary pillar

The ECB policy board ratified the Issing Committee's proposals in October 1998 and announced 'the main elements of its stability-oriented monetary policy strategy'.

The Committee had in effect decided in favour of option 2ba above. It stipulated the price level aim in terms of the rise in the euro-area HICP over the 'medium-term' (with subsequent practice demonstrating that this meant around two years), stating that this should not be more than 2% p.a.

There was no indication that the policy board had any realization that rate-pegging under its choice 2ba would have to be suspended or implemented in an abnormal way under conditions of financial crisis (see p.132).

It was left unspecified (until spring 2003) how the ECB would respond to inflation outcomes well below 2% p.a. But early policy-rate decisions implicitly filled that gap (see p. 55).

The ECB board in reaching its decision as regards the definition of price level stability including its selection of numerical reference value betrayed the trust put in it by the founders of monetary union. Albeit that the founders were wrong to have staked such an important issue for future economic prosperity of their peoples on a small group of central bank officials holding discussions entirely at their discretion in secret and instead of bringing in a wider range of decision-makers in an open process with much more time in which to implement their architectural plan.

The announced construction (by the ECB) of an alarm system based on money supply monitoring which would be sensitive to danger over a long-run frame of reference transcending the two-year definition of price stability was largely fantasy. And in particular there was no careful specification of one such danger – speculative temperature swings in credit and asset markets which culminate in severe economic disequilibrium and related waste (sometimes described as 'asset price inflation' and 'mal-investment').

The decision on policy framework as described put at great risk the achievement of monetary stability. Serious monetary disequilibrium – full of damaging consequences for the real economy – could result from an over-strict pursuance of the price-level aim as defined.

The ECB board appears (from the evidence available) to have been at best complacent about the possibilities (as raised for example by the Austrian School) that a positive productivity shock coupled with price level path targeting over medium-term periods (say two years) could lead to a credit bubble or that a negative terms of trade shock (in particular a big jump in the price of oil) similarly coupled could lead to depression. Nor did ECB policymakers realize that monetary instability could be symptomless in terms of statistically measured goods and services price inflation while manifesting itself already in dangerous fashion via asset price inflation. And there could be notoriously long lags between monetary disequilibrium occurring and the symptom asset price inflation (or goods and services inflation) becoming apparent in convincing form.

The evidence reveals no awareness on the part of the ECB about the possibility of benign pro-cyclical moves of the price level (see p. 44). In consequence the ECB became inclined to spot illusory threats of inflation falling 'too low' (as in 1999 and 2003) and to suffer more generally from 'deflation phobia'.

All these deficiencies in official perceptions explain how the ECB in its first decade became the engine of huge monetary instability.

No shelter from 'English-speaking' monetary instability

The ECB, in following a quasi-inflation targeting regime as instituted by the Issing Committee, was in great company. (The term 'quasi' is used to acknowledge that the ECB's formal description of its policy framework includes a 'monetary pillar' even though this never become a well-drawn component of any detailed architectural drawing).

The Federal Reserve and Bank of England were committing very similar types of errors.

That was no excuse for failure.

The ECB as a new institution driven by the idea of setting a high standard of monetary excellence and carrying out the mission of sheltering the new monetary union from 'English-speaking instability' (francophone writers use the term 'Anglo-Saxon') should have done better than its peers.

The Bank of England, after all, had been at the bottom end of the scale in terms of monetary performance during the 1970s decade of the Great Inflation. It enjoyed less independence then from the government than in the recent past, so it did not quite make history in being the worst performer (in terms of inducing credit bubbles and burst) during the debacle of monetary policies around the world wrought by 'inflation targeting'.

Professor Issing does show some possible disquiet about the company in which he found himself in stating (Issing, 2008) that his secretly deliberating committee decided against following a monetary framework in any significant way embracing the strict inflation targeting pursued by the Bank of England. In writing about the work of his secret committee, Issing comments:

> Of particular value to us (the committee) were the visits by prominent experts who combined an academic background with central bank experience. For instance, we were able to discuss the whole spectrum of issues relating to inflation targeting with one of its proponents, Bank of England Governor Professor Mervyn King. [...] Inflation targeting was well on the way to becoming the 'state of the art' in central bank policy-making. What could have been more obvious than to follow the example of these central banks (which had adopted inflation-targeting) and the urging of leading economists? There are persuasive reasons why the ECB at the time took a different course.

Professor Issing mentions UK and New Zealand by name but is too politically correct to refer to the quasi-inflation targeting of the Federal Reserve. In any case it was only four years later, in 2002, that the leading academic proponent of inflation targeting, Professor Bernanke, was appointed by President George W. Bush as Governor of the Federal Reserve Board. Six years earlier (1996) though, Professor Janet Yellen, then a Board Member, had won a debate within the Federal Open Market Committee (FOMC) in favour of the proposition that 'price stability' should mean 'inflation at 2% p.a.', persuading the initially unconvinced chairman, Alan Greenspan.

The new event from an historical perspective was that the ECB, as successor to the Bundesbank in the role of leading European monetary authority, followed by its actions (but not fully by its announcements) the crowd of popular (and deeply flawed) monetary opinion, even though its senior officials appreciated some of its fallacies (though not in terms of a thoroughgoing Austrian School refutation!). The protestations of the ECB's chief policy-architect through the early years, Professor Issing, that his institution remained distant from the crowd, were largely meaningless.

How different the ECB's performance during the monetary madness of the early twenty-first century was from the Bundesbank's stellar record in distinguishing itself from the dominant popular monetary opinion during the Great Inflation of the 1970s! Would the old Bundesbank (before bending to the imperative set by Chancellor Kohl of attaining the EMU destination on schedule), operating counterfactually without the encumbrance of EMU, not have remained nearer to past performance?

Milton Friedman had warned long ago that setting the aim of monetary policy in terms of a stipulated price level outcome over a two-year period (or any other short or medium-term period) would reduce the accountability of the central bank (see Friedman, 1966). For the outcome in any such period could be attributed only in part to central bank policy, given the range of white noise and non-monetary factors outside the control of the central bank which potentially affects short- and medium-term measured inflation rates. Hence there would be a wide range of plausible excuses for failure to achieve the aim. Instead, central bankers should be made responsible for something over which they have a considerably greater degree of control – the path of the money supply (and in the case of the monetary base that control is 100%).

In fact the ECB had a fair degree of success in meeting its stipulated 'medium-term' target for the price level during its first decade, with the average rate of inflation barely above 2% p.a. And so Milton Friedman's warning about lack of responsibility amid a plethora of excuses did not in fact become relevant during that period. It would have been better if the ECB had missed the price target (in the direction of prices undershooting) and its officials had discovered why this should be broadcast as good news!

Indeed more relevant in practice than Friedman's concern about responsibility was the Austrian critique that price level targeting especially over short- *and* medium-term periods, even if successful in its own terms, could go along with the emergence of serious monetary disequilibrium which would be the source of a highly destructive virus to the economic system, asset price inflation. The Austrian School economists would accept that a price level aim should be set over the very long-run (as occurred endogenously under the pre-1914 international gold standard). But their 'very long-run' was far and away beyond the medium-term as conceptualized by Professor Issing's secret committee and even further beyond the medium-term as implemented in practice by ECB policymakers.

The Austrian critique leads on to a further accusation in the present indictment.

Faulty monetary framework leads to three big policy mistakes

In choosing to define price stability as inflation (measured by HICP) at *not more than 2% p.a. on average over the medium-term* (in practice policymaking during the first decade of EMU is wholly consistent with medium-term meaning a two-year period despite the existence of many textual references in official publications and speeches to longer time-horizons) – supplemented by a further 'clarification' in spring 2003 that too low inflation, meaning more than a tiny margin below 2% p.a., would be contrary to the aim of monetary policy – the ECB substantially raised the likelihood of serious monetary disequilibrium ahead. This would be the source of two possible economic diseases – asset price inflation and consumer price inflation.

Indeed, allowing for 'good' price level fluctuations up or down related simply to the business cycle in which a recessionary phase might well last as much as two years, the notion of a two-year period for measurement purposes was palpably absurd.

In practice the ECB Board followed what was to prove disastrous monetary fashion in the UK and the US (albeit that the Federal Reserve did not yet formally adopt explicit inflation-targeting, mainly out of concern that this could become a point of leverage for greater Congressional control over its policy decisions). ECB officials who pretended that the small actual differences between their own policy framework and that of the Federal Reserve were more than technical or linguistic and that the 'money pillar' component of its monetary alarm system had any operational capability were at best in a state of self-delusion.

As a matter of semantics, as we have seen, the ECB denied right from the start that it was following the fashion of inflation targeting. In subsequent refinements (of its communication regarding the framework) the ECB stressed that its policy decisions were based on two pillars (first, medium-term inflation forecasts based on the highest quality of econometric work carried out by its staff and second, money supply developments considered in a long-term time frame including possible implications well beyond a two-year period) and so distinguished itself from some other central banks which targeted a given low inflation rate over a similar time-period (two years) without any separate cross-check to money supply growth.

Crucially, however, in common with all inflation-targeting central banks, the ECB stipulates a precise formulation of a stable desired average rate of rise in the price level over a fairly short period of time (it is mainly semantics whether this is a two-year period as officially for the Bank of England or the 'medium-term' as for the ECB) rather than acknowledging that the price level should fluctuate by a considerable amount over the short- and medium-run consistent with price level stability in the very long-run. Indeed that is what happened under the international gold standard – when there were occasional way-out years in which the price level rose by 5% or more, as in the UK during the Boer War, and long stretches of price level rises or falls, but in the very long run, price stability reigned.

Some ECB officials, including notably Professor Otmar Issing, were undoubtedly aware of the dangers in pursuing price level targets over short-term or medium-term horizons and realized that monetary disequilibrium could indeed manifest itself in asset price inflation (including credit market over-heating) well before any goods and service price inflation might emerge (and emergence might never occur if the bubble burst first). In practice, however, ECB policymakers, including Professor Issing, were not sufficiently sensitive to these risks and apparently failed to realize that asset price inflation disease could be present in fairly virulent form for some time before any reliable diagnosis could be made.

The unreliability of any monetary indicator in the new world of EMU including the framework of monetary control designed by the Issing Committee threw the policymakers off the scent (of any credit and asset bubble in the making). This unreliability was one factor in the failure of the ECB to specify a serious long-run dimension to monetary policymaking.

In the first decade of EMU, three episodes of monetary disequilibrium – (1) 1998 Q4 through 1999 (see p. 55), (2) 2003–2005/6 (see p. 60) and (3) 2007 H2 to 2008 Q3 (see p. 131) – were to result from the ECB's adoption of a 2% p.a. inflation target (in official terminology a price level path over the medium-term).

Each episode of disequilibrium was grave in its own way, with the third entering the competition for the worst monetary mistake in European or global financial history since the early 1930s.

The monetary error of 1998–9

Right at the start of EMU, the official aim of the price level rising by 2% p.a. (or a little less) over the medium-term came in for some immediate practical clarification, in a deeply unsettling fashion. When the ECB opened its doors, inflation in the euro-area was down at 1% p.a. If seeking to minimize monetary disequilibrium, the ECB would have done better to aim initially for a continuing level of price increase around that level rather than immediately seeking to breathe in a higher rate of inflation. And if medium-term meant five to ten years rather than two, then there was nothing to worry about in inflation now being at near zero!

After all, with the information technology revolution in full swing, oil prices at a two-decade low and terms of trade improving rapidly as cheap imports from Eastern Europe and China ballooned, a policy of driving inflation back up to 2% p.a. would surely be wildly expansionary by any Austrian definition! ECB officials remained perma-bears on euro-area productivity even with the IT revolution; perhaps in part because the data available in several European countries almost certainly failed to pick up the full extent of its contemporary spurt. That statistical failure, however, did not apply to Germany in particular, where the statistics office by this point in time practised 'hedonistic accounting', according to which the prices of goods and services were adjusted downwards in line with quality improvements including those now emerging in consequence of the IT revolution.

In addition there is the general point that the price level should move pro-cyclically even under a monetary regime which specifies the aim of absolute price level stability in the very long run. This (1998) was a year of recession or near-recession in the euro-area. The German economy in particular was suffering the headwinds from the emerging market debt crisis which had erupted first in South and East Asia the previous year and then in Russia.

During the boom periods, manufacturers in the highly cyclical industries (especially automobiles) should be charging high margins to compensate in part for the loss which they incur in business recessions. Indeed in a well-functioning market economy firms in highly cyclical industries should tend to have relatively low debt and high equity in their capital structures so as to contain the danger of bankruptcy during recession. Vital equity is attracted to cyclical industries on the basic premise of extraordinarily high profit during boom-time and such equity in effect insures labour and bondholders against recession-destruction of income and capital. And during the recession, the fall of prices in the highly cyclical industries to below normal levels are an inducement to contra-cyclical spending by financially fit firms and households who take advantage of low prices now compared to when prosperity returns.

Inflation below 2% p.a. in 1998 should not have been construed by the ECB as a reason for exceptional monetary ease. Benign cyclical fluctuation of prices on its own could explain a dip of the recorded rate of price increase below the long-run average rate aimed at as the anchor to inflation expectations. The monetary decisions of the ECB at that time hinted at the extent to which the newly constructed monetary policy framework was indeed flawed.

There is some evidence (see Chapter 4, p. 59) to suggest that the ECB in early 1999 was concerned that inflation had already fallen into a 'dangerous low zone' – dangerous in the sense that if the next recession (beyond the cyclical recovery generally forecast for 1999–2000) was to become severe, the central bank would very quickly find that conventional monetary policy reached its limit to provide any stimulus (once risk-free nominal rates fell to zero).

If the ECB were indeed greatly concerned on this score, there were three ways of dealing with it boldly. The first way was to aim for a considerably higher inflation rate (say 3–4% p.a.) during the next economic recovery and expansion phases (of the business cycle). If successful, then in a subsequent severe recession deeply negative risk-free rates could be reached in real terms even though under conventional monetary policy money market rates (even risk-free) could not fall below zero.

This option (aiming for steady-state inflation at say 3–4% p.a.) is discussed in *"The Global Curse of the Federal Reserve"* (Brown 2013). Its unsuitability to the circumstances of EMU or indeed to any other currency area (sovereign state or monetary union) is detailed. And in practical terms there is surely no great likelihood of such an inflation rate being reached in just one cyclical recovery. There are several general grounds for rejecting higher steady-state inflation.

One of these grounds has been hinted at already. The higher the long-term average inflation rate that is taken as reference benchmark by monetary policymakers, the more paralysed becomes the inbuilt recovery mechanism during recession or a transitory fall in many prices coupled with the expectation that these will re-bound in the upturn (that expectation justifies spending in the depths of the recession by the financially strong, when cyclically sensitive prices are at their lowest, – see p. 44). There is no evidence, though, that anyone in the ECB gave any attention to this mechanism, let alone believed that it could play a role in driving the economy out of the recession or near-recession of 1998.

The second bold (again not good!) option (for the ECB in confronting a hypothetical danger of monetary policy paralysis in severe recession) was to draft a contingency emergency scheme that would be on the shelf ready in time for possible use were the next recession to prove severe. This scheme would allow risk-free rates to fall to deeply negative levels in both nominal and real terms and yet be consistent with aiming for very low inflation or absolute price level stability over the very long run. One powerful criticism of this option is its bestowing of huge discretionary power on monetary policy-makers (when to introduce the scheme, when and how to end it) which would add to the climate of monetary uncertainty.

The third bold option – and the wisest according to subsequent analysis here – was to shake off deflation phobia and realize that a pro-cyclical move of prices (reaching a low-point in the depths of the recession, then expected to rise back to normal level) could stimulate economic recovery even in the situation where the use of the conventional monetary tool (adjusting nominal interest rates downwards) were no longer feasible due to the proximity of the zero rate boundary. The ECB would help educate euro-citizens that in the new stable monetary order there could be some periods of time during which the price level would fall but that subsequently the price level would recover in line with the stipulated objective of long-run price stability. Expectations of price level recovery would mean that low nominal interest rates would become negative in real terms and stimulate spending.

No contingency planning, no boldness

The ECB did not draft any contingency plan for deep recession or financial panic. (Much later, in 2013, then President Draghi announced that the ECB had a negative interest rate scheme 'on the shelf', most likely to be used in the next existential crisis of EMU rather than simply a cyclical downturn). Instead right at the start of monetary policymaking (in late 1998 and early 1999) it sought bureaucratic safety in seeking to lift inflation a little from the then 'low level' (relative to the aim for the price level over the 'medium-term').

Inflation, though, running at 2% p.a. instead of 1% p.a. makes only a small potential difference to the extent that risk-free rates, especially those for the medium and long-maturities most relevant to investment decision-making, in real terms can fall below zero. So long as the zero rate barrier remains firmly in place the path followed by short-maturity risk-free market rates during a severe recession or panic could be constrained still at a well-above optimal level. The continuous state of inflation gets in the way of the key pro-cyclical price level mechanism (price cuts during the recession together with the expectation of price level rebound afterwards) which potentially plays such an important role in generating a subsequent recovery. (In general, the lower frequency of big price cuts would mean less of a spending response.)

Given the problems (instabilities) which accompanied getting inflation up from 1 to 2% p.a., it is just as well the ECB was not bolder on that particular score, aiming for a higher inflation rate than 2%)!

Monetary policy blunder triggered 1999–2000 euro crisis

A consequence of the ECB's implicit decision in 1999 to drive inflation higher towards 2% (the euro-area CPI was then rising at around 1% p.a.), which was put into operation by reducing the officially pegged money rates to very low levels and so driving short- and medium-maturity market rates well below neutral level despite the absence of any severe economic disequilibrium in a recessionary direction, was to bring about the huge overshoot downwards of the euro, fuelling a later troubling increase in inflation (to above the target level) which crippled euro-area economic recovery prospects in the very early-2000s.

ECB policymakers puffed and fumed about many subjects during the precipitous decline of the euro in 1999–2000. ECB President Duisenberg, in Don Quixote fashion, took on the title of Mr Euro shooting in all directions. But there is no evidence to suggest that the ECB's top official and his policymaking colleagues realized even in part they were largely to blame through the pursuit of a destabilizing monetary policy, that of breathing a higher rate of inflation into the euro-area economy.

At a time when the euro was a totally new currency, incipient weakness could be interpreted by anxious investors as revealing only feeble fundamental demand for the euro as a store of value given its potential flaws. Hence a monetary blunder by the ECB in triggering an initial fall (of the euro) could become the source of a confidence crisis in the new currency, which is what occurred!

ECB follows astrology (econometrics based on dubious data)

Also the speculative temperature in real estate markets in some member countries did begin to warm (most of all in Holland at this early stage of EMU but also elsewhere) around this time (1999–2000). In most cases, though, the temperature rise was from low temperate or even cool levels (as for France). In any event, the ECB in choosing to target the movement of a particularly simplistic definition of the price level (euro-area CPI), which excluded almost altogether the price of housing (whether in capital or rental terms), removed itself one stage further from housing market developments.

ECB policymakers realized the problems of definition with euro-area CPI (and how it would fail to pick up a rise of residential space occupancy costs, surely an important component of the overall price level for goods and services) but made no urgent effort in the following years to bring about an improvement.

Yes, there were research papers, speeches and working groups (including national statistical office representation) on the issue, but no strong direction from Frankfurt to get things moving! The hesitancy to back intuition (admittedly in short supply, it seems, around central bank policymaking tables, including that in Frankfurt) about the big picture and instead to follow statistics of evident low quality (as in the case of euro-area productivity and indeed of CPI), while emphasizing the output of the 'high-quality and high-powered econometric model' constructed within the Economic Research Directorate, were flaws in policymaking by the Frankfurt-based monetary bureaucracy which appeared repeatedly (and most dramatically in 2007–8, see pp. 131–2).

Monetary error of 2003–5

Then there was the second 'breathing in inflation' error when in spring 2003 the ECB indicated its concern that year-on-year rises in the HICP might soon fall significantly below 2%. Yet considerations of overall monetary equilibrium at the time suggested that observed price level rises should have fallen well below 2% and that such a fall would still have been consistent with 'price level stability' in the very long-run (not the misleading 'medium-term' of the ECB official-speak), even where this were defined as a path where prices on average, say over a 10-year period, were around 10–20% higher than over the average of the prior 10-year period (the equivalent of an average price level rise of say 1.5% p.a.).

It is true that ECB officials remained dubious about the hypothesis of a secular increase in productivity growth. This hypothesis was an important basis of the Austrian critique that the rate of price level rise, appropriately adjusted for quality improvements as in Germany (but not in several other smaller member countries of EMU), for several years should be well below any very long-run aim for this. Another basis for that same critique was the view that the IT revolution was lowering the equilibrium level of nominal wages for performing routine-type jobs which could now be replaced in considerable part by computers and cheaper foreign labour. This downward pressure on wages in an important segment of the labour market should have gone along with the path of goods and services prices falling for some considerable time below its long-run trajectory. The attempt of the monetary authority, in this case the ECB, to resist that undershooting would fuel asset price inflation.

In sum, the big picture was still one of IT revolution in progress and even cheaper imports from China and other emerging market economies whether in East Asia or Eastern Europe. Together these should have gone along with a period of euro-area inflation below the long-run aim of 2% p.a. (though the extent of undershoot might be under-estimated in so far as statistics offices in the smaller member countries failed to practise hedonistic accounting and these latter were actually sharing in the productivity spurt so recognizable in Germany). And nowhere in the ECB analysis published at the time does there emerge the notion of a benign cyclical swing downwards in the price level (or of the rate of price level increase falling below the long-run average aim for this). The cyclical situation, though, was evolving from 2003 onwards, as the euro-area economies in aggregate started to re-bound from the recession of 2001–3.

The spring 2003 re-affirmation and tightened specification of an explicit 2% p.a. inflation target (forward-looking over a two-year period) by the ECB coincided with dramatic monetary news in the US.

The Federal Reserve under the special prompting of Professor Ben Bernanke (appointed a governor in 2002) decided in favour of a policy of 'breathing inflation back into the US economy' for fear of inflation falling too far (towards zero rather than near the unofficial target level of 2% p.a.). This was the first time in US monetary history that the Federal Reserve shifted policy towards deliberately raising the rate of inflation (from an already positive level).

The key role of Ben Bernanke in pushing for the implementation of this policy is found in the transcript of policy discussions of that time published in full in May 2009. Professor Bernanke was particularly impressed by the 'paralysis of deflation' in Japan, evidently unaware of the possibility as highlighted later by Professor Sakakibara that this country never suffered monetary deflation (defined as a fall in the price level driven by monetary disequilibrium) at all in the 1990s. The alternative explanation – to monetary deflation – for the transitory episodes of a falling Japanese price level during the 'lost decade' and beyond was the combination of first a benign cyclical fall in prices during recession and second a good deflation driven by both rapid economic integration between Japan and China and the IT revolution.

The doomed 2003 revision of ECB monetary framework

The ECB's announcements in spring 2003 (in effect a clarification that the ECB would seek to forestall any significant dip of the price level path as measured over two-year periods significantly below 2% p.a. and would be as vigilant in this as in preventing any rise above) got less media notice (still substantial!) than the Federal Reserve's. This was at least in part understandable as the rate of increase in the euro-area CPI was coasting at around the target level (albeit that the price level in Germany was virtually stable in underlying terms – see below). Hence the policy shift was less obvious in Frankfurt than in Washington (where it was not a question of forestalling a possible decline in inflation below its present level in line with target level – as in the euro-area – but of pushing up the rate of price level increase from a rate – around 1% p.a. – already deemed to be too low).

The ECB in effect reiterated (in spring 2003) that it would block the equilibrium forces emanating from accelerated productivity growth, terms of trade improvement, accelerated globalization made possible by information technology, business cycle weakness, which were pressing the rate of price level increase down below 2% (as would have happened if market rates were following a path closer to neutral level rather than being driven far below by present and expected future rate-pegging in the money market). Yet this was a period when the IT revolution was still in full swing, even if its effects were not being fully registered by most statistics offices in the member countries outside Germany. Hence for a second time (as in its opening formulation in 1998 as described above) the ECB, in revising in spring 2003 its monetary framework, totally failed to distance itself and tread a different path from the flawed policies being adopted on the opposite side of the Atlantic (and the English Channel).

The 2003 decision to resist any fall of inflation seriously below 2% p.a. was a critical factor in the creation of asset price inflation and its culmination in credit and real estate bubbles.

The 2003 decision was taken in a situation where on some measures (excluding the price of public goods and services) the underlying price level in Germany was indeed falling slightly. The IMF, headed by an ex-senior finance official in the German government (Horst Koehler), and advised by Chief Economic Counsellor (Kenneth Rogoff), was warning ominously about the dire state of the German economy and about 'deflationary dangers' there.

The coincidence of a dark mood concerning German economic prospects with a monetary blunder at the level of the euro-area as a whole is one piece of evidence (among many others) in support of the next point in the indictment.

ECB makes policy for Germany, not for euro-area

At several critical junctures for ECB monetary policymaking, German-centric factors have influenced decision-making to an extraordinary extent (well beyond the weight of the Germany economy in the total euro-area economy).

Professor Mundell's quip that in a monetary union policy is made for the largest member (for example, New South Wales in Australia, Ontario in Canada) applies also to the euro-area despite all the protestation of European political correctness. Further evidence is reviewed in detail in subsequent chapters to support this charge at three crucial periods. The first of these three periods was on the eve of the euro's launch and during its first year (1998–9) when one influence behind the decision to ease monetary policy despite overall solid economic expansion amid a golden low rate of inflation at the euro-area level was the underperformance of the German economy. This underperformance was in part due to the continuing slump in the construction industry following the post unification boom (bubble) and in part to the repeated upward adjustments of the Deutsche mark during the life of the now defunct European Monetary System (EMS), well beyond what could be justified by differential inflation.

The second period encompasses the reformulation of monetary framework in spring 2003 already described and the subsequent three years or so experience of over-stimulatory (non-neutral) monetary policy continuing despite symptoms of monetary disequilibrium, such as real estate and credit markets heating up in Spain, France, Italy and several smaller economies.

These events occurred when Germany was still experiencing a construction sector downturn and its real estate markets were still soft. From a business cycle perspective, Germany was in a relatively weak situation compared to the other euro-area countries. There was concern within Germany about business investment remaining weak overall due to the re-location of production into cheap labour countries to the East (most of which were soon to come into the EU). Inflation as measured in Germany was at the bottom end of the range for euro-area members. German banks were, with the benefit of hindsight, getting heavily drawn into the warming up global credit markets (both within Europe and outside), but that was not registering on any market or official monitoring device.

The third period during which German economic conditions assumed over-proportionate influence on policymaking (with the Bundesbank President, Professor Axel Weber, and the ECB chief economist, Professor

Jürgen Stark – himself an ex-Bundesbanker – both very influential) was in the aftermath of the first big credit quake of summer 2007 and continuing into almost all of 2008 (except possibly for the last few weeks of that year). It seemed then to the Bundesbank (and to the main forecasting institutes) that the German economy was still in a strong growth phase despite the big slowdown elsewhere in the euro-area (and beyond).

In the first quarter of 2008 coincident economic indicators (these lag somewhat behind reality!) suggested Germany was in a boom driven by exports to the oil-exporting countries (including Russia) and other commodity exporters (in the midst of a commodity bubble), Eastern Europe, and China in particular. (Later events and data were to show that the Bundesbankers were remarkably slow in realizing the downturn of German overall business conditions, which had set in already in spring 2008. And their concerns about the oil price bubble spilling over into wage–cost inflation – a perennial fear among the Bundesbankers – turned out to be fantasy).

It is too early to judge whether the ECB rate cut of November 2013 at a time when the Bundesbank judged the German economy to be operating at near full stretch, implemented despite the opposition of the Germans in the ECB Council (the Bundesbank president and the German board member) and their close allies (Dutch and Austrian central bankers), should be regarded as an exception to the rule or the start of a new trend. Chancellor Merkel's continued refusal to back the Bundesbank's position on EMU issues (first the Greek bail-out, later the outright monetary purchase program – see Chapter 7) might have contributed to this loss of German influence within the ECB. More generally what has been perceived by Bundesbankers, ex-Bundesbankers and their allies within the ECB policymaking council, as the best monetary path from a German-centric viewpoint has not always turned out to be so when Time has made its full revelation. And this applies in particular to the failure of the Bundesbank along with the ECB to realize the extent of the credit bubble which was building up in the euro-area from 2003 onwards, the particular role in that of the rapidly expanding inter-bank market, and the fact that German banks were becoming dangerously exposed even though the real estate market in Germany remained cool or cold.

German savings surplus swamped infant euro-credit market

It would be wrong to put all the blame for the euro-roots (there were strong US roots also!) of the global credit bubble at the door of the ECB or even more narrowly of the Bundesbankers and ex-Bundesbankers and their allies who have sat as policymakers around its table.

Some part of the blame can be attributed to flaws in the very essence of EMU.

The coming together into monetary union in 1999 of Germany, where the savings surplus was set to bulge (a corollary of continuing construction sector wind-down and transfer of some stages of manu-facturing production to the newly opened-up cheap labour countries to the East), with large countries (especially Spain) where construction activity was set to boom and savings deficits widen (households there responding to the historic opportunity of low interest rates superseding the high interest rates which had been associated with pesetas, liras and until recently French francs) was bound to create testing conditions for central bankers, bankers and financial markets. All three failed the test. The biggest failure was monetary. The invisible hands of market forces can be counted upon to distribute efficiently surplus savings in one area of a monetary union to deficit areas (whether inside the union or outside), but only in the context of monetary stability. In fact the ECB presided over growing monetary instability.

The one-size-fits-all monetary policy meant that the price level would climb fastest in those countries that were now in the swing of construc-tion boom and where savings deficits were expanding. The rise in price level would be at a much lower rate (if even positive) in the main country (Germany) moving in the opposite direction (savings surplus rising). Correspondingly real interest rates (as measured with reference to relevant national price level expectations) in the economies in construction boom and widening savings deficits could bizarrely fall to significantly negative levels. This fall of real rates in Spain and other savings-deficit economies exposed them to the danger of violent business cycle fluctuation (at first boom, later bust) along the route to full integration with Europe.

The formation of monetary union in itself was virtually pre-programmed to increase the potential divergence of savings surpluses and deficits between Germany and the other countries. Without union, a lower level of interest rates in Germany than elsewhere (especially those European countries in big savings deficits), with that rate differential between the Deutsche mark and foreign monies reflecting both exchange rate expec-tations and exchange risk premium, would have kept the divergence (in equilibrium) between savings surpluses and deficits across Europe within tighter limits.

Those tighter limits are not self-evidently a 'good thing'. In terms of neoclassical economic modelling, the removal of barriers (including exchange risk) to capital flows leads to a more efficient allocation of resources between the countries participating in the union. Scarce capital goes to a greater extent towards the biggest investment opportunities. (On the other hand such benefits might be outweighed by the costs of sacrificing monetary independence).

In practice the explosion of recycling in the form of German savings surpluses being channelled into the savings deficit countries (the largest of which by far was Spain) inside and outside EMU (especially Eastern Europe) went along with a growing potential credit problem. In principle this problem would be exacerbated by monetary instability in so far as it generated asset price inflation meaning considerable irrational exuberance at large.

Were the lenders to (including depositors), or equity investors in, those intermediaries who were active in the transfer of capital (out of the savings surplus countries, especially Germany, into the savings deficit countries) taking sufficient note of the credit risks involved (related to the capacity to service debt of the borrowers in the savings deficit countries)? Were the intermediaries charging sufficiently for assuming the credit risk and controlling their exposure to this risk adequately? And was the ECB – or any other authority with responsibility within EMU – on due alert to the dangers of potential malfunctioning, especially overheating of credit markets in the euro-area, related to this recycling process and thereby even more determined to foster conditions of monetary stability?

An important element in the flow of capital was German banks lending surplus funds (excess of deposits over loans) into the Spanish banking system – sometimes on a secured basis (via the purchase of so-called covered bonds where the loan from the German financial institution to the Spanish bank was secured by a portfolio of mortgages on Spanish real estate).

Subsequent events starting with the credit quake of summer 2007 revealed that the banks, and investors in or lenders to the banks, stimulated into varying degrees of irrational exuberance by monetary instability, underestimated the risks and overestimated the likely returns related to such 'inter-bank loans' within the euro-area context or indeed as between the euro-area and EU countries outside the euro-area (in the latter case this had nothing to do with the transfer problem generated directly by the coming together of savings surplus and deficit countries in monetary union). The largest of the latter group was the UK.

Under the complex rules which described the procedures for ECB money market operations, the new central bank's secured lending operations extended to subsidiaries in the euro-area of non–euro area banks and the security could take the form of eligible assets in any EU country, even if not a member of monetary union (by far the biggest example was the UK). Hence a British bank subsidiary in France (or any other euro-area country) could present parcels of asset-backed paper based on UK residential mortgages for discounting at the ECB.

British banks became huge borrowers in the exponentially growing euro-money markets towards financing the UK real estate and credit bubbles. They covered the currency mismatch (between euro borrowing and Sterling lending) by entering into sterling–euro currency swaps (buying pounds spot for euros and selling the pounds forward for euros).

The ultimate buyers of pounds in the forward market (from the British banks) were most plausibly in many cases the carry traders who were shorting the yen (and sometimes Swiss francs) against high coupon currencies (in this case the pound) so as to gain thereby from the large interest rate spread between the two currencies. The carry trade in the yen was booming because the Bank of Japan was steering an ultra-easy monetary policy so as to prevent its currency appreciating against the dollar in the context of the Greenspan-Bernanke Fed trying to breathe inflation back into the US economy. The counterpart sale of pounds in the spot market came to a considerable extent out of the mega-trade deficit of the UK.

No diagnosis of monetary disequilibrium despite rising credit market temperature

There is no evidence from ECB statements (including speeches by its Board members) during the years of booming euro-credit business in all its forms that officials realized the speculative temperature in euro-credit markets was climbing fast and likely to culminate in a bubble or burst. And there is no evidence that officials realized the importance of monetary stability in its widest sense towards reducing the danger of temperature rise, or the particularly high level of this danger which emanated from the starting situation of EMU.

Nor is there any evidence that the ECB was monitoring the particular credit risks which emanated from the huge savings divergence between Germany on the one hand and the countries in construction boom (and real estate boom) on the other (including the UK, via the channels described).

ECB officials could claim that monetary policymakers had no role in spotting bubbles in advance and should come in only to clear up afterwards. That after all was the so-called Blinder doctrine followed by the Federal Reserve under Alan Greenspan and subsequently Ben Bernanke. But the doctrine was flawed. Even if central bankers were no better than anyone else at spotting possible bubbles they should by profession realize that monetary disequilibrium is the fuel to possible rises in speculative temperature many of which do not end up in bubble but nonetheless result in considerable economic waste (malinvestment and ultimately a sickness of equity risk appetite). And in the pursuance of monetary stability the central bankers should allow market forces to operate freely in determining market interest rates, without continuously hectoring as to where they intend to peg money market rates over time. The invisible hands would tend to pre-empt violent temperature rises even before central bankers or anyone else could be sure that these have occurred.

The ECB should have done better than the Federal Reserve.

One aim of the EMU was to conduct monetary policy in a way superior to that which was possible before union given the new degree of freedom from external influence (attributable to an enlarged monetary area). No independent European well-designed and well-tested monetary doctrine emerged.

Instead the ECB in practice largely copied the flawed US framework of monetary control, and to such an extent that critically it failed to react to growing symptoms of severe monetary instability in the form of temperature rise in credit and asset markets.

The ECB had no power directly to cool credit markets via raising margin requirements or minimum loan to value ratios, in contrast to some such authority (albeit very clumsy and never used in modern times) possessed by the Federal Reserve. Much more importantly (than blunderbuss control actions), the ECB could have been vigilant that the 'machinery of money' was not getting out of control, taking account of the danger that credit markets could be warming up, even though overall inflation was still running at 'no more than' 2% p.a. ECB Board Members could have given speeches highlighting the dangers of the situation and remonstrating with private capital markets to use more acumen in judging the value of bank equity and debt; or they could have remonstrated with the national central banks to raise margin requirements on risky real estate lending.

None of this happened. One reason was what we might describe as *euro-nationalism* (defined p. 71) and euro-euphoria.

ECB officials wrongly diagnosed many of the possible symptoms of rising temperature in credit markets as indications that the euro was indeed taking off as international money and that euro financial market integration was flourishing.

This wrong diagnosis was not limited to the ECB.

Capital markets – and especially equity markets – applauded (and rewarded in terms of share price) banks which were rapidly expanding on the assumption that they were seizing the opportunities in a brave new world of euro-led financial integration, rather than realizing that hidden leverage and increasingly risky and under-priced credit positions were being assumed. Froth in capital market prices stemming from below-neutral interest rates fuelled the positive feedback loops about which the behavioural finance theorists wrote. Banks and investment houses which piled into the government debt markets of Portugal, Greece, Ireland and Spain, to earn a little extra income compared to what they could get on German government bonds, and in many cases doing so on a highly leveraged basis, gained popularity with their stake-holders (as reflected in their share market performance or in the new client business which flowed to them). There was little room in markets fired by monetary disequilibrium for long-term doubts about future solvency to affect present prices. Amid the safe interest income famine created by the Federal Reserve and ECB there was a desperation for yield.

Euro launch spurred irrational exuberance about banks

The launch of EMU did not make it inevitable that such inefficient use of knowledge and bad judgement (as just described) should occur in European capital markets concerning the apparent successes of rapidly expanding bank groups and the quality of credit. But such dangers rose with the launch.

The creation of a new monetary regime, EMU, just when the temperature in global credit markets was about to start rising under the influence of growing US monetary disequilibrium, and its accompaniment in the form of drum-beating (whether by officials, analysts, journalists) about the big new opportunities which financial market integration in Europe would bring, increased the danger of various psychological behaviour patterns becoming prevalent. These are described by behavioural finance theorists and summarized under the well-known catch phrases of speculative displacement, irrational exuberance, learning processes. They help power credit bubble formation. The ultimate source of power though is monetary disequilibrium which leads to these psychological patterns becoming prevalent.

ECB officials out of misguided pride became cheerleaders in the credit warming process. They were too ready to read euro success and broadcast this rather than first examining more sinister explanations for the apparent good news. A particular illustration of this was the unqualified praise which ECB officials gave to the outward signs of rapid financial market integration in Europe – whether fast growth in the inter-bank and wholesale overnight money markets, or the growth of a euro-denominated corporate bond market, or in the rapid diversification of government bond portfolios (for example Dutch or German investors disposing of domestic government bonds and buying slightly higher yielding government bonds issued by the periphery zone countries) together with the narrowing of yield spreads between the different government bond markets. If not cheerleading they should have been worrying why the bond markets were no longer discriminating between sound and unsound member government debt profiles through time and asking whether this was symptomatic of monetary disequilibrium.

In praising uncritically the take-off of the euro-denominated corporate bond market (on one occasion the claim was that new issues were now outpacing those in the US), ECB officials failed to realize that an extraordinarily large share of such paper was being issued by banks (flashing red as regards leverage ratios) and the extent to which the bonds were being bought by highly leveraged non-bank financial intermediaries (especially hedge funds) at remarkably low credit spreads. In effect their search for evidence of euro-success led them astray in their monitoring of speculative temperature (and solvency risks) in the euro-area financial system for signs that the disease of asset price inflation was present.

The integration of two big countries into EMU right at the start – Italy and Spain – where typically high interest rates and other restrictions had held back mortgage credit growth for decades before set the stage for financial intermediary institutions in those countries to experience rapid business growth. In turn the high profits growth for the leading banks in Spain and Italy helped fuel the speculative temperature rise in their equity markets along with their climb (by aggressive merger and acquisitions) to the top (in size) of leading euro-wide institutions.

There is no evidence that the ECB or capital markets became wary about the risks implicit in the rapid ascent to euro-area (and indeed global) stardom of Spanish or Italian banks. Instead the capital markets fell into the trap (in part created by monetary disequilibrium) of reading rapid expansion of domestic banks in Spain, Italy or elsewhere in the euro-area as evidence of a genuine renaissance in the 'European financial space', applauding the emergence of newly efficient and profitable global players.

Such exaggerated optimism in the context of 'speculative displacement' (the term is found in the Aliber–Kindleberger analysis of bubbles followed by their bursting and refers to a big change in the economic or political environment which is followed by a jump in Knightian uncertainty which sometimes eventually stimulates various forms of irrationality), always in part fuelled by monetary disequilibrium, is a well-known feature recognized by students of bubbles through the ages (see Kindleberger–Aliber, 2005). In this case, the replacement of various second-order high-coupon currencies by a new global currency, the low-coupon euro, was the speculative displacement.

Euro-nationalists and Quai d'Orsay gain control

The excitement created by the new money and the opportunities which it could bring to financial institutions in the integrating European space was distinct from *euro-nationalism*. This latter phenomenon features in particular enthusiasm about the reduction in US hegemony – economic, financial and geo-political – which EMU might achieve.

Euro-nationalism, perhaps an inevitable outgrowth of EMU, has led the ECB into expensive errors with respect to its G-7 diplomacy and has also gone along with a systematic under-estimation of European economic vulnerability to US economic and financial developments.

In fact euro-nationalism, with its evident pitfalls, was pre-programmed as a feature within the ECB by the virtually pre-arranged appointment of Jean-Claude Trichet as the second President.

According to the deal between French President Chirac and German Chancellor Kohl at the May 1998 EU Summit, Germany's strong preference as President, Wilhelm Duisenberg, was to be succeeded by Jean-Claude Trichet with the change-over to take place well before the end of the eight-year term of office.

Already identifiable as a euro-nationalist from his long career as top French economic diplomat, it was predictable that he would use his office to push forward an agenda long popular in the Quai d'Orsay (French foreign office) of combating US monetary hegemony.

This agenda was a component of the wider French policy aim described as multi-polarity, evident for example in the special relationship – albeit intermittent – between Paris and Beijing.

M. Trichet's big opportunity to push forward the euro-nationalist agenda came with the Dubai G-7 summit in autumn 2003. In the context of an already weak dollar against the euro (which the ECB was attributing to the US mega current account deficit and its counterpart in 'too low US savings' rather than to the fundamental source of US monetary disequilibrium), M. Trichet embraced the case (suddenly being put forward by the Bush Administration responding to protectionist pressure in Congress most of all vis-à-vis China) for East Asian currency appreciation.

The idea of breaking up the dollar bloc in East Asia was superficially attractive also from a trade viewpoint for Europe, which could gain competitiveness (in Asia) from the 'inevitable' (in the view of M. Trichet and his economist advisers at the Banque de France) appreciation of currencies there. That would help compensate for the toll on European export competitiveness from the dollar depreciation that had been occurring. And so M. Trichet formed an unholy alliance with the currency populists in Washington to demand a break-up of the Asian dollar bloc, meaning in particular that Beijing should unpeg its currency against the US dollar and make sure it climbed – far from inevitable if all exchange restrictions were to be lifted and official intervention halted simultaneously!

In dealing with China, M. Trichet had to be duly sensitive to Paris's special relationship with Beijing. In consequence, he and his colleagues in French diplomacy presented themselves as forging a middle way – advocating a milder path of currency adjustment than the path Washington neo-mercantilists were putting forward!

ECB joined fateful Washington assault on Asian dollar bloc

There is no evidence to suggest that any serious debate occurred around the ECB policymaking table about whether it would be of overall benefit to the euro-area for the Asian dollar bloc to disintegrate. And even if there had been a debate, there is no record of a strong alternative view within the ECB. No policymaker there was publicly taking issue with the mantra about global imbalances and the prescription that Asian surplus countries should take steps (including an appreciation of their currencies) to lower their savings surpluses while Washington implemented 'structural policies' to raise the US level of savings. And no one was arguing instead that the fundamental malaise (including the fall of the dollar) was US monetary disequilibrium as generated by the Greenspan Fed now under the influence of its new board member from Princeton University, Ben Bernanke. This collective failure is a big blot on the ECB's policymaking record.

What was the alternative view which could have been considered, and might well have entered the European policy debate, in an environment less closed to hostile criticism?

A robust and frictionless capital outflow between the huge savings surplus countries of East Asia and the biggest savings deficit country the US – such as would occur within the context of a dollar bloc where exchange risk was only slight – was beneficial also for Europe. The break-up of the dollar bloc in itself would introduce huge new uncertainties into the global flow of funds. In principle the emergence of exchange risk between East Asia and the US would mean a fall in the equilibrium level of interest rates in the former and a rise in the latter together with a rise in the East Asian currencies and fall of the US dollar.

Who, though, had the least idea of where the new equilibrium levels would be? In the interim there was likely to be an extended learning process in the marketplace, such as accompanies any such major 'speculative displacement' (in the Kindleberger–Aliber sense of a huge change in the economic, financial or political environment – see p. 71). Surely the danger loomed of this process fuelling speculative runs (especially in the dollar exchange rate)?

Was there not enough monetary uncertainty in the world already through the launching of EMU and the change of monetary frameworks announced by both the ECB and the Federal Reserve in spring 2003 without adding the break-up of the Asian dollar bloc to the list?

Dollar plunge leads ECB policy astray in 2004

The further plunge of the dollar which developed as a consequence of the 'successful' ECB–Washington demarche at the Dubai summit (towards breaking up the Asian dollar bloc) and of the growing US monetary disequilibrium (as the Greenspan/Bernanke proceeded to raise its interest rate peg at a glacial pace from an abnormally low level) led ECB monetary policy seriously astray and laid the seeds of a future global force of instability – an explosive bubble in the yen carry trade.

There is an accumulation of evidence to suggest that one factor at play around the ECB policy board which delayed any tightening of monetary stance already in 2004 despite evidence suggesting excess monetary ease (including the heating up real estate markets in several member countries) was the strength of the euro against the dollar, itself exacerbated by the break-up of the Asian dollar bloc.

During the episode of intense dollar weakness in 2003–4, the ECB put too much weight on the exchange rate (primarily of the dollar against the euro) in terms of judging the overall appropriateness of its monetary stance and not enough on other factors (for example monetary data, evidence of – or perceived danger of – asset price inflation in various key credit or real estate markets).

The break-up of the Asian dollar bloc also laid the seeds of the future yen carry trade bubble. The Bank of Japan, out of fright at the super-strong yen triggered by the Dubai summit (on top of over-stimulatory US monetary stance), continued to pursue its novel zero rate and quantitative easing policies. Then in early 2006 the Bank of Japan introduced its own anaemic and abridged form of inflation targeting. This was used to justify manipulating interest rates in Japan along a sub-neutral path rather than boldly adopting a framework of monetary stability untarnished by contemporary fashion in the US and Europe. The engendering of monetary disequilibrium in Japan in turn stimulated powerfully the yen carry trade into the zone of irrational exuberance.

The overheated yen carry trade became one of the catalysts to credit market temperature rise not just in many East Asian countries (especially South Korea) but also in Europe (in hot real estate markets and private equity markets) and in particular in the emerging market economies of Central Europe.

European banks, riding a wave of enthusiasm in the equity and debt markets about their long-term profit outlooks as enlarged in particular by euro-induced financial integration in Europe, became aggressive participants in a new emerging market loan business (of which Central Europe was the epicentre, but also including East Asia), an area of business which US banks were avoiding this time round. In addition, European banks became huge participants in the US credit boom – including a whole range of what were to become 'toxic assets'.

This was the first time since the late nineteenth century that European investors had got sucked into a US credit bubble. With no natural dollar deposit base to match, European banks became critically dependent on funding themselves in overnight and very short-maturity dollar repo markets where the lenders were in large part US money market funds desperately seeking interest income amid the famine of safe income as engendered by the Greenspan/Bernanke Federal Reserve.

There is no evidence that ECB officials during this period (mid-2000s) were aware or pointing to the dangers related to European banks' high involvement in foreign – and especially US – credit booms. Instead they gave speeches about how in the new age of the euro, European countries had indeed gained a new degree of independence from US economic or financial shock. Exactly the opposite was the reality.

The ECB failed totally to recognize the extent of US–European financial interdependence under its watch (common exposure to a deadly asset price inflation virus of joint monetary creation). It also exaggerated the degree of economic independence that monetary union had brought.

ECB repeatedly underestimates danger (for Europe) of US recession

On the eve and into the early stages of both recessions in the first decade of monetary union (early 2001 and early/mid 2008), the ECB repeated the same error of assessing that the euro-area economy could avoid being dragged down by a sharp US downturn (disputing that the euro-area economy was subject to the same forces that were pulling the US economy down). Policy at a critical cyclical turning point fell far behind the curve.

In the case of the recession which started in the US in November 2007, heralded by the US growth recession (defined as a period of below trend but still positive growth) from mid-2006 to early 2007 and later much more loudly by the global credit market quake of July/August 2007, the ECB at first denied that the euro-area economies would follow suit. During the growth-recession phase, the ECB was firmly on the side of the economic optimists, predicting no hard landing in the US nor severe downturn in its real estate market.

In late 2007 and early 2008 there may have been some divergence of view within the ECB about the economic outlook (with the Bundesbankers and ex-Bundesbankers remaining optimistic) but key officials could agree on a continuing tough monetary stance due to their common concern that sky-high oil and commodity prices would drive up inflation. That toughness is evident from the juxtaposition of the actual risk-free interest rate (as proxied say by the one-year yield on German government bonds) rising at the same time as the credit bubble was bursting. The latter development surely meant a big drop in the equilibrium risk-free rate (together with a much wider than normal spread of risky rates above the risk-free rate).

The ECB policymakers in deciding to toughen their monetary stance through the first three quarters of 2008 completely failed to put a substantial probability on there being an oil price bubble and on this bursting endogenously. That in itself is not the most serious criticism, as we should hardly expect that monetary bureaucrats are at the forefront of identifying bubbles. More seriously they should have considered the likelihood that the spike in oil prices was a late symptom of the asset price inflation disease whose source was earlier global monetary excess. They should have known from history that by the time these late symptoms appear strong forces are likely to be already at work creating the subsequent asset price deflation (and recession). The quakes in the credit markets during summer and autumn 2007 should have alerted them to a totally different situation of emerging financial panic and sharp temperature fall in credit markets (apparent to all).

The evidence of public statements suggests that ECB officials saw the leap to the sky of oil and other commodity prices in late 2007 and early 2008 as essentially goods and services inflation. They did not conceptualize this phenomenon as most likely a late appearance of asset price inflation in one sector of the global marketplace (commodities) which had previously in this cycle remained temperate. The most likely underlying cause of the sudden temperature was severe monetary disequilibrium in the past rather than the present. Evidence of massive financial speculation in the oil market, with US investment houses playing a lead role, should have alerted ECB officials to the likelihood that irrational exuberance under the influence of earlier monetary disequilibrium was responsible. The perennial question for monetary policymakers is whether by taking action against asset price inflation which has been long in appearing they actually make the subsequent downturn in the economy worse than it would be otherwise. Records do not show that any of this was a subject for discussion around the ECB policymakers' table.

No consideration of alternative strategies in wake of credit quake

It seems that the credit quake of July/August 2007 took ECB policymakers to a large degree by surprise, even though they appreciated that credit markets had long been warm or hot in the sense of credit spreads being abnormally low. The biggest surprise to ECB policymakers was the extent to which European banks were participants in the US section of the credit bubble and how far this participation had been hidden in off balance-sheet entities, so-called structured investment vehicles or SIVs.

As the European inter-bank markets became suddenly submerged in crisis (many banks finding it impossible to roll-over borrowings in inter-bank market except, in some cases, at lofty premiums to normal rates and in other cases not at all, on August 9 in reaction to news of BNP Paribas freezing three of its investment funds and the rescue of Europe's highest profile sub-prime casualty IKB (with the high-risk debt in a SIV), the ECB ordered that the taps be opened wide – meaning that the ECB should offer unlimited funds (against eligible) collateral at the then overnight rate of above 4% p.a.

The ECB decision of 9 August 2007 (reached by telephone conference between the policymaking officials with anecdotal evidence suggesting that the Bundesbank played a key coordinating role) to make massive secured loans to any bank on demand at a rate near to the actual unchanged official rate appears to have been taken without any consideration of the main alternative plan of action and without any consideration of the exit strategy.

It is also obvious (with supporting evidence) that those making the decision wrongly diagnosed the source of the crisis as a liquidity shortage rather than an eruption of insolvency danger. Yet any reading of financial history should have suggested to the ECB policymakers that a liquidity crisis is usually linked to a solvency crisis. Some of the institutions suddenly unable to borrow are indeed insolvent. If the ECB were to now make loans to a range of institutions which turned out to be insolvent it could find itself in effect acting as a transfer agent taking funds from financially strong countries in the union to bail out insolvent institutions in financially weak countries. As illustration, already in summer 2007 there was widespread awareness of a possible credit bubble in Spain and ECB officials might have imagined the possibility that part of the Spanish banking system might turn out to be insolvent. If the ECB used the strength of its own balance sheet as effectively guaranteed by taxpayers in Germany, France and Holland, to make massive loans to Spanish banks, it would have turned itself into a transfer agent. That would be totally against the spirit of the Maastricht Treaty, which had created a monetary union without any fiscal or wider political union. Moreover the ECB was not at all obviously obliged under the Maastricht Treaty to act as so-called lender of last resort. The Treaty seemed to put this responsibility (of lender of last resort) on national authorities.

The alternative action plan would have been to immediately cut the rate on the overnight deposit facility at the ECB to zero (in response to the crisis in the inter-bank funding markets) while imposing a premium charge on secured lending above a given quota amount to any bank (and this charge would rise with the amount of excess over the quota subject to an overall limit related to the size of the bank). Larger premiums would apply to any extraordinary unsecured lending by the ECB, subject to limits on a case-by-case basis. Beyond the limits set for emergency lending (which would have been only modest), banks would have had to apply immediately for emergency assistance from their own national governments. The ECB would have resisted any pressure from governments to make loans in advance of such assistance out of justifiable caution that once having gone down that route its independence would become fatally wounded and it could be attacked for in fact imposing ultimate burdens on taxpayers in the financially strongest countries, inconsistent with the Maastricht Treaty.

Under this plan, the yield on short-maturity high-quality European sovereign bonds would have collapsed simultaneously to near zero under the pressure of those banks with excess reserves seeking any alternative risk-free outlet to leaving them at the ECB (where they would now earn zero). In the wholesale money markets, there would have been an instantaneous fanning out of rates – with those banks recognized as less weak being able to attract non-insured funds at very low rates (only a little above zero) while those seen as weak (or under suspicion) having to pay rates well above the official repo rate applicable to normal size borrowing from the ECB.

Given the wide spread which would have immediately developed between rates on low-risk deposits and higher-risk inter-bank or wholesale lending, the banks with excess reserves or non-banks with an appetite for risk-arbitrage would have ploughed some funds towards the weaker banks or towards money market-type paper (on which the yields would be well above risk-free level).

There would have been a cluster of financial institutions which could not have satisfied their funding needs even at high rates in the private markets – except to some limited degree in secured repo markets where a procedure for placing collateral including paper of so-called top quality backed by mortgages was already in place (this market itself froze up at the worst point of the crisis) – and who would have been borrowers at premium rates from the ECB up to the limits which it set for such assistance.

In turn, the ECB would have had to decide (in conjunction with national authorities in the member countries) whether to continue such emergency lending to the very weak institutions or to insist on restructuring. (The options would range from an injection of government capital to a liquidation process in which a government entity would take over a bank's loan assets while selling the deposits – the goodwill element – to another stronger bank while wiping out the troubled bank's shareholders and bondholders.)

ECB officials remained in a state of denial about the extent of insolvency risk related to the European home-grown credit bubble (hot real

estate markets in Spain, UK, France, Eastern Europe, Holland) or to a
more general participation in emerging market loans or private equity
boom and well into 2008 continued to stress that there was a crisis of
liquidity rather than potential insolvency among several major institutions. And as regards its money market operations, the ECB continued
to defy any market solution in the form of allowing spreads between
weak and less weak bank rates to widen (alongside a rise of rates on risk-
credits to non-banks), which would have produced a profit incentive to
re-capitalization.

In particular the less weak banks by issuing equity capital (a procedure which would have required full disclosure) and so reducing the
riskiness of their (non-insured) deposits (in that depositors would now
be protected by a larger equity cushion) would have been able to earn
widened margins on their on-lending whether to other (weaker) banks
or to non-banks.

Bogus separation principle

In their conduct of monetary policy from the quake of August 2007
through to the crunch of Autumn 2008 the ECB promulgated a bogus
doctrine called the separation principle. This led policy far astray from
an optimal position.

According to this doctrine, there should continue to be virtually only
one rate in the overnight market (rather than a span of rates applying
to institutions of now starkly different credit risk) and this rate should
continue to be pegged closely to the announced official repo rate. This
rate should be set as in normal times in line with inflation-targeting
requirements.

Separately, the amount of credit support operations (sterilized secured
lending to the banks) should be determined so as to maintain 'liquidity'
of the money markets and the rate applied on these operations should
be uniform for all and close to the official repo rate.

In fact, under the circumstances of inflamed risk perceptions and highly
heterogeneous credit-risk of differing financial institutions relevant even to
overnight borrowing, the separation principle aggravated disequilibrium.

In equilibrium, there would not in such circumstances be one rate in
the overnight market for all institutions. In the absence of intervention
to suppress differentials, there would be a wide span of rates – lowest for
the strongest financial institutions, highest for the weakest.

To allow the markets to function in this way, the ECB would have
abandoned the attempt to peg one overnight rate for all. Interest rates

on overnight deposits with itself would have been cut to zero. And the ECB would have added reserves (on an unsterilized basis) through open-market operation such as to meet any increased demand for excess reserves and so prevent a shortage of high-powered money developing which would have manifested itself in a wide range of risk-free rates (such as short-maturity government bonds or repo rates secured on government bonds) rising far above zero.

Quite to the contrary, at the peak of the financial crisis in September 2008, the ECB moved to narrow the band between its deposit rate (paid on excess reserves placed with it) and its marginal lending rate, re-doubling its efforts to peg one uniform overnight rate for all. Unsurprisingly this action in defiance of market forces resulted in a huge round-trip, where stronger institutions with excess reserves parked them at the ECB and the ECB in turn became the only marginal lender to the weaker institutions.

In applying the separation principle, the ECB lost total sight of a fundamental shift occurring in the pattern of equilibrium interest rates across the marketplace and so acted in a direction contrary to equilibrium tendencies, thereby intensifying the financial crisis and economic downturn.

The ECB was also acting in contradiction of the well-established monetary response during previous financial panics in history. Under the gold standard, or under subsequent paper money standards where reserves paid zero interest (the norm until the ECB's creation), the central bank would allow (unless blocked by the overriding obligation to defend the gold parity now under attack) risk-free rates on near-money assets (for example, short-maturity government bills) to fall towards zero under the pressure of funds seeking a safe haven, while pumping extra monetary base into the system so as to prevent any temporary shortage of reserves from developing (banks scrambling to increase excess reserves so as to protect themselves against panic withdrawal of funds), a manifestation of which would be a re-bound of risk-free rates of return on near-money assets such as T-bills or short-maturity government bonds.

In the presence of heightened risk aversion and increased credit risks, the equilibrium tendency was surely for the risk-free interest rate to fall relative to risky interest rates. On top, the overall lurching of the global economy towards recession (in fact US and Japanese recession had already started in November 2007 unknown to contemporary economic observers) meant that the average cost of capital across all risk-categories should surely be falling, so as to balance an increasing propensity to save with a decreasing propensity to spend.

Even leaving that last consideration aside and taking at face value (without criticism) the ECB's intent to steer market rates above neutral level so as to defend the euro-area against 'inflation dangers', it should still have been the case that the risk-free rate as represented by short-maturity government bond yields and overnight money rates (as applicable to the least weak financial institutions) would have been falling to very low levels. At the same time the risky rates applicable say to one-month or three-month inter-bank lending or repo lending secured by non-tip-top paper would have been rising.

In resisting this tendency by pegging an overnight rate and setting a high floor to the government bill rates (by offering unlimited access to its deposit facility at near the pegged rate) – and by effecting massive intervention on a sterilized basis in the term-secured lending markets (so as to stop riskier rates rising there) – the ECB acted as a destabilizing influence on the euro-area economy.

In fact, by applying the bogus separation principle, the ECB not only acted as an economic de-stabilizer but it magnified the amount of dis-equilibrium in the credit markets.

By preventing a fan of market rates widening out in the context of heightened credit risks, the ECB magnified the perceived job of 'liquidity maintenance', the misnomer for the recycling of funds on a sterilized basis (by the ECB) towards the weak institutions.

If the market had been allowed to operate freely, several channels of credit flow which in fact clogged up would have been kept clear under the power of much wider spreads.

Of course, as on so many issues, the ECB could claim that it was in good company. Other central banks, including the Federal Reserve, were following versions of the same separation principle, at least until late winter 2007/8 when the Bernanke Federal Reserve embarked on further rate cuts, albeit inadequate. As already emphasized, though, in these indictments, should not the ECB, as a new institution, have aimed to be above the crowd and especially to outperform the Federal Reserve?

In fact at this time (until late autumn 2008), reserves at the Federal Reserve were still zero interest bearing and so some of the automatic stabilizing behaviour of risk-free rates did occur there (with T-bill rates in particular falling to zero). It was late in the day that Professor Bernanke resolved to follow the ECB in implementing a regime where interest would be paid on reserves so as to strengthen his institution's power to peg money rates.

There is another issue related to the flawed separation principle and the many other listed mistakes of the ECB in this indictment.

Lack of accountability

Further flaws in the construction of EMU – in particular, the weak stand-ards set for transparency and accountability set by the Maastricht Treaty – meant that major decisions in policymaking (such as how to respond to the 'liquidity crisis' of August 2007 and the subsequent enunciation of the separation principle; and earlier in 2003 or 1998 the design or re-design of monetary framework) were not subject to challenge from inside or outside in any effective way.

ECB officials have boasted throughout the lifetime of EMU that mon-etary policymaking is transparent and accountable. They cite the press conferences that follow on immediately from the monthly policy board meeting. On closer examination these provide no serious challenge to policymakers – most of the questions are about whether a rate increase (or decrease) was discussed or not discussed; more recently since the eruption of the European sovereign debt crises there have been many questions about the details of possible bail-out plans, on the rare occa-sions that any difficult question is asked it is snuffed out by a filibuster of loquaciousness on the part of the President, frequently with some evidence of incomprehension of the exact point made by the questioner! There is no serious opportunity for follow-up questions and of course the President selects which journalists get to ask the questions!

Then there is the Monthly Report in which the ECB policymakers can explain the basis of their policy. That never reveals the nature of any debate or alternative policies that have been considered by policymakers around the table. Yes, there is some disclosure of the macro-economic forecasts and ECB members certainly take pride in the depth and sophis-tication of the econometric work. But by their nature these forecasts are mostly wrong and everyone knows they will likely be wrong. In any case, a central bank is not an economic forecasting institute (as a matter of fact their records are equally bad in general).

The interesting facts to be discovered, when it comes to transparency or accountability, are the specific alternative scenarios and risks that were discussed together with the collective thought processes (including considerations of monetary principles) which led up to the key policy decisions. The ECB has never outlined these.

There are the regular testimonies of the ECB President to the EU Parliament. But a review of all the transcripts shows no seriously critical and well-founded questions on monetary policymaking or damaging challenges for the ECB which might change the course of policy or trigger a re-drafting of the monetary framework. Has any journalist or parliamentarian ever had the opportunity or the preparedness to ask the ECB President directly why his institution made the serious error of steering an over-easy monetary policy in 1999, 2003–5, and worst of all of imposing a monetary squeeze in late 2007 and most of 2008 when a recession had already set in the US and Japan and very likely had already spread or was spreading to Europe?

The answer is no.

More important even than these flaws in accountability is the absence of any such questions during the periods the policy mistakes were being made in the hope that the policymakers would realize their mistake or that democratic pressures would be brought on them to realize these!

ECB officials pride themselves on the transparency and accountability which stems from their annual ECB Watchers Symposium, where outside renowned economists deliver papers and partake in discussion related to live monetary issues. Apparently here is indeed an opportunity for outside challenge. Yet there is absolutely no hint of acrimony or even heated exchange to be found amid the carefully crafted summary transcripts of proceedings. The symposium is put together by a Frankfurt research institute funded in part by the Bundesbank. Participation is by invitation of the institute. The tone as judged by material available is one of deference and polite exchange within a club. There is no chance of discomfort here.

In principle there could have been a national political dimension to accountability. The French government, in particular, could have appointed an intellectually provocative head of its central bank, willing to break the ranks of silent conformity in Frankfurt, to challenge policymaking consensus (see Marsh, 2009). That has not happened to date, perhaps because there was no intention of undermining a then French President (of the ECB). Italian governments, even those headed by Silvio Berlusconi, have similarly passed up any such opportunity. In Germany there was once a tradition of appointing strongly independent and intellectually challenging heads to the central bank, but this has waned through the years under the political imperatives of first German and later EMU.

ECB abstains from key role in approving new EMU members

The ECB has strenuously sought to stay outside EU politics of any description, except to when it comes to lecturing national governments on their budgetary policies or lack of economic reform policies (such as those to boost productivity) – neither of which are within its constitutional mandate.

Towards bypassing points of controversy, the ECB smothered one key issue of responsibility within its mandate. Under the Treaty of Maastricht, the ECB was to have an equal role with the European Commission in drawing up reports (each independent) on the eligibility of any applicant to join monetary union. Very early on, the ECB made clear that it had no intention of being drawn into such a political minefield, restricting its report to laying out the facts without any recommendation. In effect it passed the responsibility to the Commission and the EU Council.

The procedure which the ECB has ended up following on issues of new members joining EMU has been entirely cynical.

In May 2000, ECB Vice-President Noyer (later to become head of the French central bank) held a press conference to announce the publication of its convergence report on Greece (and Sweden). Noyer's comments and the report's summary on Greece was bland. The vice-president announced that the decision on whether Greece could join EMU would be taken by the EU Council of Ministers, who would have to hand the convergence report prepared by the EU Commission staff and the recommendation of the EU Commission. There was no mention by Noyer of the widespread scepticism at large about the quality or accuracy of the Greek data that went into the report. France was the main advocate of Greek entry into EMU just as it had been for its earlier entry into EU. In the event Greece joined EMU on 1 January 2001.

Five years later (2006), the ECB raised no objection to the EU Commission's verdict (2006) that Lithuania should not be allowed to join EMU despite this country just missing one entry test and then by only 0.1 percentage points on the inflation score (which was no miss at all if the inflation benchmark had been limited to other EMU countries rather than including an artificially low current inflation rate at the time in the UK). Rather it published its own bland factual summary on the matter with no conclusion. This was a bare-faced decision by the EU Commission, with no expert protest from the ECB, to allow Germany to get its way with its Russia policy (not worth hurting German interests by annoying Russia over extending the euro to the Baltics!).

As a matter of constitutional fact, according to the Maastricht Treaty the ECB could have broken from the Commission's stance and produced an expert evaluation free of politics which could have been used by those in the Council inclined to favour European liberalism and democracy over sucking up to the Putin dictatorship.

Three years later in 2009, the ECB and the European Commission might have been patting themselves on the back once the global credit crisis had erupted for having either by omission or commission obstructed Lithuania's entry into EMU, even though there is no evidence that a possible credit bubble figured in the Commission's case for rejecting Lithuania or in the ECB's refusal to challenge that rejection. The Baltics with their massive real estate cycles (relative to the size of the economy) and critical dependence on large capital inflows via the banking sector fell into deep recessions.

If Lithuania had been in the euro-area, the ECB would have had to extend its rescue mission to domestic banks or Russian linked banks there (against the collateral of dodgy domestic credit assets) to counter and hopefully pre-empt a damaging run of capital out of that country on the fear of a forced withdrawal from EMU. Even so, any such rescue would have been tiny relative to the size of any of the big EMU countries.

In the event, in early spring 2009, the post-bubble crisis in the Baltic countries deepened with intense speculation that Latvia would be the first forced to engineer a huge devaluation of its currency. As the IMF was called in, replenished with the promise of vast new financing as negotiated at the April 2009 G-20 summit (where France obtained remarkable diplomatic success in spearheading multilateral aid for this institution now with Strauss-Kahn – an ex–French finance minister – at its head with the explicit intention of bailing out the emerging market economies in Eastern Europe and implicitly the weak euro-area countries), the speculation started to fade with respect to the immediate future amid savage public expenditure cuts and fantastically high interest rates.

Again the ECB played a role (by omission) in passing up an historic opportunity for the EU to use monetary union as a means of solidifying the economic and political future of a region bordering on Russia where the menace from the Putin–Medvedev dictatorship had become only too clear a year earlier.

Instead of devoting half his press statement on 4 June 2009 to the ECB's latest forecasts on the economic outlook, almost certain to be wrong again, President Trichet could have used his platform to float the historic proposal that the Baltics should be admitted immediately into EMU, subject first to a 40% devaluation of their currencies. That would have worked most likely a miracle, in that interest rates in the Baltics would have collapsed and the devaluation would have given a big impetus to economic recovery there.

M. Trichet, despite his literary idealism on the subject of 'Europe' (see Brown, 2004) implicitly decided not to risk a confrontation with

Berlin (where 'Russia first' was still the leading principle at the Foreign Office) over the issue of any bold move to buttress the position of the Baltics safely outside the reach of the Putin–Medvedev dictatorship. Yet desperation of the Baltic governments to attain euro-membership had meanwhile reached a new pitch, not least in view of Russia's war against Georgia in summer 2008. Estonia was the first of the Baltics to demonstrate that it had met all the stringent conditions for entry – leaving not even a decimal point to the discretion of its EU judges as Lithuania had done in 2006 – and duly was admitted into EMU in January 2011. Latvia followed in 2014.

Self-indictment of euro-complacency

As ECB officials showered their praise on EMU at its tenth anniversary in January 2009 in the immediate wake of the Great Financial Panic (for which the catalyst was the Lehman bankruptcy) the words of President Trichet provide the final self-indictment of complacency.

In an interview with Le Figaro Magazine (7 January 2009) he exclaimed:

> The euro is evidently an advantage for those democracies that have chosen to adopt it. It has proven its stability, its resistance to shocks and its resilience in the face of financial economic turmoil. Once again, I would say, the euro has been a key factor in providing a shield against international turmoil. [...] We were the first central bank to react immediately when the international financial turbulence first appeared (9 August 2007). [...] Europe was able to take decisions even in the most difficult circumstances. [...] The euro is a big success.

The editor of the European Wall Street Journal was on M. Trichet's side. In a lead article on 2 January 2009, he wrote:

> The Single European currency, born on New Year's Day in 1999, is a rare economic shining star of the past decade.

Evidently EMU and the ECB have had powerful officials within and friends without who would speak in their defence against any indictment. We discover in subsequent chapters how that defence could stack up and with what the prosecution could respond.

4
How the Bundesbank Failed Europe and Germany

How were such great hopes dashed?

Here was a new central bank and a new monetary union which started up at the end of the 1990s. Yes, there were the cynics right at the start including Milton Friedman who warned that EMU would not survive the first serious recession. And as is often the case some of the cynics turned out to be partly right but for the wrong reasons. They had written much about misaligned business cycles and inflexible labour markets but little if anything about potential monetary instability in a union presided over by a rate-manipulating and inflation-targeting central bank unconstrained by constitutional monetary rules, and about how this could be the source of a deadly virus – asset price inflation.

In contrast the euro-enthusiasts – and they were now in charge of Europe's monetary destiny – had boasted that a new financial economic and political future dawned. The boast proved to be empty of content. Just over one decade later the monetary union was submerged in the aftermath of a credit bubble that was as bleak as – and on some accounts bleaker than – in the US! Political integration had made no progress at all, despite the claim of Jacques Delors that monetary union would be the catalyst to political union (see Brown, 2004) and in some respects had moved backwards. Financial integration had moved into reverse gear.

A flight of capital out of the government bond markets and banks in a range of financially weak member countries had brought the scenario of EMU break-up or shrinkage within the mainstream of investor vision around the globe. Embarrassed euro-officials who had been praising their own record at the official tenth anniversary events had to issue statements of denial, mainly to the pompous effect that anyone who argued for a strategic retreat of EMU into its core must be idiotic or deluded!

In this chapter the task is to study EMU in the years up to the peak of the bubble, say early 2007, and pick out the salient factors behind the ensuing malaise. In effect the present chapter assembles the evidence from this period towards justifying the indictments of Chapter 3.

Historical observations of Otmar Issing

Let us start with the evidence provided by Professor Otmar Issing, founder member of the ECB Board and its first Head of Economics and Research.

Much of this testimony can be found in his book *The Birth of the Euro* (2008), probably written in late 2007. There he states:

> Nine years on (from the run-up to the launch of EMU), the ECB can lay claim – virtually undisputed – to the success of its monetary policy. Those observers that remain sceptics at heart might at most add the qualification 'so far'. Over this period, the average annual increase in the HICP (euro-area CPI) has been 2.06 per cent. [...] Even the D-mark performed considerably less well over the period from 1950 to 1998, with a rate of 2.8%.

Well here is the statement of a single-minded general who achieved his self-selected target, which incidentally did not make much sense in terms of broad strategy, never mind the cost! As we saw in the previous chapter, the aim of monetary stability should not be interpreted as a stable inflation rate over the short- or medium-term (in fact the price level should fluctuate upwards and downwards) but in considerably broader terms which includes the absence of the asset price inflation virus. And the bill for single-minded 'success' was soon to be presented in the form of an almighty bursting of a massive credit bubble. The historical comparison (with the D-mark) on close examination includes an element of fiction alongside fact (see p. 178).

Let us start with the first big policy decision in what Professor Issing claims was a decade of monetary policy success.

First big monetary policy decision was a big mistake (1998–9)

With inflation in the euro-area as a whole running at just 1% p.a. at the start of monetary union, the ECB decided in favour of monetary easing. In early December 1998 while the national central banks were still legally in existence as sovereign policymakers, the ECB (which had grown out of the European Monetary Institute (EMI), opening its doors on 1 July 1998) arranged for an across-the-board cut of official rates by all participating countries. Accordingly the official repo rate set for the start of EMU was at 3% p.a.

In a second policy move in April 1999 the Governing Council decided to reduce again all policy rates. The main refinancing rate and the deposit rate were both reduced by 50 basis points, to 2.5% and 1.5%, respectively.

Albeit with the benefit of hindsight, this sequence of monetary easing through late 1998 and early 1999 was deeply unsettling for the new monetary union. What was so bad about inflation for a time at one percentage point below the upper limit to the inflation target? The IT revolution was now in full swing, which surely would be ushering in accelerated productivity growth globally even if the official statisticians in some EMU member countries (but not Germany) were bound to do a bad job of measuring this. In itself, accelerated productivity growth would lower the path of the price level through time which would be consistent with monetary equilibrium.

Late summer 1998 had seen the eruption of the Russian debt crisis leading on to the brief long-term capital management (LTCM)-related liquidity crisis of autumn 1998. In response, the Federal Reserve under Chairman Alan Greenspan embarked on a pre-emptive easing of monetary policy (taking a cue in part from a passing sharp fall in the equity market). All of that would have undoubtedly influenced sentiment among the policymakers around the table at the just-opened ECB. The degree of that easing by the FOMC (Federal Reserve Open Market Committee) and the slowness with which it was withdrawn has been widely criticized since – especially given its contribution to the final expansion of the NASDAQ bubble.

Could the ECB at its start not have done better than following the mood and monetary style of Washington? And in any case, in making a big rate cut in April 1999 the ECB was already six months on from the crisis action by the Fed and concerns about a possible growth recession in the US had dissipated.

Strangely Professor Issing in his book chooses to provide little insight into how the ECB might answer such criticism. He states somewhat lamely that

[m]ajor foreign markets were still suffering the effects of the Asian crisis and the repercussions of the Russian crisis of summer 1998 were

also still being felt. [...] The assessment of risks to price developments as being on the downside underlay the ECB Governing Council's decision to reduce the interest rate on the main refinancing facility by 50 basis points to 2.5% at its meeting of 8 April 1999.

A similar non-plus analysis of the monetary easing of late 1998 and spring 1999 is found in *Monetary Policy in the Euro-Area* (2001) under the joint authorship of Issing, Gaspar, Angeloni and Tristani. This account was written nearer the event and stresses the so-called 'downside risks to inflation'. The authors write:

> [O]n April 8 (1999) the Governing Council was facing a situation in which all forecasts projected the euro area inflation rate to remain around levels well within the definition of price stability in the following two years. These projections, however, were in every case the result of a sequence of reassessments, always in a downward direction, which were by themselves the manifestation of a trend leading to downward threats to price stability. While there were no expectations of the euro-area facing deflation, there was the perception of a risk that this could happen, and the main risks to price stability remained on the downside. The risk could be taken particularly seriously in light of the dangers inherent in a situation in which monetary policy operates at very low levels of inflation.

Fear of too low inflation influences ECB policy right from start

We see from the quote above that already the ECB's monetary policy in early 1999 was being driven in part by fear that inflation would enter into a dangerously low zone (dangerous in that the ECB might become powerless to provide stimulus in an economic downturn given that the equilibrium risk-free rate could fall below zero). This was a few years before such fears became enunciated by the Federal Reserve (in early 2003). The lead of the ECB in revealing deflation phobia can be explained in part by the fact that US inflation at the time (late 1990s) was further above the 'danger zone' than euro-zone (and particularly German) inflation and in part to the timing of key appointments to the Federal Reserve Board.

The strong advocate of action against 'too low' inflation in the Federal Reserve – University of Princeton Professor Ben Bernanke – was appointed by President Bush to its Board in 2002. Even so, Alan

Greenspan had been already following for many years a quasi-inflation targeting policy (he would never admit this!), failing to acknowledge that monetary equilibrium is consistent with and even requires an uneven pace of inflation or a fluctuating price level (up and down) over considerable periods of time. In particular, a phase of accelerated productivity growth (as in the mid- to late-1990s under the influence of the IT revolution and related investment spending boom) should go along with a dip in the price level to be consistent with monetary equilibrium (see p. 40). And in a weak phase of the business cycle (as in 2001–3) a dip in the price level or a lower than normal inflation rate should be considered as an essential element in how the capitalist economy auto-generates a recovery out of recession (see p. 41).

One reason why the spectre of too low inflation (not a spectre to those economists aware of the key distinction between good deflation including benign cyclical dips in inflation or the price level and monetary deflation) first appeared in Europe was the extent of monetary savagery in the run-up to EMU. In proving their credentials to join the new union – and to resist the waves of intermittent currency flight during the early/mid-1990s – many of the national central banks (excluding the Bundesbank which was not in the position of having to prove eligibility and which in any case several years earlier during 1991–3 overdid its monetary cooling in response to the inflationary dangers evident during the post-unification boom) had pursued (earlier in the decade) disequilibrium monetary policies in a recessionary direction. Also in late 1998 Germany was in near-recession (driven there by first the global trade slowdown in the wake of the Asian crisis of summer 1997 and then the Russian debt problem together with wider emerging market debt crisis of summer 1998).

There is no evidence, either in the form of contemporaneous or subsequent testimony, that ECB officials – and crucially Professor Issing – considered seriously the hypothesis that the then feeble inflation rate (around 1% p.a.), even though well below the implicit 'medium-term' target of 2% p.a., might well have been consistent with monetary equilibrium (taking account especially of the benign tendency for many cyclical prices in the economy to fall in the weak phase of the business cycle and rise in the recovery phase). Nor is there any evidence to demonstrate that those officials were aware of the danger (especially in a new monetary union) that breathing in a significantly higher inflation rate (above 1% p.a.) could cause speculative temperatures to rise across a range of asset markets (including the currency markets) with economically troublesome consequences.

In practice, by aiming to push inflation very slightly higher from the then (1999) level of 1% p.a. the ECB could not realistically hope to gain significant extra margin of firepower should the spectre of deep recession and debt deflation become reality in the next cycle. And indeed if seriously concerned with reducing such dangers in the far distant future the ECB would have done much better to concentrate on building the still effectively missing monetary pillar in its overall policy framework.

In any event, it was not long before the chickens came home to roost from the ECB's (implicit!) decision in spring 1999 to breathe a little inflation back into the euro-area economy. The euro started to decline, with the pace of depreciation gathering speed. From a starting level of 1.18 US$ the euro had fallen to virtually 0.80 US$ by October 2000, and the decline against the yen was even greater.

As a new currency, the euro was doubly vulnerable to a policy of breathing in inflation. Each leg down seemed to demonstrate to the sceptics about monetary union that the new money could not earn the trust of international investors. In the language of the behavioural finance theorists, there was a negative feedback loop.

ECB in state of denial about monetary source of euro's plunge 1999–2000

One salient aspect of the official reaction in Frankfurt to the euro's slide is that no one there made the connection with the monetary decision to breathe a higher rate of inflation back into the euro-area economy. Instead, there were a series of explanations including why the euro was not undervalued by any long-run perspective or why the depreciation in fact stemmed from the strength of capital inflows into the US to take advantage of that country's pre-eminence in the IT revolution. Increasingly officials got drawn into a debate as to whether there should be official intervention to support the euro.

The ECB President, Wim Duisenberg, irritated by his colleagues' speeches studded with different nuances on the subject of the weak euro and the benefits or not of intervention, announced that he personally and no one else took responsibility for euro currency policy – 'I am Mr Euro', he told the assembled journalists. Mr Euro had no plan, though, to restore confidence by designing a solid monetary pillar (including strict "constitutional" rules and automatic stabilizing mechanisms) to support the new construction of monetary union and prevent it from heading into crisis at some point in the not-too-distant future.

A bout of official intervention did take place eventually in autumn 2000, as undertaken jointly by Washington and Frankfurt. With the NASDAQ bubble already bursting, the Clinton Administration (and in particular its Treasury Secretary, Professor Larry Summers) saw an advantage (some cynics saw the looming Congressional and Presidential elections as a factor here) in providing some support for US equities by driving the dollar down from its elevated levels (versus the euro). But the effect of the intervention was short lived.

The strong bounce-back of the euro from winter 2001/2 went along with a reversal of relative stance between US and euro-area monetary policies. The ECB continued to be cautious about easing policy – not least because of an inflation overhang now emerging in consequence of the earlier big devaluation (on top of jumps in food and energy prices at the start of the new decade).

The Federal Reserve, in the wake of the September 2001 terrorist attacks on the US, moved to a stimulatory policy towards combating recession (in the previous year up to September 2001 the Federal Reserve had been significantly 'behind the curve' – albeit less so than the ECB – and had been very late in recognizing the onset of the economic downturn). The shift by the Federal Reserve to a stimulatory policy in autumn 2001 occurred six months after the start of recession and barely two months before the start of recovery (as dated by the NBER). Eventually in spring 2003, still disbelieving evidence of an economic upturn, the Federal Reserve came out with its aggressive version of breathing inflation into the economy. This was more explicit and focussed than the ECB's earlier version of the same policy enacted in the first few months of 1999. The Federal Reserve's new policy also struck contemporaneous observers as more radical (and expansionary) in its implications than the almost simultaneous shift in monetary framework announced by the ECB in spring 2003.

That is running ahead of our story. Let us return to how contemporary commentators viewed the weak euro of 1999–2000. The authors of the ECB's tenth anniversary edition of the *Monthly Bulletin* (June 2008) subtitle the period mid-1999 to end-2000 as 'Phase 2 – raising rates to contain inflationary pressures (mid-1999 to end-2000)'. There is (of course!) no mention of the fact that the inflationary pressures might have been a consequence of an earlier erroneous decision to breathe in higher inflation (an exercise which apparently got out of control) back in winter 1998/9 and spring 1999. Instead the authors blame extraneous events:

Over this period, sharp increases in oil prices and a general rise in import prices [was this due to euro depreciation??] continued to exert upward pressure on prices in the short term. As these increases were larger and lasted longer than previously foreseen, the risks of indirect and second-round effects on consumer price inflation via wage-setting rose significantly in the context of robust economic growth. These concerns were compounded by the development of the euro exchange rate. Its trend depreciation continued over this period, gaining momentum in, especially, the second half of 2000 when it moved further out of line with the sound fundamentals of the euro-area. As a result, the balance of risks to price stability over the medium-term was shifted upwards.

The authors of the bulletin congratulate (no surprise there!) the ECB policymakers.

It became clear that the downside risks to price stability identified at the time of the reduction of the key ECB interest rates in April 1999 no longer prevailed. With the ECB's economic and monetary analyses both pointing to upside risks to price stability, the Governing council raised the key ECB interest rates by a total of 225 bp [basis point] in a series of interest rate hikes between November 1999 and October 2000, bringing the minimum bid rate in the Eurosystem's main refinancing operations to a level of 4.75% in October 2000.

And the authors of the bulletin do not judge policy by the counterfactual – how much better would the outcome have been if the 225 bp rate rise had all taken place by the end of 1999, or if the starting rate cuts had not been made at all in late 1998 and in April 1999.

The counterfactual experiment should not be limited to euros and cents of lost GDP over the business cycle as a whole. There was also the damage in terms of the related plunge of the euro at its start (attributable to over-easy money) and higher-than-otherwise inflation slowing down the growth of trust among euro-area citizens in the new money.

As we shall see, this possible lack of trust played a role in restricting the freedom of choice of the ECB when it came to reformulating the monetary framework in 2003, making it more difficult to abandon quasi-inflation targeting and to embrace sounder principles of monetary stability.

ECB's policy mistake of 1999–2000 handicaps response to 2001–2 recession

Reverting back from counterfactual to actual history, we arrive at the ECB's response to the global recession in the wake of the IT bubble bursting. Issing and his fellow authors (see Issing et al., 2001) describe this period as phase 3, 'Downward Adjustments to Key ECB Interest Rates – early 2001 to mid-2003'. They applaud the ECB's 'grand old duke of York tactics' (not a term used by the authors and stems from an English nursery rhyme: 'he marched them up to the top of the hill and he marched them down again, and when they were up they were up, and when they were down they were down!'):

> In the course of this period, the Governing Council lowered the key ECB interest rates by a total of 275 basis points, with the minimum bid rate reaching a historically low level of 2% in June 2003. This is the lowest level of interest rates seen in Europe since the Second World War.

It seems that the authors exclude Switzerland from Europe for the purpose of this statement.

One critical issue missed is whether the ECB's refusal to countenance a sharper fall of money interest rates during the period of the actual recession (2001–2) stemmed from the earlier mistake of having breathed in too much inflation during 1999–2000. The tone of contemporary official commentaries do reveal anxiety about dislodging the anchor to stable low inflation expectations already loose as a result of that earlier episode.

The second critical issue is whether the ECB should still have been easing policy (as against tightening) in early 2003 given the then explosive growth of money supply which itself might have been seen as one indicator of incipient speculative temperature rise in credit and real estate markets (otherwise described as asset price inflation).

The authors slur over that second issue, admitting that the rapid growth of M3 (which was accelerating from mid-2001 onwards) was a source of concern, but pointing out that the surge in the money supply was explicable by portfolio shift ('the incidence of sizeable shifts in private investors' portfolios away from shares and other longer-term financial assets towards safe and more liquid monetary assets included in M2'). The authors do not comment on the explosive growth of M1 (especially from mid-2002 on), driven in part by very rapid growth in the overnight inter-bank market – itself an early indicator of possible asset price inflation. (M3 is the broadest measure of money supply, including non-bank holdings of short-maturity government bonds and certificates of deposits; M2 is somewhat narrower, including time deposits with the banks but excluding bonds and certificates; M1 includes only sight deposits and cash in circulation, including overnight deposits held by institutional and corporate entities). Without further ado they move on to a discussion of 'Phase 4 – No Changes to Key ECB Interest Rates (mid-2003 to end-2005)'. In doing so they pass over the monetary framework announcements of spring 2003 in which the definition of price stability was 'clarified'.

Long day's journey into monetary madness, spring 2003

Coincidentally, early 2003 was a watershed in US monetary history (see Broaddus, 2004). And also in UK monetary history, with the Bank of England, albeit under closer government instruction, but with no evidence of disagreement, shifting its policy framework in similar respects to the US and euro-area. At the conclusion of its May meeting (6 May 2003), the Federal Reserve Open Market Committee had expressed concern, for the first time, that inflation might decline too far:

> The probability of an unwelcome substantial fall in inflation, though minor, exceed(ed) that of a pickup in inflation from its already low level.

For those in the know, the newly appointed Governor, Professor Bernanke, a specialist in the Great Depression (who had concluded that the blame for this lay primarily with lack of forceful enough monetary intervention to prevent a severe recession turning into depression) and ardent advocate of inflation targeting, had persuaded Chairman Greenspan and his colleagues that the US economy now (in the wake of the earlier NASDAQ bubble-and-burst) was in danger of entering a 'Japan-style' deflation.

Federal Reserve transcripts tell us that Professor Bernanke did not totally convince Chairman Greenspan in that the former's advocacy of the next step being the suggested use of non-conventional policy tools – including creation of massive excess reserves – was not successful (rejected by the FOMC), perhaps because the recovery of the economy became clear so soon afterwards.

In fact, Professor Eisuke Sakakibara was much later to argue that the very mild decline of the Japanese price level in the late 1990s and early 2000s was not at all bad depression-style deflation (what Austrian economists would describe as severe monetary disequilibrium in a deflationary direction or as monetary deflation). Instead the right description for that episode was "good deflation" (meaning not accompanied by monetary deflation) attributable to jumps in productivity per man-hour and improvements in the terms of trade stemming from rapid integration of the Japanese and Chinese economies.

Journeys into monetary deflations in history are characterized by an on-going process of money creation lagging far behind money demand in real terms. In principle at a later point when expectations of the continuation of price level declines have become prevalent, and are matched by projections of persistent feeble growth or actual contraction in money supply, there may no longer be any present monetary shortage. Long-run price declines fully expected and matched by monetary developments in the same way as long-run price increases fully in tandem with monetary expansion are not evidence of monetary disequilibrium, but they are inconsistent with the aim of price level stability in the long run.

Many economists argue that there was indeed such a monetary journey into deflation in Japan during the period 1989–93 when Bank of Japan policy was extraordinarily tight (see Brown, 2002). But that monetary disequilibrium was not accompanied by an actual fall in the price level. It is plausible that the episodes of gentle decline of the price level many years beyond that could have been due to the real forces described by Professor Sakakibara in his revisionist account of the so-called 'lost decade' and, as such, had no monetary content. There were also short periods of falling prices (again non-monetary in essence) related to cyclical downturns. The evidence, from consumer surveys and from the long-maturity bond markets, does not support the emergence in Japan of extrapolative expectations of continuing price declines over the long-run (see Brown, 2013).

As regards the US situation in early 2003, the fall of recorded price level rises to around 1% p.a. was much better explained by normal, and economically efficient, pro-cyclical behaviour (dominated by prices in the highly cyclical sectors of the US and global economy – including commodities) than any hypothesis of sinister monetary developments. Critics argued that the new Governor from Princeton University had become 'obsessed' with the Great Depression to the extent of giving an unrealistically high probability to a recurrence and that moreover he had not learnt the most important lesson of all – about the Federal Reserve's mistakes during the boom period which preceded the Great Depression (see Brown, 2013 and Lowenstein, 2008).

Early 2003 was also a critical period for the evolution of the ECB's monetary framework. Two days following the critical May 6 FOMC meeting (after which an immediate press release detailed the decision), the ECB held a 'press seminar on the evaluation of the ECB's monetary policy strategy'. This consisted of a slide show by ex-Bundesbanker Professor Otmar Issing (now the chief economist on the board of the ECB). The first and most important point was that the Governing Council clarified its quantitative definition of price stability.

> Price stability shall be defined as a year-on-year increase in the Harmonized Index of Consumer Prices for the euro-area of below, but close to 2%.

The new element here was 'close to' whereas previously the degree of tolerated undershoot had been left unstated.

As before, price stability was to be assessed over a 'medium-term' horizon, but meaning in practical terms (though not expressly stipulated) around say a two-year period. Other points – less important – in the slide show included semantics about whether the ECB was targeting inflation (according to Professor Issing no – but in practice yes); and semantics about the role of money supply path monitoring in the so-called 'two-pillar approach' to implementing (don't mention the word!) inflation targeting.

Professor Issing's notorious slide show

There were two particular points of interest to come out of Professor Issing's slide show as regards the role of monetary analysis in the policy-making framework.

First, he repeated the assertion (so well-known since first public explanation of policy framework just prior to the start of EMU) that monetary phenomena deserve separate attention from the econometric-type analysis which formed the first pillar as triggers to the raising of an alarm bell in the corridors of the central bank. Conventional forecasting models do not capture fully the signalling capacity of monetary phenomena, whether within the two-year horizon relevant to econometric equations, or beyond. Monetary analysis provides a means of cross-checking from a longer-term perspective the shorter-term indications from the economic analysis which forms the 'first pillar'.

Second, Professor Issing commented directly on bubbles:

> Excess money may provide additional information for identifying financial imbalances and/or asset price bubbles, which ultimately may impact on price developments.

The impression from this second remark was that financial imbalances and asset price bubbles were not a problem in themselves except in so far as they had implications for the meeting of the long-run price objective (inflation target by any other name). That was far removed from the Austrian concept in which severe monetary disequilibrium could occur without emitting a symptom in the form of goods and service prices rising. Rather the symptom might be just asset price inflation (or deflation) – and by the time this symptom could be confidently diagnosed the disease might already by well-advanced. And for the Austrians severe monetary disequilibrium, albeit without symptom in the form of goods and service prices rising, was not anything to be dismissive about. Its consequences were dire in terms of economic costs – including in particular the waste (mal-investment and sickness of equity risk appetite) of the bubble-and-bursting process.

For example, out of the monetary disequilibrium in the US during the early and mid-1920s, there developed a powerful asset price inflation virus which emitted symptoms in the form of strong speculative temperature rise in credit and real asset markets (see Rothbard, 1972). This was attributable to the Federal Reserve under the domination of Benjamin Strong holding down money rates well below the high neutral rate reflecting the contemporaneous technological revolution that had occurred alongside broad stability of goods and services prices. (These prices on average would have fallen under conditions of monetary equilibrium). Germany, the second largest economy in the world in the late 1920s, was also in severe monetary disequilibrium at the same time.

The German monetary disequilibrium – characterized by prevailing market rates far below the high neutral level reflecting the shortage of domestic savings relative to enhanced investment opportunity in the aftermath of war and hyperinflation – stemmed from the fixed link of the Reichsmark to the US dollar as stipulated by the Dawes Plan (1924). Indeed, in that Germany was effectively part of the dollar zone we should discuss monetary disequilibrium for the whole zone rather than just a part of it: US interest rates were below the neutral level for the zone as a whole and this meant that symptoms of asset price inflation appeared both in the US and in Germany – wherever there was a good speculative story (inside the US or outside). The level of US rates should have reflected at least in part the high neutral level of German rates. The Benjamin Strong Fed's manipulation of rates at a low level prevented that from happening (see Brown, 2013). US investors, stirred into irrational exuberance by monetary disequilibrium in the US, became avid buyers of apparently high- yielding German securities. The carry trade boomed (a feature of asset price inflation, see Chapter 1, p. 19). The speculative story was the economic miracle in the Weimar Republic. US banks, their appetites for risk fed by the sky-high price of their equities, were at the forefront of the boom in lending to Germany. The overall result was fantastic asset price inflation in both Germany and the US without upward pressure on the overall price level in either country. And yet the bubble would inevitably be followed by a burst, meaning that monetary excess might never show up in goods and services prices.

There were no references to the possibility of severe monetary disequilibrium without the accompaniment of an actual rise in the price level in Professor Issing's speech and slide show. Instead, there was much reference to the possibility of 'deflation'. Professor Issing emphasized that there was a need for sufficient safety margin to guard against risks of 'deflation', hence the revamped wording of the price aim.

There was no comment by Professor Issing to suggest awareness of the key distinction between monetary deflation (initiated by a severe monetary disequilibrium in which money supply is growing well below the demand for real money balances) and various forms of non-monetary deflation driven declines in the price level (related to terms of trade improvement, productivity growth acceleration and cyclical fluctuations) which could well be symptoms of a well-functioning capitalist economy with no monetary disequilibrium.

This re-vamped and expanded description of the monetary framework was disconcerting in several respects. Perhaps most disconcerting of all was the fact that the ECB was moving even further away from an ideal monetary framework which would recognize that the achievement of monetary stability transcended, and could indeed be frustrated by, an intense focus on price level stability (or low inflation stability) over short or medium periods of time.

One might have hoped that now the ECB had been open for almost five years, it could build on the grown trust of euro-citizens concerning their new money to back away from such a concentration on movements of the price level over the short- and medium-term.

Instead, the policy framework reformulation made the medium-term profile of the price level an even greater focus with less room for flexibility than before (price level rises now had to be held close to 2% p.a., not falling significantly below that figure).

Yes, the mistake of the ECB (unrecognized in official statements) in pursuing excessively easy money policy in its first year or so had squandered some opportunity to build trust (in stability of the new money) among euro-citizens. Nonetheless, some progress had surely been made.

The innovation of setting an implicit lower bound to inflation (as well as the upper bound) implied a reinforcement of inflation targeting (though Professor Issing denied staunchly that the ECB was an inflation targeter) which could increase the risk of severe monetary disequilibrium in the Austrian sense. If changes in real variables (such as productivity acceleration or terms of trade improvement or passing cyclical weakness) were driving the price level down or up, the ECB by combating those pressures, would induce monetary disequilibrium (of which a key eventual symptom could be asset price inflation or deflation, respectively, with all the associated misallocation and eventually waste of economic resources).

The ECB was evidently in the same intellectual culture as the Bernanke/Greenspan Federal Reserve and the Bank of England, in which asset price inflation (speculative temperature swings in asset and credit markets) had no bearing except in so far as it had implications for the prospects of attaining the inflation target. This is one of the discredited 'Ten General Principles' of Professor Bernanke (see Brown, 2008).

Perhaps there were nuances and throw-out remarks that suggested Professor Issing had an understanding that monetary stability involved much more than what he revealed at the slide show. Nothing implied, however, that these reservations would seriously influence policymaking, notwithstanding the already accumulating possible symptoms (for those who looked) of asset price inflation.

In the course of his presentation, Professor Issing made a point which unwittingly hinted at a further element in the deflation phobia afflicting himself and his colleagues. He defended the lower limit to inflation (of close to 2%) not just in terms of avoiding the perils of deflation generally (in particular the zero rate trap) but also in terms of providing scope for relative price fluctuation within the euro-area.

In the context of 2003, Professor Issing was referring implicitly to the possibility for the German economy to experience a relative price decline (vis-à-vis other euro-area countries) without suffering actual 'deflation'. This hypothesized equilibrium path of relative prices was in line with the widespread perception that sluggish domestic demand in Germany (relative to elsewhere in the euro-area), explained by the bursting of the post-unification construction bubbles and shifting of investment opportunity to cheap labour neighbours to the East, called for some gains in its competitiveness. Hence dynamism of exports could compensate for sluggish domestic demand along the route back to overall equilibrium.

Professor Issing did not raise the possibility that the apparent relative sluggishness of domestic demand growth in Germany relative to several other countries in the euro-area could be in fact a symptom of underlying monetary disequilibrium. That would be the case if excess money alongside medium-term market interest rates well below neutral level were fuelling asset price inflation with its characteristic feature of an uneven pattern of speculative temperature rise across asset markets with those most affected concentrated in a few member countries where an exciting hypothesis (for example Spain as the Florida of Germany) could attract investors (see Chapter 1, p. 8). At this time the obvious causes for concern would have included the construction and real estate boom in Spain and the public spending boom in several small periphery zone countries.

In future it could be another member economy (other than Germany) that would find its route back to prosperity conditional on an increase in its competitiveness (decline in its relative price level). For example, at some possibly distant stage (from the viewpoint of the early 2000s) the construction boom in Spain would come to an end. But Spain as a much smaller economy than Germany could surely not count on or expect other member countries to experience sufficient price level increases so that no general fall in prices would have to occur domestically. Professor Issing's analysis of safety margin (for inflation) was in fact remarkably German-centric. Indeed Professor Issing was hinting that one defence for the decision to breathe inflation higher in 1999 (notwithstanding its consequence of sharp depreciation of the euro) was the concern that the then current rate of rise in the euro-area CPI at around 1% p.a. was too low to allow for rapid relative price level adjustment downwards in Germany without an absolute fall in the price level occurring there.

IMF wrong again! It warns about euro-deflation in 2003

Deflation risks in Europe were certainly on the international conference agenda at this time. The IMF issued a much discussed research paper on deflation ('How to fight deflation in a liquidity trap: committing to being irresponsible', Eggertsson, 1 March 2003). Kenneth Rogoff,

Economic Counsellor and Director to the IMF Research Department, wrote:

> Our indicators suggest that the prospect of deflation cannot be entirely dismissed, and the same would be true for the euro-area as a whole; although there are higher risks for Germany. Interest rates and inflation rates will remain near or at fifty year lows throughout the globe, and a sufficiently strong negative demand shock could tilt the balance towards worldwide deflation. (17 July 2003)

The IMF in its World Economic Outlook in Spring 2003, in a study put together by a special task force overseen by Kenneth Rogoff, warned that

> Germany is at high risk of deflation and Japan, Hong Kong and Taiwan are vulnerable to an accelerating pace of price declines. [...] There has been a clear increase in the vulnerability to deflation for a number of industrial and emerging market economies.

The IMF report stirred deflation phobia, warning that 'deflation is seldom benign and is difficult to anticipate'.

Professor Issing at his press conference understandably made no direct reference to the deflation-mongers in Washington who clearly had never read von Mises on 'monetary deflation'! Calmly Professor Issing went out of this way to say that little had changed in the monetary framework. The significance of the lower limit to inflation was high at the moment because real pressures (cyclical and secular) might be taking observed year-on-year CPI changes below the newly formulated lower bound. But the same situation had prevailed in 1999 – in fact even more so.

Why did you go to such trouble, Professor Issing?

In the question-and-answer session which followed the slide show, there was an inter-change between one journalist and Professor Issing which can be described as at best superficial, at worst smug.

Q: Professor Issing, you have obviously gone to a lot of trouble to produce this review, but could you explain exactly what difference it is going to make to the way you formulate monetary policy? Will it, for example, make it easier to cut interest rates? Or is it all really a matter of presentation?

Issing: First, it was no trouble. It was not always pleasurable, but it was fascinating and, for somebody with my background, it was a very challenging aspect of my work, and cooperation with our experts is always very enjoyable. The word 'trouble' is certainly not appropriate. But as the President has already said, even if we had had the same clarification back in 1998, our policy would not have been any different. So I do not expect – and there is no reason to expect – a different monetary policy on the basis of the clarification of the strategy, which was decided on today.

Q: What was the point of it then?

Issing: If you are married and after four years of happy married life, perhaps one evening you sit together over a glass of wine and think about why you are so happy all the time: nobody would say it does not make sense (laughter!!!).

What issues should have been discussed at the review but were not?

We will look at this in more detail during the trial process (Chapter 6). But already in spring 2003 the possible rise of speculative temperatures in credit and asset markets and how monetary policymakers should respond – without simply copying the conventional wisdom at the Federal Reserve or the Bank of England – might well have been on the agenda. This did not mean a proposal to target asset prices but rather to consider whether monetary instability in its widest sense (to include possible but not yet provable asset or credit market inflation) might be forming.

Also of relevance could have been a thorough look at the issue of whether the extra comfort provided against the risks of monetary policy paralysis by setting a floor to inflation of *closely below 2%* was at all significant or desirable.

After all in a serious financial crisis or deep recession (or both), the optimal path of real risk-free interest rates (in terms of a safe yet reasonably fast journey back to overall economic equilibrium) for, say, short and medium maturities would surely pass through substantially negative territory. Now if the prevailing rate of inflation at such a time were 1–2% due to the choice of an inflation target of 2% rather than 0–1%, then consistent with the zero rate boundary remaining in place real risk-free rates in the first case could fall to say –1.5% rather than –0.5% in the second. But is that difference really significant?

Surely the much bigger concern in any re-draft of the monetary framework should have been to look again (not possible perhaps in the rushed preparation in summer 1998) at the whole question of inflation targeting.

Looking again would have gone far beyond the tired semantic exercise to demonstrate that the ECB's framework was not an extreme example of the monetary madness associated with inflation targeting in the UK or in the US. Rather there would have been a good look at the Austrian or Friedmanite critiques of inflation targeting or quasi-inflation targeting (see p. 49) interpreted flexibly enough to include the reality of the ECB's policymaking process. The re-look should have extended also to the evidence already accumulating about rising temperature levels in European in credit and real estate markets.

What warning signs were flashing?

Warning signs of monetary disequilibrium already evident in 2003–4

We have already referred to the rapid growth of M1 (see p. 95) partly on the back of a booming overnight deposit market. (This was for banks and non-banks, but only non-bank deposits included in the definition of M1.) In addition there was the explosive growth of mega banks in the euro-area, which the ECB much later (December 2008 – after the definitive bursting of the credit bubble) came to describe as LCBGs (large and complex banking groups).

It could hardly have been expected that the newly appointed ECB President, Jean-Claude Trichet (autumn 2003), would side with the vanguard of analysts concerned about a rise of speculative temperatures in European credit markets, not least given his own complex history regarding involvement or non-involvement in the Credit Lyonnais debacle. This had ended up with an acquittal in spring 2003 in a criminal trial where the charge was that M. Trichet, as top Finance Ministry Official responsible for nationalized industries, had signed off on misleading financial statements by Credit Lyonnais, no doubt influenced by the strong ties of his political chief, Finance Minister Bérégovoy, to its CEO (see Brown, 2004). In effect Credit Lyonnais had been one of the most irrationally exuberant speculators in the Volcker asset price inflation of the mid-late 1980s (which attacked not just the US but the global economy) and came to grief when that turned into asset price deflation. Jean-Claude Trichet, a stranger to the concept of asset price inflation, would never have described it in that way!

The blinding of vision extended far beyond the ECB presidency amid the rapture about the new age of financial integration in Europe ushered in by the euro.

ECB officials – and Professor Bernanke – cheer euro-banking boom

Some US 'friends of the euro' could not see European asset price inflation forming below the apparent good news of euro-driven financial integration. In the case of one 'friend', Professor Ben Bernanke, the cynic could say that his record of not comprehending the virus of asset price inflation in the US surely would suggest the same mistake when he turned to Europe! And indeed in a speech to the Institute for International Economics in Washington (26 February 2004), the then Federal Reserve Governor told his audience:

> The most important benefit of the currency union has been and will continue to be its strengthening of European financial markets. Traditionally, the efficiency and scope of these markets has been hampered by the costs and risks associated with the use of multiple currencies as well as by the fragmentation arising from international differences in legal structure, accounting rules, and other institutions. Given the rapidity and frequency of trade in financial markets, even small transaction costs can hamper efficiency and liquidity in these markets. The common currency, with ongoing efforts to harmonize financial regulations and institutions, has significantly reduced those transaction costs. Together with lower country-specific macro-risks arising from the adoption of the common currency [no mention of what these are!], this reduction in transaction costs has greatly improved the breadth and efficiency of European financial markets.

No doubt these words of praise, if he had remembered them, would have been one of the many embarrassments for Professor Bernanke when later the scenario of credit bubble and burst in the US and Europe became a reality. Just as Anna Schwartz was to accuse Ben Bernanke of having learnt the wrong lesson from her and Milton Friedman's history of the banking crises during the Great Depression (see Hirsh, 2009), it seems that he was applying another wrong lesson when reviewing financial happenings in Europe. Of course the excuse is obvious that he could not be expected to have an intimate knowledge of what was happening on the ground.

But what about ECB officials who were meant to have such knowledge? Consider a speech by Board Member Gertrude Tumpel-Gugerell, '*in honour of Mr Alessandro Profumo, Chief Executive Officer of Unicredito Italiano S.P.A., European Banker of the Year*' on 30 June 2003:

> It is my privilege today to honour Mr Allessandro Profumo, chief executive officer of UniCredito Italiano, as European Banker of the Year 2002 (a prize proffered by the 'Group of 20+1'). [...] With the euro, monetary stability has been achieved in Europe.
>
> [Can monetary stability really be judged over a three-year period?]
>
> Our attention should now be devoted to the efficiency in the usage of capital as well as in other fields. This, I believe, is an area where Europe still faces considerable challenges. [...] One of the reasons put forward by the Group of 20+1 for awarding the title of European Banker of the Year to Alessandro Profumo is his success in forging a 'strong, lean and very profitable bank'. I welcome in this decision the wish to reward success in achieving efficiency. Indeed, UniCredito ranks highly among European banks in terms of its return on equity [no mention of leverage!]. [...] The vocation of the euro is to serve, in due course, all the citizens of the European Union. In consequence there is the overriding need to further and complete the ongoing process of European financial integration. This cannot be achieved by the authorities alone. It must also be achieved by market participants themselves. In this context it must be possible for market participants to exploit the potential economies of scale generated by the broader dimension of the euro area relative to the national markets. A market for corporate control within the euro-area's financial system needs to emerge to allow the creation of pan-European players in all areas of finance. And the perimeter for integration needs to be thought of increasingly as the future Member States of an enlarged European Union. [...] The considerable investments of UniCredito in Poland, in the Czech Republic and in Slovakia [in 2000 Mr. Profumo had spent US$2billion on acquisition of four banks in Eastern Europe] in particular testify to the creation of a banking group on a scale commensurate with that of the enlarged union.

Tumpel-Gugerell's enthusiasm about financial integration is understandable but was she at all focused on the possibility that what was passing as exemplary in carrying out that aim was in reality evidence of inefficiency in European financial markets? In particular, were the equity markets, under the influence of much irrational exuberance stoked up by US and European monetary disequilibrium, over-rewarding bold expansion by various European banking groups – providing the means for this to take place – without taking due sober-rationalist note of other possible interpretations? For example were the banking groups in Spain and Italy that were spearheading the euro-banking industry expansion being rewarded with high equity prices due to rapid earnings growth within their home territory which were related to some mixture of rising leverage and rising credit market temperature? Were these high equity prices in turn facilitating the takeover of banks in staid over-banked markets? Italy and Spain had been the two large high-interest rate currencies prior to monetary union and the collapse of rates coincident with their entry into union had set off domestic mortgage lending booms.

And in the case of UniCredito, was the arbitrage opportunity of issuing equity with the benefit of a high price–earnings ratio (P/E) to pay for the acquisition of a German bank with a low P/E in fact phoney – in the sense that the low P/E may have reflected justifiable angst on the part of investors about the earnings outlook especially with respect to its real estate loans in Germany and abroad? Moreover the high P/E of UniCredito could have been a reflection of market failure to correctly assess the role of leverage in its performance. To be fair to Tumpel-Gugerell the big merger was to come later in 2005, when UniCredito made its all-share offer for HVB and its Austrian and Polish subsidiaries (Bank Austria Creditanstalt and BPH in Poland) for a total price tag of $23bn. UniCredito was offering five new shares for every HVB share.

One of the real issues already alluded to by Tumpell-Gegerell was the accelerated expansion into Eastern Europe. Were the profits in what was increasingly to be described as the 'Wild East' the fruits of pioneering a benign process of integration or of introducing a version of US subprime lending (in this case the teaser loans were denominated in Swiss francs) on a very thin (highly leveraged) equity capital base which one day would go terribly wrong?

Euro-banking empire-building

In most cases, the rapid expansion of the new mega banks in Europe went along in each case with a hero, who became a celebrity in the financial world for his or her acumen. As in the world of the hedge funds where the virus of asset price inflation penetrated the market for human talent (culminating in bubble incomes and revenue) the same was true in the banking industry. An article in *Economics and Finance* (19 February 2007) described Alessandro Profumo's objective as, to build up a European Citibank and to grapple for the world's largest markets of India and China. *'The pushing, aggressive business style peculiar to Alessandro Profumo was like a cold shower for Italian bankers'.*

In the case of Banco Santander, the Spanish bank which rose to global stardom along with the euro, the hero was Emilio Botin. According to an article in Forbes (14 March 2005), the billionaire had now fulfilled his lifelong ambition to transform a small regional bank once run by his grandfather into an international player. Already the largest bank in Latin America by assets it made a series of large acquisitions during the first six years of EMU (1999–2005) culminating in the $15 billion purchase of Britain's Abbey National in 2004 (what could be more incestuous than a bank in one of the hottest credit markets in Europe – Spain – buying a bank in probably the hottest of all – the UK?). The equity market, to be fair, had judged that takeover harshly with Santander's share price tumbling by almost 10%, but that had not caused Botin to pull back – an interesting case where executive empire-building rather than a hot financial equity market was the driving force behind expansion or what was lauded as 'European financial integration' by the eurocrats!

The phenomenon of empire building and rapid expansion of European banking groups was not limited to the euro-area (where other examples included Josef Ackermann at Deutsche Bank and Jean-Paul Votron at Fortis). UK and Swiss banking groups were all prominent in the process, and again in each case there was an individual who was personalizing the process – Fred Goodwin for the Royal Bank of Scotland, Marc Ospel for Union Bank of Switzerland.

Is it possible to pinpoint the launch of the euro as a key factor in explaining how such empire-building took place on the edge of (just outside) the euro-area? Perhaps the strongest argument in that direction can be made for the UK in that RBS, thanks to EMU, had access to a rapidly growing interbank deposit market (where funds obtained were swapped from euros into pounds), with its operations there oiled by the ECB's discount facilities, and had become a major player in the booming Spanish real estate market, itself in part a product of the euro.

Empire-building whether inside the euro-area or on its edges would not have raised, in itself, a red flag within the ECB even if top officials there had been on the look out for symptoms of asset price inflation. It had long been conventional wisdom, even before the launch of EMU, that monetary integration would be a stimulus to the formation of larger banking groups, which would be no bad thing (so the wisdom went) given that European banking had become backward in comparison with the bold new era of efficiency and high profit (and hidden leverage!) characterizing US banking, including the investment banking scene.

At the BIS, William White, who later became renowned as a lone voice in official supranational institutions warning against the dangers of inflation targeting, had written in 1998 about the forces (including the euro) which would bring consolidation in European banking over the coming decade. Definitely, though, he did not welcome this unreservedly, warning that the development would pose challenges for national regulators and other policymakers concerned with the maintenance of financial stability (see White, 1998).

Euro financial integration camouflages credit bubble

More generally there was such a general condition of optimism about how the launch of the euro and the evolution of monetary union would speed the benign process of European financial integration that it would have been hard even for the shrewdest policymaker or indeed market participant to realize that much of what was passing for integration on the ground was in reality indicative of asset price inflation as fuelled by Federal Reserve and ECB generated monetary disequilibrium. Some analysts, though, were perceptive even at an early stage.

For example Gabriele Galati and Kostas Tsatsaronis (in July 2001) were already drawing attention to some features in the rapidly growing euro inter-bank markets which were symptomatic of speculative temperature rise (greater degree of irrational exuberance), albeit not pressing the alarm bell, undoubtedly because of the overriding difficulty in disentangling the success of euro-led integration from bubble danger.

In their paper the authors focussed on the boom in issuance of corporate bonds denominated in euros and related this to the global wave of merger and acquisition activity in 1999–2000. Bonds offered a flexible and attractive means of financing transaction. More specific to the European scene was the financing of capital investments and corporate transactions related to the telecommunications sector. The single currency's contribution to these developments was in the form of widening the range of investor portfolios that could be tapped with a single bond issue, thus reducing the costs of capital market financing, compared to the pre-euro alternative of several issues in one or more national monies with a complex array of currency swap transactions alongside. The authors noted also that banks dominated bond issuance in euros – 60% of all euro-denominated bonds, a share almost double that of banks in the dollar segment of the market. Significantly the authors highlighted the booming issue of Pfandbriefe (securitized mortgages) by the German banks and the importance (to their success) of the ECB's decision to accept such paper as collateral in repo transactions:

> The success of German banks in marketing Pfandbriefe and thus increasing the range of financing tools has prompted a number of countries to introduce legislation in recent years that would support the creation of similar types of asset backed securities.

Like so many investors, the ECB failed to see through the misleading AAA labels being stuck on these asset-backed securities by the credit-rating agencies. In any chronology, though, of how Europe's credit markets heated up through the early- and mid-years of the first decade in the twenty-first century, the demonstration that ECB officials had woefully insufficient understanding or appreciation of that phenomenon only goes so far.

Yes, it is disappointing that with all the avenues of information at their command – beyond what the ordinary investor in the equity market place could assemble –the officials did no better at detecting possible danger in the form of credit market temperature rise below the wrapping of euro-driven financial integration which so flattered their whole endeavour. There can be no disappointment, though, without expectation. So the old lesson to take from this experience is that a stable monetary order must be based on firm rules that do not interfere with free markets discovering the neutral level of interest rates and whose application does not depend on any above-average intuition on the part of central bank officials. EMU, as contracted, has no such inner robustness.

ECB officials ignore explosive growth of euro-bank dollar loans

Even so the lack of any focus at the ECB at that time on the possibly sinister message from acclaimed examples of euro-driven financial integration as regards monetary stability and prosperity over the long run is striking. No ECB official hinted at any scenario analysis concerning the danger of a future existential crisis for the euro which a violent bubble-and-burst sequence in European credit markets might bring.

There is no evidence from any speech or publication that any senior official at the ECB through those years had pinpointed the reality or the risks of the explosive growth in European banks' international dollar lending funded to a large extent out of non-stable sources (for example, US money market funds or currency swaps). In practice, and in fairness, it was only six years later, well after the event, that the BIS produced its two excellent analyses of what had been happening then in its March 2009 quarterly review – *The US dollar shortage in global banking* (Patrick McGuire and Peter von Goetz) and *US dollar money market funds and non-US banks* (Baba, McCauley and Ramaswamy).

Yes, for years (from the early 2000s onwards) the balance of payments data for the US highlighted massive foreign inflows into US non-government bonds and European payments data which showed massive outflows of capital via the banking sector. To some extent, though, there was the always-ready excuse that information from balance of payments statistics is so notoriously unreliable. Though the ECB statisticians (and the co-respondents at Eurostat and in the national balance of payments offices) had made valiant attempts to assemble and publish euro-area wide balance-of-payments data, the swings in errors and omissions were so large relative to the totals reported that who could have any confidence in what tentative message they seemed to be conveying about risks in the present pattern of global capital flows.

Nonetheless it is idiosyncratic at best that the ECB through 2003 and beyond (into 2006) repeatedly banged the table so loud at international gatherings about the US balance of payment deficit and about low US savings being a source of potential serious crisis without realizing that a key channel of funds to the increasingly speculative US credit markets (which went along with a low aggregate savings rate in the US economy) came from Europe (as transmitted via the off-balance sheet activities of many European banks).

And as regards the lending boom into Eastern Europe, the ECB view (as illustrated by the Tumpel-Gugerell quote above – see p. 107) was that this was wholly a benign development accompanying the extension of the EU and ultimately the euro-zone into the 'Wild East'. In effect, officials in Frankfurt's Eurotower were wearing strong rose-coloured euro-spectacles (filtering out the dangers) in much the same way as the irrationally exuberant investors conditioned by the monetary disequilibrium in the global economy (in which the ECB was the second largest generator after the Federal Reserve). These spectacles apparently blocked out the landscape of the growing sub-prime type lending boom (effectively teaser loans denominated in Swiss francs or euros) in some parts of Central and Eastern Europe alongside a gigantesque construction and real estate bubble. Instead, the officials saw a benign furthering of economic union.

EMU flaws block emission of monetary warnings

Let us take one step back. Suppose we accept that the leading monetary bureaucrats in Frankfurt for one reason or another would remain poorly informed about any real-world developments in European or global credit markets. Were there nonetheless indicators just from within the normal range of prudent monetary control systems that should have been flashing yellow or red and to which the bureaucrats should have been responding by making monetary policy adjustments that in turn would have controlled the temperature in the credit markets? And was the ECB by its heavy-handed pegging of short-term interest rates, together with its efforts to influence expectations in the market-place about how this peg would be adjusted through time, stifling the free market forces which would tend to bring interest rates in the capital market in line with neutral? A large gap of actual market rates below neutral would fuel asset price inflation.

We come back to the flaws in the monetary framework which was designed in such a hurry during late 1998 and then revised with so little 'lateral thinking' in early 2003. If the ECB had been operating in a wholly different frame of reference from the Federal Reserve, imbued in a system of sound money (price level stability as assessed over the very long run rather than striving to make sure that inflation as measured over any two-year period did not fall too low) where market-forces could freely determine medium- and long-term interest rates without continual interference from the central bank's hubris about its intentions regarding the peg for short-term interest rates, the outcome would surely have been better than otherwise.

Trichet pursues French foreign policy in attacking Asian dollar bloc

While all alarm systems which might detect the high speculative temperatures generated by the virus of asset price inflation remained turned off in the Euro-tower, it was quite different with respect to the currency markets. Official statements and speeches from the ECB revealed growing anxiety through the early months of 2004 when the euro started to rise against the dollar, as was inevitable so long as the ECB fell behind the Bernanke/Greenspan Fed in its pace of breathing in inflation! ECB President Trichet had played a distinct (unintended) role in the dollar's general fall by allying himself (and his institution) with Washington in an assault on the Asian Dollar Bloc (at Dubai in autumn 2003 – see p. 71). Trichet and his 'cabinet' of French advisers had imagined that the assault would bring a stronger euro against the dollar matched by a weaker euro against the yen and the yuan. The direction of the forecast moves turned out to be correct, but the extent of the dollar depreciation was underestimated while the appreciation of the ex-Asian bloc currencies (including the yuan) was overestimated.

While the ECB president (and Paris economic diplomats long devoted to the cause of further multi-polarity in the currency world as part of the broader mission of reducing US hegemony as pursued by the French Foreign Office) were joining in this East Asian adventure, giving speeches on why East Asian currencies were not appreciating sufficiently and on how US citizens and their government should bolster the dollar by saving more (mechanism totally unclear, but probably running through a lower US current account deficit in some variant of partial equilibrium analysis), there was an eerie silence in the Euro-tower on the subject of monetary conditions in the euro-area. Alarm bells should have been ringing there about the dangers for Europe of monetary disequilibrium in the US! Germany's monetary guardian at the ECB, Professor Issing, should have been leading the chorus of concern and making sure that the ECB's monetary framework could provide as good a defence as possible for Europe.

Let us revert to the ECB's own scripted chronology to check what officials were in fact doing during the critical period of the Federal Reserve breathing inflation into the US economy from mid-2003 to mid-2005. This is the period the ECB in its anniversary review (June 2008) described as '*phase 4 – no changes to key ECB interest rates*'.

Why no change to ECB rates from mid-2003 to end-2005

Without comment the chroniclers state the strange facts that no sooner had this prolonged phase of ultra-low rates got under way (in 2003H2) than economic recovery started. Real euro-area GDP grew, on average, by 0.5% quarter-on-quarter in the first half of 2004, the highest rate recorded since the first half of 2000. On the external side, the growth of the world economy remained strong. On the domestic side, very favourable financing conditions, robust corporate earnings and business restructuring provided a positive environment for investment.

After some slowing in the first half of 2005, the expansion of euro-area economic activity regained momentum in the second half. So why was the real equivalent (taking account of inflation expectations) of the risk-free interest rate as pegged by the ECB still in slightly negative territory during this period, especially as the monetary pillar of the ECB's analytical framework was flashing yellow if not red? Moreover, expectations that the ECB would continue pegging money rates at such low levels for a considerable time and then only allow a gradual climb were bearing down on medium-maturity interest rates as set in the capital market.

The authors state that though headline M3 growth 'moderated substantially' through the second half of 2003 and early 2004, the series corrected for the estimated impact of portfolio shifts continued to grow at a sustained and slightly increasing rate through this period. In addition the annual rate of growth of loans to the private sector increased in the second half of 2003. And anyhow from mid-2004 onwards, headline M3 growth accelerated. The robust credit and monetary expansion from mid-2004 reflected the stimulatory effect of the then prevailing very low level of interest rates in the euro-area.

Eventually, in December 2005, the ECB resolved on a tentative 25 bp hike in the repo rate (to 2.25%) indicating that there was no presumption of further tightening and thereby continuing to bear down on medium-maturity capital market interest rates. But in the course of 2006, the ECB got more definitively into 'tightening mode' by little steps of 25 bp each time, culminating in a hike to 4% in mid-2007.

What was the ECB Chief Economist, Professor Issing, thinking about during the period of ultra-low rates (to December 2005 and beyond)?

One clue comes from his speech at an ECB Workshop in October 2005 (*What Central Banks can learn from money and credit aggregates*):

> [E]xtraordinary increases in asset prices in financial history have typically been accompanied by strong monetary and/or credit growth. This empirical relationship suggests that monetary and/or credit aggregates can be important indicators of the possible emergence of asset price 'bubbles' and thus are crucial to any central bank's approach to maintaining macroeconomic and price stability over the medium-term. [...] The acceleration of money supply growth from mid-2004 has been judged to be of a different quality to that observed between 2001 and 2003 [when portfolio shifts out of bonds and into deposits were an important explanatory factor]. On the counterparts side, stronger monetary growth has been associated with increasing demand for loans to the private sector rather than

capital flows from abroad. On the component side, higher M3 growth has been driven by its most liquid components, pointing to a significant impact of the low level of interest rates on monetary dynamics. Stronger monetary dynamics can no longer be interpreted as reflecting heightened financial and economic uncertainties, which have normalised since 2003. Since faster monetary growth appears to have been more fundamental in nature since mid-2004 than was the case between 2001 and 2003, the likelihood that strong monetary developments ultimately find their way through to higher prices must be seen as considerably higher. Moreover strong money and credit growth in a context of already ample liquidity in the euro-area implies that asset price developments, particularly in housing markets, need to be monitored more closely, given the potential for misalignments to emerge.

There is no doubt from this quote that Professor Issing was aware of the potential bad news for economic and financial stability contained in the monetary bulge. But there is some fuzziness in the remarks about whether house price or other asset price developments are in themselves cause for policy course correction or only in so far as a link can be made between these and the probable behaviour over the medium-term of the price level.

Moreover there is a total lack of urgency. It is only in autumn 2005 that Professor Issing is delivering this speech. And what is the denouement? A micro-rate rise (25 bp) occurs two months later amid a verbal barrage (to the effect that any further rise in the official peg for money rates would occur at a glacially slow pace) aimed at holding down medium-term interest rates! On available indices, house prices in Spain and France (and a range of small countries) had been racing ahead (in similar, if not greater, momentum to the Case–Shiller indices for the US) for two years or more. Yet despite the note of disquiet there is no serious indication of this development making a big difference to the planned monetary course.

Very possibly, residential real estate market developments were a background factor in the decision to raise money market rates by 25 bp in December 2005. But surely a careful analysis of the prevailing situation at that date would have suggested that the neutral rate of interest in the euro-area could well be far above market rates, albeit that no official or individual investor can have a high degree of confidence in his or her own estimation of neutral. Rather the best estimation is that which emerges via the interplay of free market forces in the money and capital markets.

The signalled glacial pace of advance of the pegged repo rate from a super-easy level to a still well below neutral level over the next year just created much further financial and economic disequilibrium. And there is a big item not mentioned at all in Professor Issing's speeches or articles – the rising speculative temperature in credit markets across the euro-area with German lenders prominent (not vis-à-vis German resident borrowers but as regards aggressive expansion of German banks into non-German loans and other assets – including the amassing of government bonds in periphery and mid-periphery zones of the euro-area despite the relevant yield spreads being at only feeble levels relative to potential risks).

Would a 200 bp higher rate in 2003–5 have pre-empted credit bubble?

One potential response of Professor Issing or any other central bank practitioner to the charge that monetary policy was critically to blame for the subsequent euro or global bubble and burst is to question whether, say, 200 bp or even 300 bp extra on money market rates would have made a critical difference to the outcome. That is a question which we take up in much more detail in Chapter 6. For now the provisional answer is 'yes, a great deal of difference'.

Why? If investors globally and in the euro-area in particular could have expected to earn 4% p.a. plus (in nominal terms) over a period of some years rather than a feeble rate of 2% p.a. or slightly more they would surely have been less desperate to bolster yield (income) by falling into the traps sprung wittingly or unwittingly by the array of financial 'innovators' in New York, London, Frankfurt or elsewhere. Why buy illiquid non-transparent paper, albeit with an AAA stamp, to get a little more return, when a good return could already be made on liquid transparent paper? Or why buy the government debt of Greece or Portugal at such tiny yield spreads over Germany without even considering seriously some dark scenarios which might become reality in the future?

With medium-term rates at neutral rather than far below there would have been less danger of froth developing in the higher risk credit market prices which would generate positive feedback loops apparently justifying questionable speculative hypotheses (such as in a world of European financial integration Greek bonds are almost as safe as German). Moreover, there would not have been such a queue of borrowers at the opposite end of the line, ready to issue all the paper being lapped up in many cases with varying amounts of hidden or partly hidden leverage, unless the going level of interest rates (with respect to low-risk and even more so high-risk credits) was well below equilibrium level.

The merchants of various types of credit paper had plentiful amounts in the store to sell because there were vibrant real asset markets along with strongly rising real economic activity – both stimulated by interest rates far below neutral level – in the world outside! The risks of leverage could not have remained disguised (except from the wilfully unseeing) if there had been a continuing roll call of bankruptcies. And the market for equities in financial intermediaries peddling the high-risk paper and in some cases taking this on to their own books would not have been in such a high temperature range with rates closer to neutral.

In sum, the ECB in its programme of adjusting its peg for its official money market rate upwards only at a glacial pace (and of clearly signalling this programme to the market so as to influence downwards medium-maturity interest rates) repeated with a lag exactly the same mistake as the Federal Reserve was making. This was a time of madness for the rate-manipulators on both sides of the Atlantic.

It would have been such a feat if the ECB had distinguished itself from the rate-pegging, (quasi-) inflation targeting and inflation breathing-in Federal Reserve. But that was not to be the case. The sales material for EMU which made much of how the new creation would bring protection against 'Anglo-Saxon' monetary shock turned out to be bogus.

The ECB official anniversary report on monetary policy during the first ten years makes absolutely no reference to this failure. It is plausible – and indeed likely – that the perpetrators of the failure were completely unaware of it!

'Withdrawal of monetary accommodation, 2006–2007H1'

The chroniclers continue into their next subsection of history under the subtitle of '*Phase 5 – withdrawal of monetary policy accommodation (since end-2005)*':

Since the end of 2005, the Governing Council has raised the key ECB interest rates by a total of 200 basis points, bringing the minimum bid rate in the main refinancing operations of the Eurosystem to a level of 4% by the end of June 2007. This adjustment of the accommodative monetary policy stance was warranted in order to address risks to price stability, as identified by both the economic and the monetary analysis. [...] As regards prices, average annual inflation was 2.2% in 2006 and 2.1% in 2007, mainly driven by domestic demand. In both years, the headline inflation rate fluctuated significantly, largely on account of developments in oil prices. In 2006 it followed an increasing trend until August, mainly as a result of substantial increases in energy prices, while the annual inflation rate fell below 2% in the remaining months of the year, largely as a consequence of significantly declining oil prices and base effects. Until the third quarter of 2007, annual inflation rates developed in line with the ECB's definition of price stability, partly because of favourable base effects stemming from energy price developments a year earlier.

In sum, a credit bubble of once-in-a-century magnitude was forming in the global economy with the European banking system deeply infected by the underlying monetary virus of asset price inflation which had its origin in the extreme monetary disequilibrium created in Frankfurt and Washington. The monetary critic of this period in reading the notes of the policymakers cannot help but feeling like K in Kafka's *The Trial* when he comes to examine the judges notepads – all he finds is scribbling (in that case, obscene!).

And just before the bubble burst, with the maximum initial impact of the Great Credit Market Quake (August 2007) felt in Europe (to the total surprise of the ECB!) rather than the US, there had been the biggest moment of madness in the financial equity market place, also in Europe. This was the takeover battle for ABN-AMRO.

Merger mania: the takeover battle for ABN-AMRO

The saga had started on 21 February 2007 when a British hedge fund, TCI, specialized in finding profitable opportunity from triggering changes in corporate control (or management), asked the chairman of the Supervisory Board (of ABN-AMRO) to actively investigate a merger, acquisition or break-up of the bank, stating that the current stock price did not reflect the true value of the underlying assets. TCI, with a small but significant shareholding in the bank (ABN-AMRO) asked its chairman to put their request on the agenda of the annual shareholders meeting (April). Four days later the President of the Dutch Central Bank (and thereby a member of the policymaking council of the ECB), Dr Wellink, was quoted in the Dutch newspaper *NRC Handelsblad* as saying that it was unprecedented that a hedge fund should call for a bank to be broken up. President Wellink warned that there could be repercussions beyond the borders of the Netherlands:

A bank is different from other listed companies. For us, that is a bridge too far.

Evidently President Wellink got no public show of support from his colleagues in the ECB – albeit that there is no evidence that he requested this! Meanwhile TCI went public with its case citing that excluding dividends ABN-AMRO had returned zero since May 2000 compared to a 44% return for its European banking peers! This stodgy bank had not been a full participant in the go-go profitable opportunities of investment banking, and TCI was determined to exploit the profit from acting as catalyst to a change in direction (towards full participation!). The CEO of Citigroup was famously to say (in early summer 2007) that when everyone else is dancing you have to get up and join in. ABN-AMRO management, according to TCI, were failing to join the dance. By getting ABN-AMRO into the dance (fully involved in the global credit bubble) TCI was to make its profit.

The rest is history – the bid from Barclays and finally a superior cash offer from a joint syndicate of three European banks all deeply steeped in the euro- and global-credit bubbles (Fortis, Santander and RBS) and all enjoying valuations in global equity markets which rested on a high degree of confidence in a never-ending rapidly growing profits stream from investment banking (albeit that in the case of RBS there had been periodic jitters about the aggressive expansion plans of its CEO on some previous occasions) and on a lack of awareness of actual leverage.

Among the big gainers were those shareholders of ABN-AMRO who collected the cash and were not tempted to join the dance by buying other financial equities! Among the big losers were the tax payers in the UK, Holland, Belgium and Luxembourg, who had eventually to foot the bill (around one year later) for rescuing two of the three consortium banks – RBS and Fortis – and of course the shareholders (and some categories of bondholders) in the consortium banks which had squandered their capital in the takeover.

The takeover could not have taken place if the financial equity markets had been operating efficiently – correctly discounting the huge risks which accompanied Europe's highly leveraged big banks (by and large the regulators ignored leverage concentrating instead on a flawed BIS bank-risk measurement system, widely described as 'Basel 2'). But the many years of serious monetary disequilibrium both in Europe and the US had sent speculative temperatures so high across the credit and financial equity markets that the normal forces promoting efficiency were now weak in this context of irrational exuberance (asset price inflation).

Incredibly in hindsight, the vote of Fortis shareholders in favour of the takeover took place almost literally on the eve of the Great Credit

Quake. Despite an ominous warning from ABN-AMRO's CEO, Rijkman Groenink (carried in *Het Financieele Dagblad*, the Dutch financial daily) to Fortis shareholders that a successful bid by the consortium would further weigh on Fortis's share price and that shareholders should vote against it, an overwhelming 90% majority voted in favour on 6 August 2007. The loud pre-quake rumblings already to be heard in the global financial market place apparently had no impact on the shareholders. Even more incredibly the following Friday, just two days after the Great Credit Quake of 8 August, RBS shareholders gave their approval.

A little more than a year later both groups of shareholders had lost almost everything. Well, we all know the saying that the Gods make mad who they want to destroy, albeit that in this case the catalyst of destruction , TCI, was laughing all the way to the bank. The much bigger question relates to the policy issues raised by this madness.

First, there is the general point that the madness could only have developed in a climate of extreme monetary disequilibrium such as had been fostered by inflation-targeting central banks on both sides of the Atlantic.

Second, if the ECB had been assuming at all any role in monitoring and responding to possibly dangerous rises in credit market temperature, then its actual performance was surely woefully inadequate.

And third, despite all the literature on efficient capital markets and empirical evidence supporting that hypothesis, huge irrationality had apparently become prevalent in a core component (financial equities) of the global equity market. The hypothesis of irrationality or inefficiency could be based in part on huge failure in the market for information, including gross asymmetries and lack of big enough incentives for investigative journalists or analysts to make discovery and publish their findings. An essential condition, however, for the inefficiency and irrationality was the monetary disequilibrium.

As regards that third issue, one plausible hypothesis was that not only ECB officials but also equity market investors had been so lulled (under the influence of the asset price inflation virus) by the music of financial integration and its potential efficiency that they had become uncritical of the underlying business models and unseeing of the growing risks which lay behind the bank profits. All three of the bidding banks had share prices which at the peak reflected an uncritical appraisal of continuing the go-go profits from a European-made component of the global credit market (Spanish mortgage boom, East European lending, UK commercial and residential real estate mortgage boom, private equity boom) and of the risks, including those built on leverage, related to these.

Some, but not all, of this in its full extent might have happened even with the most orthodox of ECB monetary policies over the preceding years (and including 2007). After all there had been a Great Bubble and subsequent Panic in the US in 1905–7 without a central bank there yet in existence. Even in that early historical episode the proverbial monetary monkey wrench had not been absent – but it was de-personalized and de-institutionalized. Instead gold discoveries together with technological progress in the mining industry, downward shifts in demand for high-powered money related to financial innovation, and huge uncertainty concerning the natural interest rate level in the wake of the San Francisco earthquake then meant much scope for mal-estimation in the market-place. An ECB operating within a rigorous framework designed to ensure monetary stability could have been similarly trumped by misfortune. In the event, however, ECB policy had been highly unorthodox as judged against the benchmark of stable monetary orders.

Yet, in the days following the Great Credit Quake of August 2007, there was much speculation and hope about how the new central bank in Europe and its US counterpart could act to alleviate the consequences. Few imagined at this early stage that the ECB, together with the Federal Reserve and Bank of England, all in their own ways, would make the consequences much worse, even though a long look at previous monetary history would have suggested such a possibility!

5
The Bursting of Europe's Bubble

The monetary policies on both sides of the Atlantic responsible for creating and spreading a powerful virus of asset price inflation through 2003–7 and then for adding to the economic and human suffering when the disease progressed to its ultimate phase characterized by steep falls in speculative temperatures (market crashes) may not have fully satisfied the definition of catastrophic. But how far short they were of that benchmark will doubtless long remain a matter for heated debate.

The turmoil and distress (whether economic, political or geopolitical) wrought by global monetary disequilibrium originating in the Greenspan–Bernanke–Yellen Federal Reserve, joined by China, Japan and Europe, during the first two decades of the twenty-first century may turn out to be of a lower order than for the years around the Great Boom and Great Depression of the inter-war years (1920s and 30s) as stemming originally from the policies of the Benjamin Strong Federal Reserve. It is arguable that there has not been the same degree of monetary nationalism this time round which so heavily contributed to the devilish chain of national political and geopolitical events in the 1930s. That is still an open question, though, given the legitimization and use of currency war by the Bernanke Federal Reserve, euro-nationalism as practised by the Trichet ECB, President Sarkozy's 'Napoleon III' moment in euro-policy (persuading German Chancellor Merkel to go along with turning EMU into a 'transfer union' in large part via the ECB expanding massively its bad bank operations) and the many years of resistance in Beijing to creating a fee market in a fully convertible yuan.

Even so, early in the twenty-first century the bust phase in Europe of the asset price inflation virus, this time created and spread by the Greenspan/Bernanke Federal Reserve and the Trichet/Issing ECB, has not featured as it did in the inter-war years a collapse of the biggest economy, Germany. Now the country experiencing the most severe bust, culminating in insolvency of both the sovereign power and the banking system, has been tiny Greece.

Yet there are echoes of the earlier catastrophe in the present-day monetary tumult (or catastrophe?) which are troubling for those who believe strongly in human progress. Yes, the renowned professor in monetary economics later to become the head of the Federal Reserve assured us on the occasion of Milton Friedman's ninetieth birthday party in 2002 that the monetary mistakes which surrounded the Great Depression would never be made again. There are grounds to question, though, whether the professor had learnt the right lessons.

No monetary progress in US or Europe?

The professor, Ben Bernanke, became the key proponent of the expansionary policy (breathing in inflation) adopted in early 2003 which played such a critical role in generating the virus of global asset price inflation in the first place, (even if the buck ultimately stopped at Greenspan's desk). Indeed, much of the 'neo-Austrian' critique (see Rothbard, 1972) of US monetary policy in the 1920s under the leadership of New York Federal Reserve Governor Strong could be repeated against the Greenspan–Bernanke Federal Reserve.

At a time when real forces (productivity surge due to technological revolution and terms of trade improvement) were putting downward pressure on the equilibrium level of goods and services prices, the Federal Reserve was setting monetary conditions such as to produce a stable or gently rising price level. In doing so the Federal Reserve created grave monetary disequilibrium with its main symptom being a sharp rise of temperature in credit and asset markets. This had already happened in the second half of the 1990s, culminating in the severe recession of 2001–2. Then the Greenspan–Bernanke Federal Reserve (Professor Bernanke joined the Board in autumn 2002) had sought to force-feed the recovery from that recession by 'breathing inflation' back into the economy while exhibiting deflation phobia to an extreme degree.

Some critics, including in particular John Taylor (2009), highlighted how ignoring monetary rules had sewn the seeds of crisis. Taylor included for criticism the flouting of his own brand of monetary rule – the so-called Taylor Rule – which is more complex than that of Milton Friedman and, unlike Friedman's, requires considerable discretion on the part of policymakers. And then, Milton Friedman's co-author of *A Monetary History of the US*, Anna Schwartz, argued that Professor Bernanke had misdiagnosed the crisis which erupted in summer 2007 as a liquidity crisis (the situation in autumn 1930) when in fact it was a solvency crisis (in the 1929–33 episode as examined by Friedman and Schwartz a real solvency issue erupted only much later on in the depths of depression – see Schwartz, 2009). That misdiagnosis led on to that fateful weekend in mid-September 2008 when there was no contingency plan on the shelf for the threatened insolvency of Lehman. John Taylor provided additional important evidence to bear on that point (see Taylor, 2009).

Finally, the critics of cyclical fine-tuning accused Professor Bernanke of having made even bigger mistakes than George Harrison, the much-criticized successor to Benjamin Strong (see Meltzer, 2004). Harrison, after all, had not stood in the way of risk-free rates generally (including T-bill and short-maturity government bonds) collapsing to virtually zero immediately following the October 1929 Wall Street Crash. The New York Federal Reserve had then supplied adequate extra reserves to the banking system (equivalently expanding the supply of monetary base) for that purpose.

In the later episode the Bernanke Federal Reserve got in the way of the powerful move down to zero of risk-free rates, engaging in a novel type of sterilized lending to the weakest banks while seeking to break the overall rate decline, out of residual concerns about meeting the quasi-inflation target in the context of transitorily sky-high oil prices. Astoundingly in early October 2008, in the darkest days of the financial panic, the Bernanke Fed announced the innovation of paying interest on reserves (an enabling bill had already been signed into law but with no intention of early use) with the express purpose of strengthening control over risk-free rates. In particular the intention was to prevent these rates from falling to zero under the influence of huge liquidity injections.

However troubling were the echoes on the western side of the Atlantic (of the mistakes in the mid and late 1920s/early 30s), those on the eastern side were even more so. As in the US, the policymakers in Frankfurt had pursued quasi-inflation targeting (no ECB official would admit to that!), blind to the real (non-monetary) forces (such as productivity growth or terms of trade improvement or business cycle dynamics) which might be lowering the price level, and sceptical of or unsympathetic towards monetary auto-piloting based on constitutional rules.

In Frankfurt's corridors of monetary power there was apparently a very low (if any) state of alert with respect to the financial and economic dangers emanating from the US, even though a key justification for EMU in the first place had been to protect the member countries to a greater extent than possible before from US monetary shock! ECB officials had responded to the unwelcome strength of the euro against the dollar in 2003–4, triggered ultimately by US monetary disequilibrium, by disabling any putative alarm system (in the Eurotower) installed to detect imminent or present US monetary shock.

Frankfurt had the excuse (for poor overall monetary policy performance) of an unreliable indicator board (with money supply data hard to interpret because of the newness of monetary union) and the difficulties of steering one policy to suit all in a union with much greater regional divergences and far less flexibility than the US, whether in terms of relative wages, prices or inter-regional labour movements. These, though, were a self-wrought problem for the participating members of the EMU. The consenting electorates who had signed up surely reckoned with significant costs to range against the potential benefits, even though some of the smooth-talking euro sales persons may not have spelt this out!

What the consenting electorates (in so far as they were asked for approval) could not have reckoned with (as a certainty as against a low-probability scenario) was the seriousness of monetary framework error and subsequently monetary policymaking error that lay ahead. Moreover during the period when speculative temperatures across a range of markets (including many in Europe) were rising under the influence of the asset price inflation virus the consenting electorates were broadly satisfied with how monetary union was functioning. The errors became the (largely hidden from popular view) source of dissatisfaction only when the phase of severe asset price deflation followed.

Summer 2007 credit quake

The story of those serious monetary policy mistakes in the post-bubble period starts in summer 2007 with the seize-up of the inter-bank money markets on 9 August. John Taylor describes this as the 'Landing of a Black Swan in the Money Market' (see Taylor, 2009). (For two excellent chronologies of the crisis see Brunnermeier, 2008 and Jordan, 2008.)

The immediate trigger to the seize-up was the announcement on 9 August by BNP Paribas, France's biggest bank, that it had halted withdrawals from three investment funds because it could not 'fairly' value their holdings now that US sub-prime mortgage losses were roiling credit markets. The funds had about 1.6 billion of euros on 7 August, with about a third of that in sub-prime mortgage securities rated AA or higher. This followed announcements in the days before by Bear Stearns that it was stopping similar redemptions. And on 2 August the German bank, IKB Deutsche Industriebank, had revealed it was in trouble because of investment in US sub-prime loans where these had been in an off-balance- sheet structured investment vehicle.

After US house prices had peaked in 2006, it became more and more obvious to some market participants that a rapidly growing number of sub-prime borrowers would soon be unable to service their debt with the amount of potential shortfall becoming ever more alarming. Prices of sub-prime-backed securities had started to ease in early 2007.

As 2007 progressed, the deteriorating sub-prime market began sapping confidence in related structured finance product markets and during the course of July 2007 had triggered a sudden general re-pricing of credit risk beyond the confines of US residential mortgage products. There was a ballooning of credit spreads in the credit-derivative markets, especially as related to higher-risk categories of credit (whether mortgages or leveraged loans to non-financial corporations). Credit spreads widened also in Europe, notably with respect to leveraged loans and mortgage-backed assets in Spain or the UK. And in the US banking industry, the worsening plight (and slide in equity price) of Countrywide, the giant aggressive California-based mortgage lender, was making it into the daily financial headlines.

All of this formed the background to a sudden and general 'seizing up' in European inter-bank money markets on the morning of 9 August 2007. The catalysts were the events which demonstrated that many of the European banks had huge exposure (hitherto camouflaged) to the US sub-prime market and especially via off-balance-sheet vehicles (so-called structured investment vehicles) which financed themselves in the so-called asset-backed commercial paper markets. Exposure to hot speculative areas of European credit markets also came into view.

ECB's panic response to money seize-up, 9 August 2007

It seems (there is no available hard evidence of discussions and, unless a revolution takes place within EMU, the practice of official secrecy means that no such evidence will become available in the future) that the ECB President, M. Trichet, alerted in his Brittany summer house to the seizing up of the European money markets, shared the view of his colleagues assembled in teleconference that this was an epic crisis of liquidity stemming in main part from the bubble-burst in US sub-prime mortgage markets, with concerns about weak European credits playing only a subsidiary role.

Some hearsay evidence suggests that the Bundesbank played the lead role in initiating and coordinating the initial response to the seizing up. This role in part may have been forced on the Bundesbank by circumstances – the lightness of the holiday staffing in the ECB and M. Trichet's absence on vacation. The hearsay evidence is consistent with the later-revealed role of the Bundesbank as staunch defender of the Separation Principle according to which liquidity provision was to be distinguished from the chosen path for the policy interest rate (see p. 79). There is no evidence that any key Bundesbank official had a premonition that by starting down this road the ECB would lose its political independence. This realization came much later – in fact in spring 2010 (see Chapter 2, p. 26) – when Bundesbank President Weber openly, but unsuccessfully, defied ECB President Trichet.

The response of the ECB to the crisis was to make unlimited funds available through the secured lending markets to all applicant banks at around the official repo rate (4% p.a.), which remained unchanged. By such operations the ECB (on Thursday, 9 August) 'put' nearly $95 billion into European financial institutions, followed by a somewhat smaller operation ($61 bn) on Friday. On the same Thursday and Friday, the Federal Reserve's Open Market Trading Desk injected funds in similar fashion, 'putting in' a total of $38 billion.

'Putting' here did not mean an expansion of the monetary base. Rather, at issue was a sterilized operation, in which ECB lending to banks experiencing a sudden shortage of funds was matched by ECB borrowing from banks in the reverse situation (those unwilling to lend out surplus funds in the inter-bank market, except possibly to a limited extent at much greater margins over risk-free rates than normal). This borrowing by the ECB could take the form of those institutions piling up excess reserves in the deposit facility at the ECB earning interest at just one percentage point below the unchanged official repo rate (at 4%), or repo operations in which the ECB would borrow short-maturity funds and lend out government bonds or bills.

What exactly were the forces triggering such huge intervention?

With the benefit of hindsight and much circumstantial evidence it has become clear that what happened on 9 August far transcended a crisis of liquidity. This was already a crisis of solvency. And, as American Enterprise Institute (AEI) scholar Alex Pollock points out, the two phenomena are inevitably linked in varying degrees (see Pollock, 2009).

The huge reported sterilized injections by the ECB involved much more than liquidity provision. They were in effect a combination of massive price-rigging operations (suppressing or containing any rise in risk premiums in the inter-bank deposit markets) and of emergency quasi-capital assistance to the weakest banks by the central banks. (The term quasi is used as there was no matching change in the banks' legal capital structure). The capital could not have been available in the given circumstances from any other source.

The solvency issue stemmed in the immediate chiefly from the unknown amount of loss on so-far camouflaged holdings of sub-prime US assets by some European financial institutions. But there was also another dimension to the solvency issue; one about which ECB officials were totally silent and apparently ignorant. This was the extent of potential loss on holdings of European financial institutions in their own domestic (European) credit markets – whether related to hot residential real estate markets in Spain, UK, France and Holland, or to private equity lending in those same countries and including Germany, or to the booming loans into the Wild East (much of which was related to hot real estate markets and booming construction sectors there), or to massive investments in the government debts of periphery-zone EMU member countries (especially Greece, Portugal and Ireland) and mid-zone countries (Italy, Spain and Belgium).

Those banks with a chronic surplus of funds (more non-bank client deposits than non-bank client loans) – as was largely the case in Germany, corresponding to that country's massive savings surplus – which during recent years had simply lent the excess into the booming inter-bank (unsecured) loan market in Europe suddenly realized that they had become greatly overextended to credit risk there. What to one bank had seemed like a low-risk overnight inter-bank loan suddenly came into view, in terms of the bigger systemic picture now emerging, as high risk.

As those less weak banks in surplus pulled their funds out of the inter-bank markets, they had a choice between deploying these in short-maturity government bond markets (of which the safest and most liquid in Europe is Bunds) or into the deposit facility at the ECB (on which interest accrued at a fixed small margin below the official repo rate). Arbitrage between these two (denominated in euro) meant that rates on both remained closely in line with, and not far below, the official repo rate.

Failure of the ECB (and Fed) to promptly diagnose insolvency

If the ECB (and Federal Reserve) had looked around hard in those late summer days of 2007 they would have discovered plenty of evidence suggesting a solvency element to the crisis. (See Schwartz, 2009 and

Taylor, 2009 for two strong critiques of the Federal Reserve under Professor Bernanke for its similar failure to make such a diagnosis with resulting huge cost for the US – and global – economy.) For example, whereas rates on repo-transactions secured by top quality government bonds between banks remained steady, unsecured rates in the inter-bank market (in so far as funds were available to any particular borrower) rose sharply as did rates on secured borrowing (repos) where the security took the form of less than tip-top government bonds (for example, AAA-rated mortgage-backed paper).

In this situation of a sudden re-appraisal of risks (meaning solvency risks) across the whole spectrum of credit including especially bank (and inter-bank) credit, the emergency decision by the ECB on 9 August 2007 to supply all bank demands for secured funds (against any eligible collateral – not just top government bonds) at the fixed repo rate (a virtually risk-free rate of 4% p.a.) was bound to create huge round-tripping.

Banks with funds flowing back, courtesy of the ECB, from the repayment of asset-backed commercial paper or from maturing inter-bank loans or from repos secured on mortgage-backed paper took the money and ran. Where did they run – mainly to the ECB, stupid! (Or otherwise into short-maturity Bunds.) The ECB was keeping the rate on its so-called deposit facility at just one percentage point below the repo rate (meaning in effect around 3%) and banks with excess funds (due to reflow of funds described) could now simply deposit these with the ECB. Some banks with excess funds available continued to lend in the overnight markets within tightened limits (and only to banks deemed safe) at an interest rate very near to the official rate of 4% p.a. as set by the ECB.

If the ECB's view about this all being a liquidity crisis was correct, then within a few days or weeks there should have been a reflux. Inter-bank lending at the old rates would have resumed and the ECB could have withdrawn its support. Of course this did not occur!

The ECB had constructed, unintentionally it seems through lack of knowledge and appropriate analysis, a whole pyramid of secured lending (most of which was against increasingly dodgy assets such as the so-called AAA residential mortgage-backed securities emanating from Spain or the UK and then the government debts of the periphery-zone member countries of EMU) to the banks under most stress at well below the rates that would have prevailed without the ECB's intervention. In several important cases (the weakest banks) the ECB had lent amounts well beyond those that would have been available at any market rates.

Meanwhile the ECB strove with total success to keep the overnight rates for those banks able to obtain funds there (albeit within shrunken inter-bank limits) very close to the official repo rate of around 4% (and of course there was arbitrage between the repo and overnight deposit markets to keep the two in line with each other). Arbitrage operations by the less weak banks in surplus meant that risk-free rates (as quoted on short maturity government bonds denominated in euros) remained close to the ECB's overnight deposit rate, at a small margin below the official repo rate.

A superior crisis response ignored by the ECB (and Fed)

The outcome brought about by the ECB's massive response of 9–10 August was very far from a market solution or from a solution consistent with overall economic equilibrium. It was also ultimately in contradiction of the ECB's own prized political independence, as the eventual run-down of its huge secured lending to weak banks would require entering into negotiations with member governments to replace its support. Some member governments could be too financially weak to support their own banks in which case the ECB would have inadvertently become the agent of a transfer union – implicitly drawing on taxpayers in financially strong countries, as guarantors of the ECB's balance sheet, to aid banks in the financially weak countries.

The monetary framework constructed at the dawn of EMU – in particular the payment of interest on excess reserves at only a fine margin below the official rate and emphasis on micro-management of micro-changes in officially set money interest rates (signalling the trend ahead) – had much to answer for in any serious investigation as to why a better solution did not materialize. What form would this have taken? Here are the main elements.

First, with a high degree of uncertainty relating to the non-transparent risks which may be residing in various banks, and yet an immediate presumption that these were heterogeneous (some banks suspected of being in much weaker conditions than others), it no longer made sense as an operational strategy for the ECB to peg one uniform overnight rate. Even in the overnight secured markets the weaker banks (those where possible solvency risks were higher) should have been paying a substantially higher rate for funds than the less weak banks.

In effect the operational strategy of the ECB would have changed from rate pegging in the overnight inter-bank deposit market to setting a quantitative target for monetary base, (now to be non-interest bearing);

something evidently not possible to implement with any precision in the midst of a panic. In broad terms the immediate supply of monetary base should have been large enough to mean that all risk-free euro interest rates (such as those on very short-maturity German government bonds) fell to zero. Alternatively the ECB could have carried out rate-pegging in the very short-maturity repo market based exclusively on top-quality government bonds (with the peg at a level well below the pre-crisis official repo rate, possibly already as far down as zero).

Second, the ECB would not have stood in the way of a wide spread forming between risk-free and higher-risk rates (depending on counterparty) whether at short or long maturities. Nor should the ECB have acted to prevent a wide spread developing between repo rates secured on top-quality government bonds and those secured on dodgy collateral (albeit AAA), such as UK or Spanish mortgages. Consistent with this 'laissez-faire' approach, allowing markets to set spreads related to solvency or credit risks the ECB would have removed various obstacles to such market determination – including in particular the now well-above equilibrium interest rate (then fixed at 3% p.a.) on its deposit facility (where banks could place excess funds) and the now in most cases generous Lombard rate (5% p.a., only one percentage point above the official repo rate) which it charged on unsecured lending.

Optimally the ECB would have reduced to zero the overnight rate on deposits with itself (regarded at this point as 100% safe), meaning that risk-averse banks could not gain interest by parking funds at the ECB; they would have had to place these in short-maturity government bonds, driving the yields on these down towards zero, or else taking on some risk and lending at higher rates. And ECB lending at the Lombard rate would have been strictly limited for any one institution (according to normal prudential yardsticks), with the Lombard rate itself set on a sliding scale with each successive tranche being borrowed at a higher margin above the official repo rate. The amount lent by the ECB against eligible collateral would also have been restricted according to normal practice and a higher rate would have been charged on secured lending against non-prime collateral than against top government collateral.

Third, the ECB in its estimation of the market-clearing level of risk-free rates of interest, which would be the basis for any quasi-pegging operation in the very short-maturity prime government bond markets or in the market for short-maturity repos secured on prime government bonds, would have deduced that this was now surely much lower than on the eve of the crisis. The rise of a whole spectrum of rates (in absolute terms) on higher risk credits surely had to have as a corollary (from the viewpoint of overall balance in the economy – including an optimal path back from present panic conditions to full equilibrium) a lower level of risk-free rates. As indicated above, in a severe crisis this market-clearing level of the risk- free rates was surely zero.

Moreover, in the new reality of financial crisis the likelihood had increased of recessionary developments being under way, adding further justification to revising down estimates of the neutral or natural rate of interest, as specified distinctly for short, medium and long maturities.

Over and above all this, it was justifiable to lower the alert on inflation and increase the alert on depression. Yes, the ECB had a predisposition towards econometric modelling. But in present circumstances of extreme discontinuity any forecast from such a process had to be treated with the utmost caution. And in any case were a recession or depression to get going that could set off a vicious circle of ever worse insolvency within the financial system.

Fourth, there would have been the pressing issue what to do with banks that could not raise sufficient funds in the markets, even at the widened spreads prevailing, and who came up against the normal prudential limits at the ECB's official windows for Lombard credit or secured credit. This was not a new issue – it can be traced back through the financial history books to the whole discussion around the role of lender of last resort. There were some novel features though in the case of EMU.

In particular, the Maastricht Treaty had not in fact determined that the ECB should act as lender of last resort. And this was for good reason. How could the ECB enter into the whole area of taking calculated gambles on bank insolvency without simultaneously becoming immersed ultimately in the politics of burden sharing between the member countries as to who should be responsible for bail-outs? If the ECB was zealously resolved to protect its independence then at any hint of a bank insolvency crisis it would have to turn the issue of support and emergency funding over to the member governments, rather than itself assuming a role as lender of last resort. In this role, the member government (or inter-government agency/authority) would determine first, whether the cash-starved institution is still solvent. If so, then it lends, albeit at a highly penal rate, while seeking a resolution (either new equity capital raising or merger). By contrast where the member government (or intergovernment agency/authority) determines that the institution is insolvent but with a going concern or net asset value which likely exceeds deposits outstanding, then a controlled de-leverage plan (imposing haircuts on bond-holders and debt-for-equity swaps) takes place linked to a re-capitalization plan.

In the dour case of deep insolvency being suspected right at the start (not enough asset value to match deposits) then there may be no alternative to immediate closure, with the deposit insurance corporation taking a lead role in disposing of assets.

If the ECB (and Federal Reserve) had gone down this route (incorporating points one to four above) of recognizing an insolvency crisis as such rather than mis-diagnosing it or mis-treating it (with an unpublicized correct diagnosis) as a liquidity crisis there are grounds for imagining that the eventual economic and financial outcome would have been better than what actually occurred. And the independence of the central bank would not have become so compromised in the process.

Instead the ECB rolled over vast amounts of loans largely secured against dodgy assets (some packaged together so as to meet the eligibility requirements of the ECB) to the weakest institutions at subsidized spreads and far beyond 'normal' prudent levels without exerting any of the standard textbook pressure for prompt re-capitalization. Simultaneously the ECB steered policy rates – and risk-free rates in general – higher, out of fear that sky-high oil prices would push up inflation.

Counterfactual monetary history of autumn 2007–8

Let us look at the counterfactual case in more detail so as to draw out how this would have been better than what actually happened (from the viewpoint of the overall economy and financial system). Suppose in reaction to the trauma of 9 August 2007, the ECB had indeed lowered dramatically the floor to risk-free rates (for example yields on short-maturity top government bonds) by cutting its overnight deposit rate to zero. This would have allowed risk-free rates to fall sharply – indeed possibly all the way to zero as had occurred during some great previous world financial panics including October 1929. That step would have been the catalyst to a wide span of interest rates (according to the risk of the borrower) forming.

Then weak but still widely deemed as solvent banks might have been able to borrow, say at 5–10% p.a., in the overnight markets and at some premium above that (to a limited extent) in the term money markets (unsecured). Repo rates fixed with respect to dodgy (non-government) collateral would have been well above the risk-free rate especially where the borrower was a weak bank. Less weak banks would have been able to fund themselves at rates much below those risky rates (with the exact rate depending on the category of collateral used, if any). Repo rates based on top government bonds would have fallen towards zero in line with the downward pressure on risk-free rates.

The ECB would have injected additional high-powered money into the system so as to relieve any shortage due to banks seeking to build up excess reserves to protect themselves against deposit withdrawals. One guide to the adequacy of the injection would have been rates on risk-free near money assets (such as short-maturity government bonds). Inadequacy would be suggested by these rates re-bounding due to banks scrambling out of anything for cash.

Note that even if the ECB had not thought through this plan of action on day one, instead supplying unlimited funds (as in fact occurred) it could have made progress towards implementing something similar in the days that followed. The ECB would have refused to roll-over repos or other lending except according to the counter-factual framework as described here.

In this counter-factual world the less weak banks would have scrambled to demonstrate their financial soundness – revealing to the marketplace the full extent of their loan and asset portfolios and the extent of the cushion (to depositors) provided by their capital base. This scrambling process is evident in that great financial panic of 1907, the last great panic before the creation of the Federal Reserve and the advent of Keynesian policy prescriptions, in which the less weak trust banks demonstrated their soundness to the rescue committee instituted by J. P. Morgan in the wake of the failure of Knickerbocker Trust Company (with a lead role played by Benjamin Strong, then Bankers Trust vice-president and protégé of Morgan, later of Federal Reserve fame or infamy for his role in the 1920s credit bubble – see Bruner and Carr, 2007 and Rothbard, 1972).

The less weak banks would have had a big incentive to go out and raise more equity capital – as by doing so they would push down their overall cost of funding (in non-insured deposit markets) to nearer the risk-free level and capture market share from their weaker rivals. Their well-cushioned (by extra equity protection) deposits would appeal to a widened base of (non-insured) retail and wholesale clients, meaning they could make a new pitch for deposit business and the long-term profits (for example, through the sale of other products) that might be associated with this. These equity-bolstered banks would have been able to carry on charging the same elevated rates according to client credit risk across a broad spectrum of their floating rate loan book.

It is true that the issuance of more equity capital could have diluted present equity outstanding if indeed (as would be probable) there were no mechanism for the original shareholders to claw back windfall gains bestowed by the re-capitalization on the holders of bank debt. Plausibly, however, that dilution would be less than the extra present value to be gained from business profit enhancement derived from being able to market for deposits with a deepened equity cushion. Note that the mechanisms leading to this outcome are weakened in the situation of government, or its agencies, issuing blanket insurance on deposits across all banking institutions, weak or strong.

What would have happened to the weakest banks which could survive only with lender of last resort assistance?

Autumn 2008 would have been brought forward to autumn 2007 in terms of the individual European member governments having to provide explicit injections of capital towards an emergency stabilization of the weakest elements within their own political jurisdictions. Yet that task would surely have been less daunting (and damaging) in 2007 than in 2008 or indeed later given the lack of intervening recession and fear of depression that emerged.

If the US authorities had been similarly pre-emptive then the train of financial history may well not have made it all the way to the Great Financial Panic of autumn 2008. And a sharp fall of the risk-free rates of interest in Europe and the US, perhaps all the way to zero already in Autumn 2007, would surely have reduced the severity of the looming downturn. Instead the ECB steered policy during the year from the First Big Quake of August 2007 on the basis of three disastrous premises.

Three disastrous premises of ECB's reaction to credit quake

The first premise was that the euro-area (and especially Germany) would be on the edge of any economic storm sweeping through the global economy in the aftermath of the First Big Quake.

The second premise was that there continued to be a serious danger of inflation in the euro-area economy and indeed that this risk had increased in consequence of the surge in oil and commodity prices (from late 2007 into mid-2008). Buttressing ECB explanations of this danger was a reference to the 'monetary pillar' (in reality never constructed) and in particular to a continuing rapid growth of bank lending as reflected in contemporaneous banking sector statistics.

The third premise was that the central bank monetary pilots, in steering the rate of interest in the overnight money market (a dubious concept at a time of extreme heterogeneity of credit risk among the banks), should focus unswervingly on achieving the aim for the price level over the medium-term (2% p.a. inflation or just below over say a two-year period) while blocking their ears to the financial storms raging around them. It should be left to the liquidity crisis management team (which included the monetary pilots wearing different hats) to use an entirely independent tool (subsidized and sterilized credit operations) to alleviate the funding stress in the banking system. The basis of the economic optimism (first premise) was German-centric. Germany continued to enjoy booming business with Eastern Europe, Russia and the Middle East oil exporters in particular through the first few months of 2008. It seemed as if the strength of the euro (reaching a crescendo in the first half of 2008 as the ECB allowed monetary conditions to tighten sharply while the Federal Reserve was in more temperate mode though far from aggressive ease) was having no serious negative influence on the German export industry. Had the Deutsche Bundesbank, since as far back as the late 1960s, not been singing the tune about how well German exports withstood a strong currency?

The second premise was built on a confusion between a lagging symptom of asset price inflation (the huge contemporaneous spike in oil prices) generated by earlier monetary disequilibrium and the actual strengthening forces of asset price deflation. This was not the first time in monetary history that central bank action against asset price inflation had come so late as only to make the subsequent asset price deflation worse (see Chapter 1). The third premise amounted in effect to the pernicious 'separation principle' (see p. 79)

Blinded by econometrics and statistics

The Deutsche Bundesbank, since 2004 under the presidency of a renowned economics professor, Axel Weber, now seemed to be putting more emphasis than ever before on the output of the economic forecasting models which continued at this stage (the first half of 2008) to be upbeat. Otmar Issing, the *eminence grise* in the ECB at the start, and to a moderate degree sceptical of econometrics according to his autobiographic account (see Issing, 2008), had retired in autumn 2006. To his term's end, Professor Issing showed neither the slightest regret nor regard for the fact that the ECB had been unable to reconstruct a monetary pillar such as had supported the temple of the Deutsche mark and Bundesbank during the heyday of their acclaim and popularity.

The warnings of Professor von Mises (1971) carried no weight in the ECB Council:

There is not, and there cannot be, such a thing as quantitative economics. The usual method employed in business forecasts is statistical and thereby retrospective. They depict trends that prevailed in the past and are familiar to everybody. They in no way answer the questions that all people, and especially businessmen, are asking. People know that trends can change; they are afraid they will change; and they would like to know when the change will occur. But the statistician knows only what everybody knows, namely, that they have not changed yet!

The data that was being fed into the econometrics model on which the ECB prided itself, supplemented by the ECB's analysis of the 'second pillar' of its monetary framework, did not produce any hint of serious recession risk ahead. Instead it was the amber or even red inflation alert light that was blinking! Money supply data was still growing strongly, reflecting in part strong increases in lending to the business sector. Could this lending surge represent a crisis-led re-intermediation, with those corporations no longer able to access the euro-denominated new issue bond market (in that the one main investor there, the credit-hedge funds, were in crisis) tapping already negotiated credit lines?

ECB and Bundesbank officials shook their heads in doubt. Figures are figures they said! On the subject of figures, though, should monetary data and the monetary pillar not be interpreted in a long-run sense transcending the econometric focus? So why was such a big point being made of the most recent money supply and lending behaviour in the midst of a financial panic? No answer!

As for the spoil-sports who came to Frankfurt or Paris and started to talk about potential asset price declines in France where, according to Organisation for Economic Co-operation and Development (OECD) indices the real estate market had been as bubbly as in UK, and more urgently in Spain or bursting real estate and credit bubbles in Eastern Europe, they were politely ridiculed. French banks had been so conservative, unlike their US counterparts. And there was absolutely no sign of weakness ahead in the French real estate market. In any case there had been no overhang of construction in the key Paris metropolitan area. And in Spain, had analysts not been warning about this for years? Moreover Spain could gain offsetting benefits from its strong Latin American connections. To suggest that the East European miracle might be largely a speculative bubble was to ignore all the solid evidence of remarkable economic progress built on solid integration with the advanced economies to the West. Perhaps the spoil-sports were early in their dire warnings about French real estate but not about anything else. Indeed speculative temperatures were to rise even further in the Paris real estate market during 2010–11 following some small fall in late 2008 and 2009. Serious asset price deflation only started to become widely suspected in 2013. And in general the spoil-sports were not pessimistic enough about the credit bubble that had emerged in periphery euro-zone government debt. In fact, most did not yet mention this topic.

The broadly optimistic attitudes about the economic outlook which could be gained first hand in interviews with monetary officials in Frankfurt at this time (spring and early summer 2008) also percolated through the official reports and autobiographical accounts of the period. Thus in its tenth anniversary report, mid-2008, the ECB editorialists wrote:

> A cross-check with the monetary analysis confirmed that upside risks to price stability prevailed at medium to longer term horizons. Money and credit expansion remained very vigorous throughout this phase (end-2005 onwards including 2007/8), supported by a persistently strong growth of bank loans to the private sector. Viewed from a medium-term perspective, the marked dynamism of monetary and credit growth reflected a continuation of the persistent upward trend in the underlying rate of monetary expansion observed since mid-2004. As such, it added further to the accumulation of liquidity which, in an environment of continued strong money and credit growth, pointed to upside risks to price stability over the medium to longer term. [...] Thus far there has been little evidence that the financial market turmoil has strongly influenced the overall dynamics of money and credit expansion.

Further evidence of the ECB's state of mind comes from the press conference on 3 July 2008, of which the main task was to explain a surprise 25 bp rate hike (taking the official repo rate up to 4.25%; money market rates were well above 5%). M. Trichet explained:

> This decision was taken to prevent broadly based second-round effects of the oil price rise (then near its peak level of around $150 per barrel) and to counteract the increasing upside risks to price stability over the medium-term. Second round effects were euro-speak for fear that powerful German union, most of all IG Metall, would set off a process of wage-price inflation by seeking compensation for rising oil prices. HICP inflation rates have continued to rise significantly since the autumn of last year. They are expected to remain well above the level consistent with price stability for a more protracted period than previously thought.

Moreover, continued very vigorous money and credit growth and the absence thus far of significant constraints on bank loan supply in a context of ongoing financial market tensions confirm our assessment of upside risks to price stability over the medium-term.

Whilst the latest data confirm the expected weakening of real GDP growth in mid-2008 after exceptionally strong growth in the first quarter [arithmetically this stemmed entirely from Germany then at the peak of its export boom], the economic fundamentals of the euro-area are sound. [...] On the basis of our current assessment, the monetary policy stance following today's decision will contribute to achieving our objective. [...] Whilst moderating, growth in the world economy is expected to remain resilient, benefiting in particular from continued robust growth in emerging economies. This should support euro-area external demand. The fundamentals of the euro-area economy remain sound and the euro-area does not suffer from major imbalances. In this context, investment growth in the euro area should continue to support economic activity, as rates of capacity utilization remain elevated and profitability in the non-financial corporate sector has been sustained.

In the question-and-answer session that followed, M. Trichet admonished:

those [i.e. the German trade unions or French public sector workers!] who think they can embark on second-round exercises, because they want to deny that there is a transfer of resources from consumers to suppliers, are paving the way for a long period of a high level of inflation, slow growth, stagnation and unemployment at a higher and higher level. There was full employment in Europe before the first oil shock, and at the end of the 1970s we had dramatic mass unemployment which we are only starting to get out of. So that is a similarity and that is why in particular we are so attached to our message on 'no second-round effects'.

ECB in 2008 believes it is the reincarnated Bundesbank of 1973!

In his usual show of verbal eloquence (some critics would say this was practised so as to stifle the opportunity for criticism!) M. Trichet had let the cat out of the bag.

The ECB saw itself as repeating the success of the Bundesbank in 1973–4, which by contrast to other central banks at the time had single-mindedly attacked virulent monetary inflation notwithstanding widespread gloom about the near-term recessionary or even depression-ary economic outlook. In consequence, Germany could bask in the sun of price stability for the following decade while other countries delayed coming to grips with the disease of inflation.

Within weeks this reading from the laboratory of history was shown to have been completely misapplied in the contemporary circumstances as Europe joined the rest of the world in a sharp deep recession and the price level in the euro-area actually declined briefly, albeit that this did not signify monetary deflation.

M. Trichet's aim to emulate the success of the Bundesbank of the mid-1970s by pioneering a distinct monetary response which turned out to be right where everyone else was wrong and so bringing long-run fame to itself and its currency turned out to be total pie in the sky! He evidently had not learnt one key fact about the 1973 Bundesbank success. That had not been based on economic forecast-ing prowess, as would have been the case if the crystal ball gazers in the Bundesbank had greater skill or luck than their counterparts in foreign central banks. Rather the success was due to the Bundesbank pioneering (coincidentally with the Swiss National Bank) a new framework of monetary control sharply at odds with the consensus wisdom of central bankers elsewhere at that time (including promi-nently the US).

The Bundesbank in 1973–4 had been the first central bank to switch to monetary base targeting and jettison Keynesian type fine-tuning. The Bundesbank pioneers, influenced by the monetarist revolution which had erupted in parts of the academic economic world, staked out an adventurous course away from the cumulative policy flaws of the recent past. They had as their aim the achievement of monetary stability. In summer 2007, M. Trichet and his colleagues had designed no new monetary framework (to replace in this case quasi-inflation targeting implemented by micro-pegging of money rates of interest) and they were certainly not monetary pioneers.

In the crude language of US presidential election campaigning, one could say, 'No, M. Trichet, no Professor Stark, you are not Dr Emminger and Dr Schlesinger!' That may well be an unfair comment to make but it would be the stuff of a more democratic and transparent monetary policymaking process.

The heightened concern about inflation which M. Trichet voiced in his (now) notorious July 2008 press conference is puzzling in several respects. Just a month later, after the first violent move down of the oil price as the commodity bubble burst, M. Trichet told the subsequent regular monthly press conference on7 August 2008:

> I consider that the peak in the price of oil and commodities was abnormal and did not correspond to what would be an equilibrium price. But we will see what happens. We have to be, again, totally humble in the presence of facts and figures, and we will see what happens. I think 'high and volatile' is a good description, a good way to capture things in the present situation.

But where was that humility as regards price-level forecasts to be found the month before (July) when he was admonishing labour unions not to seek wage awards which compensated for oil price movements. Indeed the unions (and wage negotiators) appeared to have greater understanding of the volatility of the oil price than the European central bankers in that there is no evidence in retrospect for the first half of 2008 of any wage-price spiral getting under way. And on the question of how to respond to CPI jumps related to the oil bubble a significant (but not radical!) difference could be found between the ECB and Federal Reserve at that time in their steering of monetary policy (otherwise so similar).

The Federal Reserve did not respond to the oil price bubble by raising its peg for short-term money rates though it did in spring and early summer hint at the possibility that this may have to rise, thereby having a perverse influence on market interest rates for, say, medium maturities. If these latter rates had been free of the influence of such expectations of manipulation they might well have fallen in line with an efficient market estimation of neutral level (see below). The particular concern of policy-makers around the ECB table, by contrast, appears to have been that the $150 oil price might immediately dislodge the anchor to stable and low inflation expectations formation in the euro-area, particularly in the heavily unionized German auto industry.

Economic reality was totally different from the perception of the monetary policymakers – not least in that the US and Japan had already entered recession the previous November (2007), although that date was not fixed until a year later by the statisticians. Recessionary forces with their source in the bursting of the global credit bubble had already become very strong, albeit not registered in the backward-looking real economic data and puzzling monetary data, in the euro-area. Indeed one research group – the Centre for Economic Policy Research – was to claim much later in March 2009 that the euro-area had in fact entered recession in January 2008 if applying the same metrics to that determination as the National Bureau in the US. The spike in the oil price turned out to be a seriously lagging indicator of the business cycle.

Though the Federal Reserve in spring and summer 2008 did not join the ECB in the mistake of an alarmist response to the so-called oil price-induced 'inflation' scare, critics fault it for treading still a deeply sub-optimal path. In particular, as Leo Hetzel (2009), a senior adviser to the Richmond Federal Reserve Bank, points out, the Federal Reserve's repeated references to a possible looming rise in its peg for the Federal Funds rate drove term money market rates higher through spring 2008. The growing gap between these term rates (together with short- and medium-maturity bond yields influenced by expectations regarding Federal Reserve rate pegging) and the presumably falling neutral level contributed materially to the severity of the recession already in the summer quarter of 2008 (Q3) before the Lehman collapse. Hetzel writes:

> What caused the appearance of a deep recession? The explanation here highlights a monetary policy shock in the form of a failure by the Fed to follow a decline in the natural interest rate with reductions in the funds rate. Specifically, the absence of a funds rate reduction between April 30, 2008 and October 8, 2008, despite deterioration in economic activity, represented a contractionary departure. Moreover the FOMC effectively tightened monetary policy in June by pushing up the expected path of the federal funds rate through hawkish commentary. By June 18, futures markets predicted a funds rate of 2.5% for November 2008.

Hetzel points out that it was not just the Federal Reserve encouraging expectations of higher rates at this time. There was also the example of the ECB and Bank of England. And then there was the BIS which in its annual report published in June 2008 called for higher rates. This recommendation was disappointing for some fans of BIS chief economist, William White, who had been for many years a rare contrarian in the world of central banking, arguing against the follies of inflation targeting. But in this case, the BIS authors failed to recognize that the asset price inflation (featuring also credit inflation) virus about which White had written was already progressing into the phase of asset price deflation. In this transition the virus could attack still one or more new markets – in this case oil – but the central banks ideally should not respond to that late symptom (see p. 9).

Again, as discussed earlier in this volume (see p. 51), the issue is not whether the ECB was piloting monetary policy marginally worse or better than the Federal Reserve, but its complete failure in the mission of developing a superior monetary framework to the highly disequilibrium-prone US one whilst bolstering Europe's defenses against US monetary virus attack.

ECB's analysis of inflation danger from high oil was deeply flawed

The modest difference in attitude between the Federal Reserve and ECB towards oil price developments was not a new feature of 2008. For several years back (since energy prices started to rise at the beginning of the decade), the Federal Reserve had focused on a core measure of price level rise (the private consumption deflator excluding food and energy) whereas the ECB had insisted that its focus should remain the overall measure (in the case of the euro-area including food and energy, but excluding almost totally any imputed rental equivalent of house prices). And no consensus existed among economists outside the central banks as to what measure of inflation should be adopted for the purpose of steering monetary policy.

There were two main arguments for focusing on the core measure.

First, oil (and food) price changes over short periods could be violent and self-reversing. Hence, if the central bank were trying to assess the underlying rate of goods and services inflation it was best to filter the short-term changes in oil prices out of the reckoning.

Second, in line with the Austrian School teachings, the objectives of price level stability in the very long run and monetary equilibrium did not require (and might indeed be inconsistent with) price level stability over the short- or even medium-run. During periods of negative resource shock (such as would be symptomized by a jump in energy prices) not allowing money to become a source of disequilibrium would mean accepting a transitory rise in the price level and conversely during periods of positive resource shock (such as a big improvement in the terms of trade or a jump in productivity) there should be a transitory fall in the price level.

The Federal Reserve, in focusing on core inflation measures, was influenced mainly by the first argument. At no point in that institution's almost 100 years' history have Austrian ideas gained any traction or even any written mention in its policymaking.

The ECB in choosing to stress the overall inflation measure (without taking out the volatile food and energy component) bizarrely made implicit reference to Austrian school teaching but came to a policy conclusion at total odds with it. The authors of the ECB monthly reports on several occasions made comments to the effect that yes, there was a trend rise in energy prices – an inevitable consequence of China's rapid growth; but by the same token China's entry into the global economy was a source of significant downward pressure on the price of manufactured goods (a terms of trade gain). These two real source effects – according to the ECB – would broadly offset each other in trend terms. So yes, monetary equilibrium might imply price level stability over the medium-term notwithstanding real source upward pressure on prices from growing oil shortage.

The problem in this synthesis of real effects – including oil – on the price level (by the authors of the ECB report and apparently reflected in ECB policy discussions) was that the huge jump in the price of oil during the second half of 2007 and the first half of 2008 could hardly be described as in line with an underlying trend. Only the trend component of the oil price rise should have been netted against trend terms of trade improvement when calculating actual upward pressure on the price level from real sources during this period. Most of the actual oil price rise should have been treated as a real resource shock, even after netting out other real related forces on the price level.

The author can say, on the basis of meetings with ECB officials, that there was some sympathy for seeking to decipher the underlying rate of inflation without the white noise of oil price spikes. But there was a concern that any such doctoring up in public would be the beginning of a slippery slope away from the absolute respect by all 'social partners' for price level stability. It was best from this perspective to keep measurement simple. That would have been fine if actual decisions on policy interest rates took the core measurement (rather than the headline price level change) into account without this being publicly stated. There is no evidence of such 'sophistication'.

Rather, at a time of growing recession around the globe including the euro-area (a wide recession in the euro-area was not yet generally recognized albeit that there was no doubt already about a downturn in Italy), in July 2008 the ECB raised its policy rate, and rates on virtually risk-free money market rates rose upwards in step (rates on unsecured inter-bank loans – to the limited extent that these could be arranged – rose by somewhat more, but the corresponding risk premiums were compressed well below where these would have been under the hypothetic alternative monetary policy described above). These term money market rates were the basis for many loan rates fixed under rollover contracts in commercial borrowing agreements.

Perhaps under a sane monetary policy some of the higher risk borrowing rates would have risen in absolute terms consistent with equilibrium tendencies. But the risk-free rates so heavily influenced by the present and prospective rate-pegging operations of the ECB (or Federal Reserve) should surely have plunged even during the oil bubble (if they had not already done so in autumn 2007). The response from Frankfurt monetary officials to any such suggestion was that lowering the official rate or reducing its visibility (by allowing a wider market determination of the interest rate structure) would interfere negatively with its supreme task of assuring price stability (according to the refined definition of 2003).

Bogus separation principle becomes ECB mantra

The separation principle had become a mantra – one policy tool (the pegging of the overnight money rate) for preserving price stability and one policy tool (a mass of subsidized sterilized lending collateralized against increasingly dodgy assets) for dealing with the 'liquidity problem in the banking sector' (in fact an insolvency problem, but not yet admitted as such).

It is the first time in monetary or financial history that the separation principle was applied. And that first time event was related to another first time event – the intensity with which central banks in Europe and the US were now seeking to fix short- and medium-maturity interest rates (rather than leaving these to market forces) and to target an exact level of inflation over a short period of time (say two years). In previous great financial panics, the central bank did not stand in the way of risk-free rates generally (including rates on near-money assets such as short-maturity government bonds) falling towards zero (under the pressure of a general flight into safety by investors) unless they were constrained to do so by a threat to the national currency's exchange rate or gold parity (under a fixed exchange rate system or international gold standard – see Eichengreen, 1997). The euro is a freely floating currency not subject to such legal constraints on monetary action in crisis.

Two main obstacles now stood in the way of risk-free rates falling.

First, there was the payment of interest on reserves (until the start of EMU almost all major central banks paid no interest on reserves at any time) coupled with a total lack of flexibility in savagely cutting that interest rate in financial crisis.

Second, the ECB was applying the 'separation principle' in a way to veto swamping the system with extra reserves (high-powered money) as would be required to prevent a pre-cautionary surge in demand for reserves inducing a monetary squeeze (see p. 136).

No exit plan from crisis intervention following 2007 quake

Now it would certainly have been no surprise if, in secret, ECB officials throughout winter 2007/8 and spring/summer 2008 had been in desperate communication about the exit problem (how to run down massive ECB lending to the financially weak institutions) with national finance ministries, including those in EU countries outside EMU whose banks via branches in the euro-areas had heavily availed themselves of ECB 'liquidity help' (the UK was the outstanding example of such a country). If there was to be no exit then the ECB's independence from governments could be compromised in the long-run as the financially strong nations could resent the implicit transfers from its taxpayers into making good deficits on loans to weak borrowers elsewhere. The ECB could find itself under pressure to inflate these deficits away, meaning that the burden would be more widely shared across all member nations.

How would the ECB one day shrink back its balance sheet to normal level and extricate itself from massive secured lending operations to the weakest banks? These operations now threatened to transform the ECB into the 'European Bad Bank', with its assets composed to a considerable degree of dubious loans and its liabilities implicitly guaranteed by taxpayers in the financially strong countries. All of this jarred with the contention, fundamental to the Maastricht Treaty, that sovereign countries could enter into monetary union without this becoming a 'transfer union' (citizens in one member country making aid payments to citizens in other member countries) which in principle would demand solidarity as found only in political unions. But the members of the EMU had not joined in a political union.

Yes, the ECB loans were secured. But if the ECB refused to renew those secured loans and grabbed the collateral it would trigger widespread insolvency from the viewpoint of the banking system as a whole. The weakest banks had no possibility of refinancing themselves from private sources. And given the dodgy nature of much of the collateral, what could the ECB realistically obtain for it in a fire sale? Yes, the ECB could enter into negotiations with member governments seeking their action to recapitalize banks with public funds, so allowing them to raise funds again in the private markets (which could then be used to repay the ECB). But the weak periphery-zone governments might not be able themselves to raise finance on the scale required for such supportive action.

In fact the only exit (for the ECB from secured lending to the weakest banks during the crisis) was an EU-wide effort to facilitate a restructuring of the banking system (the weakest banks would disappear). The solvency problem would be all the more difficult to address if in the meantime ECB policies contributed to a steep recession. Here was another big reason for caution in anti-inflationary zeal.

No evidence of such discussions at this early stage (spring and summer 2008) has filtered out into the public domain. The plunge in US and European bank stocks in summer 2008, an obvious indicator of a deepening insolvency crisis was not sufficient to provoke any change of monetary policy tune in Frankfurt.

The Separation Principle remained supreme.

Lehman bankruptcy causes rate-fixers in Frankfurt to dig in

Even when, in autumn 2008, the Lehman bankruptcy and threatened insolvency of AIG eventually triggered a rash of bank insolvency crises in Europe (the first crisis point being Fortis, followed in quick succession by middle-size banks in Germany and France and then one of the largest UK banks) the rate fixers in Frankfurt could not immediately let go.

In fact the rate-fixers tightened their grip! Simultaneous with an internationally coordinated 50 bp rate cut in early October 2008, the ECB announced that it was narrowing the bands either side of the official repo rate within which money rates could float as set by its marginal deposit rate and marginal lending rate. The narrowing was apparently prompted by the Bundesbank which was concerned about the ECB losing strict control of market rates and thereby allowing a greater than optimal easing of monetary policy under present turbulent conditions.

By narrowing the gap of the marginal deposit rate below the official repo rate to just 50 bp the ECB continued to set a high floor for the broad span of risk-free rates for short-maturity top euro-government bond markets and for government-bond secured repo rates. These continued at well above 3% into the period of intense crisis.

No wonder that record round-trips took place in the form of the less weak banks depositing excess funds at the ECB which in turn lent them out at subsidized rates (and beyond any normal prudential limit) to the weakest banks. This was such a far cry from what would have occurred under a classical monetary system in which high-powered money (deposits at the central bank and bank notes in circulation) was all non-interest bearing.

In the 'classical system' risk-free rates on near-money assets (for example, Treasury bills or their equivalent) would have been driven down by a flight into safety and the central bank would have been busy pumping in high-powered money to pre-empt any shortage of this developing amid the panic. The architects of the ECB's monetary framework had almost certainly overlooked that danger (the perverse overriding of automatic stabilizers during a financial crisis) in their ordaining that deposits at the central bank should pay interest.

Indeed, under the classical monetary system (with no interest paid on reserves) risk-free rates would come under downward pressure most likely before the full crisis was to erupt, as investors sought safety. The spread between the risk-free rate on, for example, short-maturity government bonds and money market rates is in that system a leading indicator of crisis. And in the thick of the crisis, the collapsed level of risk-free rates stimulates banks and others with surplus funds to lend into the now riskier or illiquid segments of the money market.

The action of the ECB shoring up the risk-free rate to above 3% p.a. in the depth of the financial crisis (October 2008) is evidence that the separation principle was still reigning intact and consistent with little sympathy among policymakers around the table especially on the part of the Bundesbank President, Professor Weber and ex-Bundesbanker Professor Stark for the hypothesis that the profound shock had driven down the equilibrium risk-free rate to near zero or even negative levels at the same time that high-risk rates had risen.

The econometric modelling so highly valued in ECB policy deliberation could not provide any insights in the situation of financial panic. (It is plausible – but there is no evidence to support this – that the Bundesbank economics staff was somewhat behind real time in realizing the slump now occurring in the German economy in consequence of its special vulnerability to a precipitous fall in world trade induced in considerable part by a freezing up of many trade credit channels). Indeed nothing suggests that the policymakers judged that a broad span of rates should emerge to reflect the present unusual degree of heterogeneity in credit quality and liquidity in money markets.

The monetary officials in Frankfurt were still apparently in the mode of thinking that setting an adjustable peg for one interest rate, the overnight rate, was the only way to implement policy and that strict monetary control meant keeping all market rates as close as possible to that overnight rate while steering expectations as to where the peg would be moved further ahead. The proposal to target instead the monetary base under such unusual circumstances and allow money rates to be freely determined (amid considerable heterogeneity) in the market just did not come on to the policymaking agenda.

The bogus separation principle was to re-emerge during the Italian debt crisis of summer 2011. As waves of capital flight buffeted Italian government bonds and, to a lesser extent, Italian banks, markets drove down the yields on risk-free assets – in this case short-maturity German government bonds. But so long as the ECB kept its overnight rate paid on reserves at just a small margin below the repo-rate (of 1.5% p.a.) this set a floor to the decline in the risk-free rate. Relatively strong banks in Germany or elsewhere chose to re-lend a growing surplus of deposits to the ECB and to reduce holdings of short-maturity German government bonds (on which yields were falling). If the ECB had cut its overnight rate on reserves promptly to zero that could have kick-started some on-lending of surplus funds to Italy. As German short-maturity bond yields fell to virtually zero that would have taken some of the strain off the Italian government bond market. But the ECB had just raised its repo rate in June (2011) after many months of deliberation about rising risks of inflation related to sky-high energy prices (a possible symptom of the asset price inflation virus stemming from the Bernanke Fed's QE programmes). Any early reversal was out of the question! Instead the ECB initiated a vast new security purchase programme under which it now bought Italian government bonds to help restore normal monetary transmission within EMU.

Insolvency crisis in European banking deepens, late 2008

Let's return to the solvency crisis in Europe which was continuing to deepen through autumn 2008. The ECB persisted in applying the tools appropriate to a severe liquidity crisis. In any case the ECB on its own could not arrange remedial action for a deep solvency crisis. If this was to include public sector financing of a recapitalization process for the weak banks then governments had to become involved.

The most intense pressure was in the US dollar funding markets. European banking groups had huge short-term dollar borrowings outstanding in the repo markets where a chief lender had been the US money market funds. The freezing up of those funds and massive demands for repayment in the aftermath of the Lehman bankruptcy (and other simultaneous credit events) had had a violent knock-on effect to Europe.

European banks scrambled to pull back dollar loans (on maturity) from the rest of the world (especially where repayment could be effected easily as from South Korea and Russia) to alleviate their immediate shortage of funds. In turn the ECB arranged vast swap lines with the Federal Reserve so as to provide dollar funds to cash-starved European banking groups (see Hördahl and King, 2008). The solvency crisis in European banking, however, transcended this issue of funding interruption. And indeed if the banks now short of dollar funds once provided by US money markets were of undoubted tip-top quality they could readily have replaced these from other sources.

At the end of the line there was growing anxiety (among non-secured lenders) about the extent of possible loss not just on the now much publicized holdings of European banking groups in US credit markets (mortgages, levered loans, etc.) but also on loans against real estate (where some regional markets such as Spain and the UK were already displaying signs of distress) and on loans to the emerging market economies in the Wild East (much of which was secured on once-hot real estate markets and in euro or Swiss franc denomination). The potential problem of huge investment by European banks in periphery-zone sovereign debts did not yet feature in financial commentaries.

As national governments closed in to salvage banks from insolvency (starting with the Dutch and Belgian governments taking over Fortis at end-September 2008) an EU summit in October 2008 agreed that individual governments should introduce packages of re-capitalization or emergency loan guarantee operations to be determined in detail at a national level. In effect, the much-vaunted financial integration fostered by the launch of the euro had come to an end and gone into reverse – at least in respect of the banking systems.

Will a weak EMU member government default?

Bank salvage operations implemented at the national level were bound to put downward pressure on the credit-rating of governments in the euro-area where the public finances were already in weak condition or where the extent of aid to the banks was very large relative to economic size (or both!). In principle, the credit rating of governments in the euro-area was more immediately sensitive than that of governments outside the euro-area, which still retained ultimate sovereign power over a national money-printing press to the deterioration in the state of public finances – including the contingent liabilities taken on in guaranteeing the banking sector or the implicit losses incurred in paying well above market price for banking assets. In practice, though, that heightened sensitivity (of credit ratings to the state of public finances) should not apply to the sovereign debt of core EMU countries (let us say France, Germany and Holland) as in the ultimate the ECB would surely print money to avoid a default within the core.

In principle, if sovereign credit risk is defined in economic terms to include deliberate partial default by the government (including the central bank) unleashing an inflation shock (including devaluation of the national currency) to write down the real value of government debt, then the distinction between the credit risk of governments with and without access to a printing press becomes blurred. After all, the Weimar Republic did not default on its debt in 1921–3 according to a technical legal definition, in that the printing press was used to service all obligations punctiliously, but in reality there was a default. In practice though there are important differences.

In case of a sovereign government with its own money, or a government of a core EMU country, doubts about eventual deliberate real partial default via inflation do not translate fully into a present spike in long-term interest rates or equivalently a massive tumble in today's nominal price of government bonds. The means of generating monetary inflation involves keeping money rates of interest far below neutral for a prolonged period. Long-term interest rates are an average of short-term rates expected on a roll-over basis from the immediate present to far-out dates and thereby give those depressed money rates a substantial weight in the averaging process. Instead the pressure of default risk in the form of deliberate inflation is likely to be felt most of all through an immediate decline of the sovereign government's currency, unless all sovereign governments are following the same policy of default by inflation.

By contrast, in the case of a sovereign government with no effective access to a national printing press (as for a government of a periphery-zone EMU country) a rise in default risks translates directly into lower bond prices and even into a total funding crisis (in a market panic it may not be possible at all for the government to issue bonds) and wider financial crisis (in that banks and other financial institutions hold large amounts of government bonds, now slumping in value, to match fixed money liabilities).

A danger scenario for EMU began to be painted by a few market analysts around this time in late 2008 in which crisis driven by fear of insolvency would erupt in one of the weak government bond markets and spread by contagion to other weak government bond markets. This scenario did not yet get a wide airing and amazingly there was not as yet any spotlight on Greece. According to the scenario, depositors with the banks in those political jurisdictions subject to substantial default risk might flee out of fear that the debt crisis would bring down the banking system in that political jurisdiction or trigger an exit from EMU. The vulnerability of the banks would reflect their holdings of poor quality assets (including private loans and domestic sovereign debt) together with the fact that the sovereign government might not be in a position to provide support.

Perhaps the financially fragile government involved could summon the needed political consensus (within its country) to effect a package of draconian budgetary cutbacks (tax increases and expenditure decreases). Yet these might fail to build confidence if investors saw them as the implementation of Brüning-style depression economics with the budget deficit becoming ever wider (at least relative to the shrinking size of the economy) despite the best efforts (because tax revenues plunge and unemployment benefits soar) and political risks increasing. Much would depend on whether the fiscal cut-backs were concentrated on government spending which had become bloated during asset price inflation without resort to incentive-killing tax rises and other measures enfeebling the appetite for equity risk (foreign or domestic).

Brüning was the Chancellor of Germany during the depths of the depression from 1930 to 1932 who instituted savage budgetary cuts under emergency decrees, legally bypassing the need for Reichstag approval. Some critics have argued that he followed this path of driving the German economy into the grave towards proving that the reparations bill was impossible to pay. Against the background of soaring electoral support for the Nazi party and with the US equity market in its severest stage of asset price deflation there was no appetite for investment risk in Germany. In 1932 the Treaty of Lausanne effectively brought reparations to an end.

Under such re-incarnated circumstances the only alternative to a forced exit from EMU might be a mega financing loan from the stronger governments – either directly or via an agency created for that purpose. But would the political will exist in France, Germany, and say the Netherlands, to accomplish that? Again that question was in very embryonic form if it were heard at all during winter 2008/9. There were grounds for hoping, in any case, that the global financial and economic climate would increasingly favour equity risk-taking which could help towards economic renaissance in the member countries forced to take the path of severe budget austerity.

We turn in a future chapter (Chapter 8) to a more detailed analysis of how the weak government could be forced to exit EMU and include a description of how a revised treaty could provide for this explicitly.

As a matter of historical record, though the possibility of forced exits from EMU had entered the range of scenarios viewed by some investors in spring 2009 and become a focus of media attention, it was still a long way from the mainstream, not to enter there until the Greek debt crisis erupted in early 2010. Greece's debt problems were still not being picked up by market radar.

ECB debates minute rate adjustments as recession deepens

By spring 2009 the ECB had almost exhausted the scope for conventional monetary easing. Risk-free rates in nominal terms were at last below 1% (near zero for some money market operations, somewhat higher in the illiquid one-year German government bond market).

In December 2008, a broad coalition of policymakers around the ECB table had unusually won the argument against the Bundesbank (there is no proof of this given the rules of secrecy under which the ECB operates, but the hypothesis rests on a collection of anecdotal and media reports) and been successful in bringing about a re-widening of the interest rate corridor such as to allow short-maturity risk-free rates to fall by as much as 100 bp (rather than 50 bp) below the belatedly declining official repo rate. Subsequently in early 2009 as the repo rate was trimmed further, the Bundesbank was successful in arguing against a cut of the overnight deposit rate to 0% and so the corridor narrowed to 75 bp. It was not until the Spanish debt crisis of mid-2012 that the ECB cut its overnight deposit rate to zero. Most probably the willingness of the Bundesbank to concede a widening of the interest rate corridor at the end of 2008 stemmed from the accumulation of evidence that the German economy was now in slump of greater severity than in France. In fact, in December 2008 the euro-area was in a great recession and financial panic where the neutral interest rate level in real terms across short and medium maturities was surely negative. In the world of the gold standard negative real rates at severe cyclical low points came about via a fall in prices coupled with expectations of an eventual recovery of prices as business conditions improved. In the monetary framework of Dr. Issing there was no such automatic mechanism at work.

There was no evidence that ECB policymakers realized how powerless their box of contra-cyclical tools becomes in severe recession when inflation expectations are feeble or non-existent. They exaggerated the potential effectiveness of non-conventional options although they were less enthusiastic about these than their Fed counterparts. Their best contribution to recovery would have been to underpin confidence in long-run price level stability while explaining carefully to the public that meanwhile some decline in goods and services prices is a key part of the process by which the self-recovery forces of the capitalist economy operate. Instead ECB officials continued to refer in robot fashion to implicit inflation-targeting as built into the framework of monetary policymaking 'perfected' in spring 2003, even though by now the flaws in the framework should have become evident. At the August 2009 monthly press conference President Trichet told reporters that although year-on-year price level rises had turned negative, these would return towards the target of '2% or close to (from below) 2%' over the medium-term.

ECB officials did not admit that the recovery would depend most of all on self-corrective forces of non-monetary source. The best hope here was that the steep drop in international trade brought about by the post-Lehman freeze of the global financial system would reverse itself as freeze now gave way to thaw. Businesses would cease their emergency slashing of inventories (once back into line with sunken sales volumes) and capital spending programmes. And hopefully the equity markets might lead a recuperation process.

If investors in equities had confidence in a better future, companies would be able to justify investment projects with pay-offs over the long run (where this future income would be priced in present value terms by equity investors) even though present profit prospects were dismal. Justification would take the form of the simple answer to a simple question – does the adoption of this capital-spending programme bolster the value of my equity?

With the Bundesbankers in particular expressing caution, the ECB policymakers continued through spring 2009 to debate the merits of a further 25 bp rate cut, as if the distinction between a risk-free rate of 75 bp (the then level of yields on three-month German government bills) and 50 bp or even zero would make much difference to anything when the neutral level of short and even medium-maturity risk-free rates was transitorily far below that and in deep negative territory! The big mistakes had already been made!

ECB refuses to admit any mistake in crisis

No one, though, would have heard the word mistake, in M. Trichet's keynote address in mid-march 2009 on *'What lessons can be learned from the economic and financial crisis?'* (speech at the '5eme Rencontres de l'Entreprise Europeenne' organized by La Tribune, Roland Berger and HEC, Paris). His introduction was promising:

> Tonight, I would like to examine the roots of the current crisis and the policy responses which are taken to address it and to inspire a new sense of direction.

Unfortunately, no illumination was to follow!

> In the last ten years we saw a dramatic shift in influence away from entrepreneurship in the real economy to speculation and gambling in the financial sector. The assumption and the hedging of genuine economic risk gradually ceased to be the main concern of international finance. [...] At some point, the financial system seemed to be no longer there primarily to hedge existing economic risks, but more and more to create and propagate risks on its own.

[*Author's comment*: M. Trichet seems to be referring here to the rise in speculative temperature – sometimes describe as irrational exuberance – which is an essential feature of asset price inflation. He does not name the phenomenon he describes as such (the virus of asset price inflation) and does not realize or admit that the source (of this virus) is monetary disequilibrium created by the ECB and Federal Reserve].

The credit boom had three multipliers.

- First, ill-designed compensation schemes for loan managers reinforced the shortening of lenders' horizons. In the eyes of many loan managers, the short-run gains from an expansion of credit obscured the need for any consideration of the potential losses that their institution could incur over the long-run.
- Second, the complex structure of securitized products made it difficult for the ultimate holders to assess the quality of the underlying investment.
- Third, international imbalances and their potential to encourage liquidity creation on a global scale acted as the macroeconomic – and perhaps most powerful – multiplier. A chronic shortage of savings in some of the world's advanced economies was funded by an excess of savings in other parts of the world. These global macro-economic imbalances contributed to the creation of international liquidity and therefore further fuelled credit and debt accumulation.

These three multipliers went into reverse – suddenly, although not unexpectedly – sometime in the middle of 2007. Liquidity dried up. [...] The ECB moved pre-emptively. It ensured the continued functioning of the money market at the very first signs of the turbulences in August 2007. We have not shied away from action at any time since then. Our actions have been early, resolute and broadly based!

Who could M. Trichet have been hoping to fool, unless the worst fears were true about the European central bankers now inhabiting an ivory tower totally removed from the real world?

There is absolutely no mention at all in M. Trichet's speech of the cardinal error of the ECB, together with the Federal Reserve, moving in spring 2003 towards a super-easy monetary policy out of deflation phobia. M. Trichet does not concede that the ECB failed to be alert to the danger that its low interest rate anti-deflation policies through 2003–5 could be germinating and spreading the virus of asset price inflation; nor does he regret the only glacial pace of tightening through late 2005 and 2006; nor does he admit the failure to distinguish between a liquidity or solvency crisis in summer 2007 and the suppression of all private market forces which might have brought about an early re-capitalization of the healthier parts of the financial system; or the implicit rejection of stabilizing monetary action found in previous great financial panics (risk-free rates falling being allowed to plunge and huge injections of monetary base to meet raised demand for reserves and currency).

Instead there is the old pre-EMU French prejudice against Anglo-Saxon finance, the dogma about global imbalances (US savings deficits, East Asian savings surpluses) and financial casinos (in London and New York) being the source of a US-centred global credit bubble. The story defies all neo-classical economic textbook accounts of how the invisible hand of market forces if left unrestricted and if operating under conditions of monetary stability should cope with the transfer of capital from parts of the world where savings are plentiful relative to domestic investment opportunity into those parts where the reverse holds. The total silence is deafening on the tightening of euro-area monetary conditions through 2008H1, the ECB's driving the risk-free rate of interest to well above 4% p.a. when recession had already started in major parts of the world (including the euro-area) and the misplaced reading of history (imagining a phantom danger of wage-price inflation).

The ECB's chief economist and board member Professor Jürgen Stark (ex-Bundesbanker) did not provide any more clarification when he spoke in March 2009 to a German-Luxembourg economic conference.

Thankfully, he kept away from any historical account as to how the crisis came about. But his analysis of how the ECB was now conducting monetary policy could only mystify.

In fairness Professor Stark started by making the reasonable point that though the price level may be falling (due to sharp declines in oil prices) this was not deflation (a persistent broad-based and self-sustaining decline in the overall price level reinforced by anticipation that prices will decline further in the future) but disinflation (linked to a transitory movement in relative prices). If he had had more time he might have added a cyclical drop in the price level to the disinflation list (suppliers in the most cyclical sectors of the economy cutting profit margins at the depths of the recession and re-building them during recovery). But then he started to tread the murky waters of the separation principle:

> To better understand the scale of our interventions in the interbank money market, one needs to appreciate its importance in the implementation and transmission of monetary policy. Money market interest rates, especially of short maturities, mark the starting point in the transmission of monetary policy. They determine the marginal costs of refinancing of the banking sector and thereby act through the bank lending channel. Money market interest rates are a key factor in determining the entire yield curve and thereby are crucial for the expectations channel of monetary transmission.

Professor Stark leaves no doubt about what his attitude would have been (and presumably was!) to any suggestion, if made (and there is absolutely no evidence or reason to believe the suggestion was ever put forward at the ECB's policy meetings), that in the wake of the 7 August quake, a wide span of rates should have been allowed to form, with the risk-free rate falling towards zero and risky rates (for example to the weaker banks) rising. Any such messy outcome would have blurred (in the viewpoint of Professor Stark) the signalling from firm rate control by the ECB.

We can also see that Professor Stark was a key opponent of any idea to widen the corridor between the overnight deposit rate and the marginal lending rate in late 2008 (and why M. Trichet had to stall questioners at the November and December press conferences as to why this was not happening despite massive round-tripping, saying that it was 'under review'!).

Professor Stark then ventured into the liquidity-solvency debate, by implication suggesting that the ECB's massive interventions from summer 2007 onwards had been for liquidity purposes. He quoted the maxim:

> Central banks can alleviate liquidity risks, but they cannot address the perceived solvency problems that impair the financial system.

So why had the ECB spent the year or more from the 7 August quake lending more and more on a secured subsidized sterilized basis to the weakest banks in Europe when it was apparent to almost all (except perhaps at the ECB) that there was a serious solvency issue?

The sterilization occurred via the ECB conducting reverse repo operations in the market – in effect lending securities and borrowing funds from non-banks and the stronger banks – so as to offset the loans to the weakest; and in a bizarre decision the ECB as late as June 2009 decided to amplify this sterilization operation by making the same overall amount of funds available now for one year (rather than as previously for six-months) at a below-market rate, at least with respect to the weakest banks, of 1% p.a.

There is no record in the ECB transcript of a question to Professor Stark on the futility and indeed deceptiveness (in terms of public accountability) of such lending to the insolvent!

Implicitly Professor Stark offered a bizarre defence of why the ECB had driven the risk-free rate of interest higher in spring and early summer 2008. If it had not been for the (avoidable) US shambles of allowing a big investment bank to blow up, the euro-area was not on course for a recession:

> The crisis started in Summer 2007, as losses in the US sub-prime mortgage market, a relatively small segment of the US housing market, triggered the ongoing financial turmoil. However, its impact on the global economy remained relatively limited until the summer of 2008. However after the collapse of Lehman Brothers last September, the tensions in global financial markets escalated to a full-blown financial crisis and thereafter turned into a global economic crisis. The severe global economic downturn has now become much more synchronized. The collapse in global trade has amplified the adverse impact from the financial turmoil and caused emerging market prospects to deteriorate drastically.

Was the source of the problem really just a small section of the US housing market? Or was Professor Stark blind to the much bigger picture of a global credit bubble of which the US sub-prime mortgage market was just one component and for which the ultimate source was a monetary madness which embraced the ECB as much as the Federal Reserve?

As regards this gentle economic slowdown environment in the first half of 2008, were Spain and Italy not already in serious recession? Indeed from January 2008 the whole euro-area was subsequently identified as in recession. And yes, most analysts would undoubtedly agree with Professor Stark that the Great Panic following the Lehman bankruptcy was the immediate catalyst to a 2008Q4 and 2009Q1 slump in business activity around the world (driven by a near freeze-up of international trade credit and many other forms of credit, especially those where the now defunct 'shadow banking system' had been important). But how could Professor Stark still in March 2009 justify the only gradualist adjustment down (the previous autumn) of the peg for the overnight rate and all the efforts to prevent a sharper fall at that time in the risk-free rate (at first narrowing the corridor around the repo rate in September 2008, subsequently allowing it to return to the previous norm under the sheer weight of the round-tripping which the move triggered)?

And was the main justification for what rate declines did actually occur really the avoidance of a bigger decline of inflation over the medium-term (the next two years) below the target level of 2% p.a.? Or did the justification lie in the much more urgent objective to prevent severe monetary disequilibrium such as would arise from sustaining market rates for short and medium maturities at far above the almost certainly now lowered neutral or natural level?

That severe monetary disequilibrium may or may not have ended up with inflation in the euro-area undershooting the target as set by the ECB. Even without such undershoot, would not all the other pain of monetary disequilibrium, including financial institutions failing and severe recession or slump together with precipitous asset deflation, justify bold action now? And did not the survival of the euro itself in present form not depend on alleviating monetary disequilibrium? Otherwise how could a forced exit from EMU of the periphery-zone countries (Portugal, Ireland, Greece and Spain) be prevented?

A French diplomatic coup to diffuse existential crisis, spring 2009

ECB officials remained effectively silent on the issue of existential crisis of the euro as recession deepened through early 2009. This is understandable to the extent that the same officials realized that survival of the euro-area in its present wide form (as against a narrow union of France, Germany and Holland) might depend ultimately on the willingness of electorates in France, Germany and Holland to make transfers to the foreign governments within EMU at high risk of defaulting.

Even so, there were some forms of support which might not require such willingness – either because they could be camouflaged from electoral view (such as the ECB providing cheap 'liquidity' to Spanish, Greek, or Irish banks – a non-exhaustive list!) or because they were forthcoming from other sources, as for example the IMF. This Washington institution, now under French ex-Finance Minister Strauss-Kahn, hit it lucky in spring 2009, obtaining huge new resources from China, Japan and the US. Only a few months before there had been widespread chatter in G-7 circles about whether there was any rationale for the IMF's continued existence, so incompetent had been its analysis and actions during the global credit bubble.

French economic diplomacy enjoyed crowning success at the G-20 summit in London in April 2009, where the main resolution was a re-capitalization of the IMF. All participants in the G-20 summit realized that the main destination of re-vamped IMF lending would be European countries in distress. The most obvious distress stories were in the 'Wild East' (ex-communist countries of central/Eastern Europe). But the more perspicacious delegates at G-20 knew that not far behind in the queue for assistance would be the periphery-zone members of EMU.

The new Obama Administration, inaugurated January 2009, promised to obtain the necessary approvals for IMF funding from the US Senate (no difficult questions asked as to why Germany was still the number one exporter to Iran). Treasury Secretary Geithner had ascended the ladder of official stardom via the first rung of IMF apparat. He and the rest of the Obama economics team (including the Federal Reserve chief, Professor Bernanke) had been traumatized by the fallout from the Lehman collapse and saw it now as self-evident that anything similar must be prevented in Europe; they were in no mood or mind to contemplate laissez-faire solutions. Moreover a deepening European banking crisis would most likely mean a sharp fall in the euro which would dash the Obama economics team's plan to use a weak dollar towards promoting US recovery. Japan and China signed up to massive loans to the IMF at least in part towards keeping the peace in currency relations with Washington.

Less understandable than the traumatized state of the Obama economics team is the glibness with which ECB officials repeated the mantras that exit from EMU was impossible or disastrous and that euro-membership had spared the weak countries from much greater pain. For example, when asked about exit pressures on weak governments at his press conference in mid-March 2009, M. Trichet answered as follows:

> As regards your question on the issue of members of the euro-area that could be in extreme difficulty, first of all the euro-area is an area where you have considerable automatic help through the very existence of the single currency itself. For instance the balance of payments deficit, if any, is financed automatically by virtue of belonging to the euro-area. Let us not forget that. I say regularly when I am asked more direct questions that I do not comment on absurd hypotheses [any mention of exit is absurd!]. I have confidence in the capacity of the governments of the euro-area in line with their own pre-eminent responsibility to convince their own people and markets that they are going in the right direction and that they are credible as regards the medium- to long-term path for sound fiscal policies.

The critic could question the notion of automatic help being bolstered by the existence of EMU. If Spain were now in slump and its private sector savings deficit plunging (as construction spending collapsed, non-real estate companies also cut back outlays and households' propensity to consume fell) the net inflow of capital from the rest of the world especially the euro-area (which inflow Trichet describes as 'balance of payments deficit') would decline in line (adjusted for the simultaneous widening of the public sector deficit). Membership of the euro-area meant that the decline in the 'balance of payments deficit' would be less gradualist than otherwise. If Spain had its own currency, nominal interest rates there could fall below the level in the euro-area. Devaluation, if reflected in higher inflation expectations, could bring real rates speedily into negative territory. Hence the contraction of the private sector savings deficit would be slower than inside EMU.

The cheapness of the Spanish currency (together with expectations of a potential eventual re-bound) would act as a magnet for foreign financing allowing its savings deficit to stay larger for longer (despite negative real rates). And why was the notion of Spain leaving the euro absurd? After all during the era of the gold standard, countries left gold. The mechanics would be broadly similar for exit from the euro-area, even if comprehensive details had to be sorted out regarding the launch of a new 'Spanish peseta'.

At last ECB refuses to join the crowd: it rejects quantitative easing

Another big topic at press conferences during the two quarters of economic slump which followed the financial system freeze-up of early autumn 2008 was why the ECB abstained from following other central banks (first the Federal Reserve, then the Bank of England) in adopting a policy of 'quantitative easing'. This meant expanding the monetary base (excess reserves in particular) aggressively once the risk-free interest rate had fallen to the zero rate boundary with the aim of providing further stimulus to the economy.

There was a perfectly respectable intellectual case to be made for the central bank not venturing down this particular path. It would be better to allow good cyclical deflation to work its wonders – a fall in prices to a below-normal level during the recession matched by expectations of a rebound of prices into the recovery and expansion phases. Hence low nominal medium-term interest rates during the recession would be negative in real terms taking account of the likely rebound in prices further ahead.

Yes, the ECB could follow the Federal Reserve and buy massive amounts of government bonds in the secondary markets, though there would be the ticklish question of deciding which bonds of which governments would form part of this operation. Would this include the government debt of the periphery-zone members (of EMU) where prices were already reflecting some significant risk of default or EMU exit? But beyond that 'technical' problem, why would the banks respond to a flotsam of extra reserves by increasing their risky loans rather than just parking these at the ECB in its overnight deposit facility earning there even a slightly positive interest rate until 2012 (see p. 32) and levying increased charges on their deposit customers? If the banks lent out the money at rates which did not fully reflect raised risk premiums and increased risks (at a time of deep recession) and to an extent which went beyond the maximum leverage ratios appropriate in any case (where these are determined in particular by deadweight bankruptcy costs and moral hazard) they would find their equity prices plunging as investors in the bank took fright.

Yes, non-conventional monetary tools (different from those available to the Federal Reserve or ECB) had already 'worked' in Communist China during the first half of 2009 in producing a lending boom of fantastic proportions, with banks commanded by Beijing to meet loan quotas. But this was not a model to follow in a market economy and political democracy. The financially repressed depositors on which the Chinese banks depended for their survival had no effective voice. And a command-driven lending boom not based on market price signals would surely not bring about the efficient deployment of new capital so essential in the long run to steer the Chinese economy on to a path of economic prosperity and away from a path of bubble-and-busts with so much collateral damage.

After a financial panic and deep recession in a market economy such as those in Europe, Japan or the US, it is likely to be the financially fit firms which lead the process of recovery, drawing on funds from the equity and bond markets. The more fragile firms who are particularly important as borrowers in the bank credit markets emerge as effective demand there at a later stage in the recovery. By that point the optimal path of market-clearing short and medium maturity risk-free interest rates may well have entered again positive territory. Bank lending growth would be consistent then with rising bank equity values – in that risk premiums and the risk level of many borrowers have decreased since the panic and its aftermath.

Quantitative easing in itself might well cause expectations regarding the price level over the medium term (say three to five years into the future) to shift upwards even before strong recovery becomes evident, on the basis that the central bank by moving even further away from a conventional monetary system with its known rules would be likely to make serious mistakes much further down the road, most plausibly in the direction of inflation. That anxiety about potential inflation, inflamed perhaps by the central bank committing itself to holding rates down at abnormally low levels for an 'extended period' (with the likelihood that they will not be raised in line with inflation when it emerges) might frighten some financially fit households into spending now rather than run the serious risk of their monetary assets depreciating eventually (in real terms). But it is far from clear that these stimulus effects would be particularly powerful. The strongest effect might be downward pressure on the currency. That pressure could be increased by the central bank buying massive quantities of government bonds, raising thereby the spectre of long-time monetisation as the eventual 'solution' to a deepening crisis in public finances. The floating of such a policy strategy by ECB officials, even if in their hearts they had no stomach to carry it out, would conflict with their 'sworn' mission of price stability according to the Maastricht Treaty.

In fact ECB officials have shown no enthusiasm for proceeding down the track of quantitative easing. Their pursuance of that route has been driven by institutional (including political) factors which have favoured bail-outs to insolvent banks and sovereigns via the ECB balance sheet rather than via EU institutions. But nor have they been enthusiastic promoters of laissez-faire solutions driven by some initial good cyclical deflation. The officials did not make the case that exit from recession should be powered to a considerable degree by natural forces of recovery (deep price discounts encouraging consumers and businesses to bring forward spending, bold speculators in the equity market supporting prices there at levels that priced at a reasonable level expectations of returns in periods beyond the present recession from new capital expenditure, so allowing projects to be adopted now, recuperation of international trade and business confidence led by thawing of the financial system freeze).

Speeches of ECB officials during this time did describe the likely problems of quantitative easing (for example, see Bini Smaghi, 2009), albeit tending to put great focus on possible losses for the ECB in holding the assets bought rather than on inherent flaws in theory! And if so concerned about losses, how could some of the same officials already in spring 2010 be advocating huge buying (by the ECB) of Greek sovereign debt now transformed into junk or lending through the ECB's back door on the collateral of increasingly dubious periphery-zone government debt? The less in-depth speeches emphasized the point that the central bank should ignore all cyclical fine-tuning and just concentrate on the long run, without analysing the particular issues related to quantitative easing (see Stark, 2009). But there was no evident coherent shift anywhere in Frankfurt away from the collection of hypotheses that lay behind the monetary framework designed in 1998 and refined further in 2003. A shift in particular away from the misconceptions of quasi-inflation targeting would have differentiated policymakers in Frankfurt from those in Washington or London.

In designing a new framework – a distinct European alternative – the ECB would have stood to win (if vindicated by history!) the sort of esteem which the Bundesbank won in 1973 from not following the wisdom of the global central bankers club. Instead, there was a buzz which just sounded like excess caution, intellectual laziness or both – and of course the policymakers had still not exhausted conventional policy tools by allowing risk-free rates to fall to zero. A question-and-answer session at the early March 2009 press conference (of the ECB) is revealing:

Q: With the main refinancing rate at 1.5% do you think you are getting close to the limit? Last time you said you considered 0% rates inappropriate? Do you still think so?

Trichet: I confirm what I have already said. We see a number of
            drawbacks associated with a zero late level. [...] As regards
            non-standard measures, there is no pre-commitment for any
            kind of non-standard measure. I exclude nothing, it would
            be the decision of the Governing Council and we are looking
            at it.

Q: You have just said you are studying the implementation of
            non-standard measures. Does that mean you are studying
            the process by which you might implement them or you are
            studying the need for them?

Trichet: We are discussing of course both the need and the process.
            And any decision would suppose that we see the need and
            that we agree on the process.

The reader can judge for him or herself what the ECB was up to, but
none of this interchange would encourage confidence among investors
in the monetary policymakers at a particularly dark hour in European
financial history. Perhaps the ECB was at last refusing to follow the
latest US monetary fashion (this time quantitative easing, previously
quasi-inflation targeting). But did the officials in the Eurotower realise
the challenges that would lie ahead were the Federal Reserve to use
its non-conventional policy tool as a weapon of undeclared currency
war? It was too bad that the Frankfurt policymakers by their previous
mistaken policies had left the euro-area in such a weakened economic
condition. How much better it would have been if the ECB had forged
its own and better-designed way right from the start of monetary union!

6
Guilty Verdict on the European Central Bank

It is time to 'give the floor' to what the leading officials in the project of EMU have said and continue to say in its defence (or more aptly, in trumpeting its success). A ready-made early brief on their behalf came from Stephen Cecchetti and Kermit Schoenholtz and was published in late 2008. These authors (the first was Economic Adviser and Head of the Monetary and Economics Department at the BIS, the second is professor at Stern School of Business, New York University) conducted a series of 17 extended interviews between June 2007 and February 2008 with a range of current and former high officials at the ECB, and with other policymakers and scholars who viewed the evolution of the ECB from privileged vantage points outside the institution.

The authors of the brief concluded:

> We share the assessment of our interviewees that the ECB has enjoyed many more successes than disappointments. These successes reflect both the ECB's design and implementation. Looking forward, we high-light the unique challenges posed by enlargement and, especially, by the euro area's complex arrangements for guarding financial stability.

Plan of the trial

The plan in this chapter is to first, extract the main features of the positive case made in the Cecchetti–Schoenholtz brief, raising some doubts along the way. Second, we look critically at alternative direct testimonial evidence available from leading ECB officials, including in particular speeches and press conferences. Third, we seek to weigh up the evidence (including the weight of material since the brief was published) and consider in particular one key issue. How far, even given the policies of monetary disequilibrium pursued by the Federal Reserve, could the ECB have steered its own monetary policy in a way so as to lessen the severity of global asset price inflation and to spare the euro-area economy from wild temperature swings in credit and real estate markets?

Leading central bankers and ex-central bankers in Europe and the US continue to press their claim either explicitly or implicitly that monetary policy played little or virtually no role in the debacle of credit bubble and burst. They deny responsibility for the awesome economic damage, both short- and long-run, wrought by the virus of asset price inflation during the past decade. Indeed some leading central bankers still dispute or ignore the reality of this disease and its monetary origins. (In private conversation, there is some remarkable capacity for self-criticism below the top in both the Federal Reserve and Bundesbank. And within the Federal Reserve System such self-criticism has found its way into print in regional research output – see for example, Hetzel, 2009.)

Does that official claim of central bank innocence stand up to scrutiny? Or is this continuing official denial of responsibility for the economic debacle one aspect of a further troubling concern – that the central bankers have abused their independence?

This concern is particularly relevant to EMU where central bank independence is rooted in the Maastricht Treaty. Those roots originate in the German ordo-liberal school's concept that institutions essential for the benign functioning of the market economy should be insulated from the turmoil of political democracy. Yet if we find that such insulation is not a sufficient condition for monetary stability, then there is a strong case for examining radical remedies.

First entry in the defence of EMU – it has survived!

Let's revert, to the first entry in the positive case (as summarized in the Cecchetti–Schoenholtz brief) for EMU.

EMU made it successfully past the starting line! Otmar Issing (one of those interviewed) stressed this particular point in his comments to Cecchetti–Schoenholtz:

> There was a clear view from a number of outside observers that we would fail and that it would be a disaster in any respect.

The authors of the report continue with this same point:

> As late as 1997 there was widespread scepticism about whether EMU would begin on schedule as a broad union and in some quarters

whether it would happen at all. Yet, here we are a full decade later and there are 15 countries where the euro is legal tender. The 21 members of the Governing Council of the ECP make monetary policy for a region of 320 million people with a GDP of roughly a9 trillion. And it is hard to find major fault with what they have done over the past decade.

Evidently the authors of the brief were not thinking of the indictments and the commentary found in the earlier chapters of this book! But let us look at the narrow claim that EMU had a successful birth.

Was a successful birth an accomplishment?

Without doubt a lot of able organizers took part in the process of launching the euro. There was no equivalent to a monetary blackout due to a mega-technical hitch. That is undoubtedly a cause for pride or at least a sense of relief among those making or fitting the nuts and bolts. The monetary version of the Titanic did not fall apart on its first voyage. The vans arrived on time with the new banknotes, there was no robbery, and the distribution occurred ahead of schedule! (The authors of the brief relate an interviewee's comment that 'this enormous logistical process went more quickly and smoothly than many had expected. Most of the legacy currency was replaced within a matter of weeks, rather than months'.) The clearing system for inter-bank transfers worked efficiently. The ECB could peg an overnight interest rate immediately. Its operational framework for implementing monetary policy (strict control of a very short-term money market rate) did not encounter any serious technical glitch.

This pat on the back for the monetary union engineering corps and its supervisors is to lose sight of the big picture. The absence of glitch or hitch in no way demonstrates that creation of the new monetary system was an act of progress. Such demonstration would require matching, as a first step, the record to date of monetary union with the heterogeneous intentions of its advocates. Then there would be an assessment of how it performed relative to the alternatives – whether contemporary regimes in other parts of the world or, counter-factual, regimes in Europe – and in absolute terms.

Yes, despite some reservations, most of all in Frankfurt, the train to EMU made it all the way through to a broad union (including in particular Spain and Italy) rather than stopping at the earlier destination of narrow monetary union including France, Germany, Holland, Belgium and Luxembourg. But as subsequent events turned out, including especially the extent of destruction wrought by the asset price inflation virus in the 'periphery zone countries', would it not have been better if the train had stopped one station short of that final destination? An essential condition for a smooth journey to the end destination of broad union was the establishment of a stable money regime under which the virus of asset price inflation could never become powerful. Yet the planners of the EMU train ride had failed to secure the track.

Defence claim 2: Euro as good a store of value as its predecessors

A second claim of success comes from a comment by Jean-Claude Trichet, quoted by the authors of the report:

> The main challenge we saw was to transfer to the new currency what had been promised: namely, that it would be as confidence inspiring, as credible, and as good a store of value as the previous national currencies had been.

The authors of the brief, Cecchetti and Schoenholtz, buttress M. Trichet's claim:

> The policy tests facing the ECB at its inception were numerous and daunting. It is evident that the ECB faced an extraordinary challenge as it sought to inherit from the start the credibility of its most successful predecessor central banks. There also were great risks, as there would be no honeymoon or grace period. Any significant rise of inflation expectations or of inflation risk premiums in the run-up to EMU might have branded policy a failure even before the ECB began to exercise monetary control. [...] There was concern whether the powerful NCB Governors – and their large staffs – would overwhelm the ECB, and potentially undermine the euro-area focus of the new central bank. [...] And the ECB was to begin operations in an environment of overt scepticism. [...] The broad membership of EMU, which included several formerly high-inflation countries, raised doubts about credibility.

The authors quote Alexandre Lamfalussy (a key figure in the creation of the euro, first as President of the BIS during the period when the Delors Committee was meeting regularly there to draw up its blueprint for monetary union and later as the head of the EMI, the predecessor of the ECB) as saying:

> I feared that they would have technical problems of all kinds. Ultimately I was wrong. The implementation went extraordinarily smoothly.

They also relate a comment from Otmar Issing:

> What really shocked me (when I arrived) was the lack of any reasonable information (data, etc). We were preparing monetary policy for totally unchartered waters.

A problem with the claims of survival and no technical hitch

There is a problem with all of these self-congratulations just recited. The claim that the ECB or EMU was successful because the new money is as good as the old (the Deutsche mark) in terms of goods and services inflation and because really bad scenarios (of considerable likelihood) were avoided where most citizens in the euro-area would have been much worse off than under the old monetary regime is bordering on the impudent! Why should a model European money have been subject at all to the curse of monetary inflation? And why did none of the self-congratulators consider the virus of asset price inflation (one type of monetary inflation) that now emerged in a more dangerous category than under the old Deutsche mark regime? Moreover, if there was really such a large probability of various bad scenarios becoming reality (and the best that could be said about the new money is that it is as good as the old) then why were those advocating the project of EMU doing so in such unequivocal terms?

Did M. Lamfalussy, for example, act in accordance with the highest democratic principles in deciding not to go public with his forebodings of chaos? It was not a time of war when secrecy concerning all disaster scenarios might be justified.

Was there a flaw in the European democratic processes that the leading officials and ex-officials were not quizzed under oath about the risks that were being run? If the democratic processes had been alive and the truth about risks revealed, including the key fact the launch may well turn into a glitch-laden disaster), would the citizens-to-be of the euro-area have continued to support the train going forward towards monetary union, even in those few countries where referendums had been held and they had originally voted for the Treaty of Maastricht?

The inclusion of the previous high-inflation countries in EMU (Spain, Italy, Portugal, Greece, Ireland) did prove an initial success in terms of citizens in those countries having a domestic medium-of-exchange which was superior to their old (whether pesetas, liras, or drachmas) in some respects (in particular as regards the extent of long-run inflation danger and liquidity). Citizens of all member countries, with the possible exception of Germany, now enjoyed a wider range of highly liquid instruments to choose from without incurring exchange risk or exchange transaction costs. In any overall appraisal, however, we should consider the costs of that success.

A prominent cost was the economic damage wrought by the virus of asset price inflation – the bubbles and subsequent bursts in credit and real estate markets (the bubbles, bursts and damage being spread unevenly across the new monetary union) – in so far as the particular severity of this disease could indeed be traced to flaws in monetary union and serious mistakes in ECB policymaking.

Claim 3: ECB developed a state-of-the-art forecasting apparatus

The authors of the report do not consider the cost of monetary disequilibrium attributable to flaws in EMU, most ostensibly because they wrote their report before the most devastating phase of the bubble-bursting process. They continue instead with their claims of technical prowess, focussing next on the forecasting tools which the ECB assembled from a zero starting point:

> The ECB has developed a forecasting apparatus that is at the state-of-the-art in the central banking world – and as previously mentioned – routinely publishes its staff projections. In addition the broad research program of the ECB has reached a status that puts it at the frontier of applied policy analysis alongside the best research efforts of other leading central banks and academic institutions.

It was too bad that with all that it had at its command, the ECB made in its first decade three big monetary errors. First, easing in late-98/early-99 because price level rises during a period of economic slack were running at 'only 1% p.a.', ushering in a sharp decline of the euro and significant monetary inflation; second, fuelling a credit and asset bubble through 2003–6 out of concern that the newly refined inflation 'target' might be undershot; and third, pushing risk-free rates up to almost 5% half a year into the global recession – including Europe – which started in winter 2007/8 out of anxiety about the 'inflationary potential' of oil price rises and contributing thereby to the intensity of the economic downturn and the extent of financial system distress.

Claim 4: ECB has been a good European, ignoring national interests

The authors of the brief go on to reveal that in their discussions with present and former senior 'euro-officials':

> There was unanimity amongst ECB insiders that country-specific factors were irrelevant in the policy rate-setting process even at the start of EMU. Having feared a greater role for national interests, some interviewees reported reacting with surprise and satisfaction at that time. Others suggested that the long process of preparing for EMU – including joint preparatory work at the EMI – had fostered a broad consensus among euro-area central bankers about the objectives and implementation of monetary policy that underpinned the ECB's behaviour.

We have all heard the quote from Shakespeare's *Hamlet*: 'the lady doth protest too much!'

Of course, the policymakers were all good Europeans! Yet how was it that at critical junctures Germany's situation seemed to get a dominating weight in policymaking, more than just due to that country accounting for around 30% of euro-area GDP and thereby influencing significantly overall euro-area aggregates?

In winter 1998/9, the fact that the German economy was one of the most affected by the passing slowdown in world trade following the autumn-1998 mini financial crisis (related to Russia's default, the troubles of LTCM, and continuing retrenchment in East Asia in the aftermath of the debt crisis which erupted there in 1997) had at least some relation to the Bundesbank taking the lead in the policy easing at that time (see p. 56).

It is also plausible that the unfavourable relative cost and price level at which Germany became locked into EMU, with so many of the other member currencies having obtained big real devaluations vis-à-vis the mark in the years before, and the business malaise which accompanied that situation played a role in making German policymakers on the ECB Board over-complacent about the big decline of the euro in 1999–2000; failing to see this as a possible symptom of monetary disequilibrium.

And the later fact that Germany was not experiencing any temperature rise in its real estate and credit markets and its price level was flat (or even slightly falling) surely contributed towards the middle one of the three large ECB errors (2003–5), when overall monetary conditions remained excessively easy.

The export boom in Germany which continued into the first quarter of 2008, together with a doomsday concern of German monetary policy-makers about the power of unions (IG Metall in particular) to push up wages in response to oil-price hikes, help to explain the third error (2008 – see p. 64).

Claim 5: EMU achieved price stability and economic stability!

The Cecchetti–Schoenholtz brief was published just around the tenth anniversary time for EMU and so it is no surprise that some of those interviewed were in reflective mood. Anniversaries are a time for looking back and forward. Bundesbank President Weber expressed the view to the authors that:

> I think the success is the high degree to which price stability has been achieved [...]. Long-term inflation expectations have been stable and low and anchored at the level defined as price stability.

Hans Tietmeyer, founder ECB policy-board member in 1998 and Bundesbank President (1993–9) states to the authors of the brief that:

> From the beginning, the ECB was seen inside and outside the euro-area as independent and credible.

The then (in early 2008) New York Federal Reserve President Timothy Geithner (subsequently Treasury Secretary under President Obama) told the authors:

> Since the ECB has been setting monetary policy, it has not produced a sustained period of sub-par growth; the euro-area has not experienced greater volatility of economic growth; and there has certainly not been any erosion of inflation performance. All this suggests that the ECB is performing well.

A problem with the claim of stability

Um! The Bank of France and Bundesbank had both achieved inflation of 1% p.a. or less before the start of EMU. What did the creation of EMU and the ECB offer French and German citizens that they did not have already in terms of stability?

In fact, as highlighted in earlier chapters, the ECB was most probably more receptive to the monetary preachers warning that 'inflation might fall too low' than a still-sovereign Bundesbank would have been. There was no resistance within the ECB to the sirens of a false IMF-alarm on German and indeed global deflation risks in 2003. And it is hard to believe that the German government would ever have been an ally of the IMF in swaying the 'Old' Bundesbank against its better judgement. By contrast, in spring 2003, Berlin, Frankfurt – including the 'new Bundesbank' and Washington – had all been in step about the phoney danger of deflation.

And at no point was the Bundesbank an inflation targeter or quasi-inflation targeter, as the ECB became, carrying the danger of creating deep monetary disequilibrium. As for the record, the Bundesbank over more than a decade (1975–87) pursued a target for the monetary base (central bank money stock), putting much less emphasis than the ECB on rigid pegging of the overnight money market rates (see Leaman, 2001). The old Bundesbank studiously avoided any signalling to markets of the likely future path of any pegging operations (such signals influence market rates for longer maturities). That was consistent with a set of principles emphasizing monetary stability to which a stable price level over the very long run would be the accompaniment but with no hang-up about delivering stability of a CPI over a two-year period and with no manipulation (deliberate or unintentional) of interest rates (for short, medium or long maturities) away from neutral level. The erosion of principles at the Bundesbank came largely in the run-up to EMU (and even previously during the consummation of German Monetary Union) when the leadership of that institution became increasingly subject to the overriding European (and German union) objectives of Chancellor Kohl, buttressed by his choice of a monetary chief likely to be compliant with those objectives.

Counter-factual peril: the old Bundesbank would have done better!

It is always dangerous to undertake counter-factual history-making. Even so, it is hard to imagine that without monetary union the member countries either singly or together would have gone down the road of breathing inflation higher. If the monetary order had remained unchanged – with the Bundesbank enjoying hegemony – there might have been some one-off exchange realignments in the late 1990s so that the mark would have fallen in value vis-à-vis some of its main partners. The German price level would not have been under any downward pressure in that event. In any case there is no reason to believe that a staunchly independent and self-confident Bundesbank, not weakened by a train journey to GMU (German Monetary Union) and then EMU, would have been inclined to follow currently popular monetary practice as set by the Bernanke/Greenspan Federal Reserve and praised by the IMF.

The ECB, however, as a new institution, had no such self-assurance or indeed inclination to defy fashion as set by the Federal Reserve. There was no 'old guard' within the new central bank, steeped in alternative monetary doctrine, and ready to do battle with the latest version of monetary populism. The Schroeder Government was siding with Washington on deflation risk and the need to counter it. ECB officials were enjoying their time in the sun as issuers of the new global money and as partakers in the brainstorming of the annual Federal Reserve research symposium (at Kansas) or like events where the ten Bernanke principles of inflation-targeting (a follow-on from the Blinder doctrine whereby the central bank should ignore temperature upswings in asset and credit markets, concentrating instead on goods and services price changes) formed the essential text of the popular gospel (amid some dissent, most notably from the BIS chief economist, William White). The old Bundesbankers, by contrast, may have decided to just stay at home! (See Brown, 2008, for a statement of the ten Bernanke principles.)

The Bundesbank at this time (2003) was at low ebb in terms of leadership, direction and exercise of influence. The current president, Ernst Welteke (the successor in 1999 to Hans Tietmeyer, the Bundesbank president who had never raised interest rates and had remained loyal to Chancellor Kohl throughout the five years running up to the launch of EMU, see Marsh, 2009) had been a blatantly political appointment by Chancellor Schroeder. Welteke's rise to the top had run from head of the SPD faction in the Hesse Federal parliament, to regional board member of the Bundesbank (appointed there by Hesse Prime Minister Eichel), to head of the Bundesbank (appointed there by Chancellor Schroeder on the advice of his finance minister, Hans Eichel).

In a counter-factual world in 2003 with a sovereign Deutsche mark and a 'non-corrupted' Bundesbank still calling the monetary shots for Europe, it is hard to believe that any of the other central banks on their own would have followed the lead of the IMF or Bernanke/Greenspan Fed in deciding to breathe inflation back into their individual economies. If monetary deflation were in fact to materialize (despite the best efforts of the respective central banks to achieve monetary stability) in any of these countries outside Germany, a quick effective counter-measure could be a downward adjustment of their currency against the Deutsche mark. There would be no need to take pre-emptive action now to bolster the inflation rate!

So what did Messrs Weber and Tietmeyer actually believe that the ECB had brought to the party? (see p. 174). The authors of the brief do not tell us! As regards Tim Geithner's comment (see p. 174), presumably he would not have made it six months later into the European Slump of winter 2008–9!

It is also dubious whether Professor John Taylor would have made his flattering comment quoted in the brief if interviewed a few months later:

> The biggest success of EMU to date has been to set it up from scratch, to deal with the inherent difficulties of communication and different traditions, and to have a policy apparatus which is basically working well in terms of interest rate decisions. That has to be viewed as a major achievement. It's the first time anything like that has been done.

Surely Professor Taylor as assistant secretary of the Treasury in charge of international affairs under the first Bush Administration (2001–5) was aware of the ECB's decision in spring 2003 to follow its own version of breathing inflation back into the economy, just as the Bernanke/Greenspan Federal Reserve was doing at the time? And indeed in his critique, published in 2009, of the Federal Reserve's role in the bubble-and-burst he makes explicit reference to the monetary errors in the euro-area at the same time. These are cast, however, simplistically in terms of whether the short-term interest rate as pegged by the central bank was above or below the level specified by the 'Taylor rule' as calculated for each individual member countries. Taylor does not apply a more general concept of monetary disequilibrium including the virus of asset price inflation, though incidentally those member countries where the 'one size fits all' official interest rate stayed for a long time (during the early/mid 2000s) far below where his rule would indicate are those where speculative temperatures in credit and real estate markets reached particularly high levels.

It is far less clear whether Paul Volcker (not interviewed by the authors of the brief) was so familiar with euro-history when he praised EMU in late 2008 (Volcker, 2008). He told the assembled dignitaries at a conference held in honour of Helmut Schmidt, the German chancellor under which the train to EMU started with the launch in 1978 of the EMS, that

> Today, on the 30th anniversary of the EMS, the world economy faces a new and severe challenge reflected in the volatility of the US dollar and extraordinary pressure on the international financial system. In the midst of the great uncertainties, there is no doubt in my mind that Europe and therefore the world is better able to cope with that crisis by virtue of having achieved a common European currency.

Perhaps this was the type of glib praise which Paul Volcker might have re-considered later if in full possession of present and subsequent facts just as Milton Friedman might have revised subsequently his praise in 2006 (at age 94!) of Alan Greenspan, congratulating him as the Federal Reserve president whose record had refuted his long-run view of that institution as a perennial source of monetary instability.

Claim 6: A bogus comparison of inflation before and after EMU start

The authors of the brief (Cecchetti and Schoenholz) completed their work before the full financial panic developed which formed the backdrop to Paul Volker's favourable comments about EMU. They quote the fact that over the period from 2001 (assuming that ECB policy typically affects prices with a time lag of about two years) until the latest datapoint available at the time of writing (in early 2008), HICP inflation averaged 2.3% p.a. For comparison, in the pre-EMU period of 1991–8, headline inflation averaged 2.6% p.a. (but why do they exclude 1999, a year of very low inflation, from the pre-EMU performance measurement, on the same two year principle?):

> Even in Germany, which boasts the pre-eminent pre-EMU inflation track record, inflation has been lower and far more stable in EMU: under the Bundesbank, German inflation averaged 3.4% from 1965 to 1998 (with a standard deviation of 3.4%), while German inflation since 2001 has averaged 1.8% (with a standard deviation of only 0.6%).

Thank you for nothing!

What is the relevance of citing inflation in Germany during the period of the Great Global Inflation of the late 1960s and 1970s, from which Germany made an early exit but only after the final crash of the Bretton Woods system (including its brief Smithsonian sequel) in March 1973 allowed the Bundesbank to follow an independent monetary policy?

As to the stability of the inflation rate, that should be a source of suspicion (like the stable returns provided by the Ponzi-schemer!). Central banks that find they are piloting under 'ideal weather conditions' of a stable price level for goods and services (or a stable low rate of price level rise) without interruption should be on raised alert that their policies are introducing severe monetary disequilibrium into the system. The avoidance of throwing a monkey wrench of money into the machinery of the economy – by not creating gaps between neutral and market rates – requires some instability in the price level or in the rate of price level change over the short- and medium-run!

Claim 7: ECB did well in the context of 'trying circumstances'

The authors of the report go further in their dubious praise of the ECB's 'inflation record':

> In light of the trying economic circumstances of the past decade, the achievement of low and stable inflation in the euro area most likely reflects good monetary policy, not good fortune. Since its inception, the euro-area experienced large price shocks from developments in energy, commodity and currency markets – not unlike in the Great Inflation episode.

Well, yes, inflation over a very long period – high or low – is determined to a large extent by the monetary regime and how monetary policy is conducted under that regime. But where were the 'trying circumstances'? On two big occasions (1999 and 2003) the ECB deliberately followed a policy of breathing inflation higher. The catalytic role of large price shocks (which may well subsequently reverse), better described as real resource supply shocks, in setting off a long-run process of monetary inflation or deflation is highly questionable. And in the short-run, the various types of real shocks, including sudden resource shortage, or big improvement in terms of trade, affecting an important price (such as energy) should be reflected in overall price level swings if indeed severe monetary disequilibrium is to be avoided.

The Austrian School pointed out long ago that central bank policy action to combat price level swings due to real changes in the economy (for example, terms of trade swings, an acceleration or deceleration of the productivity growth trend, real resource shock or cyclical fluctuations) is a recipe for monetary disequilibrium of which the chief symptom (after a potentially long and variable time lag) might well be asset and credit markets overheating or cooling down excessively, otherwise described as asset price inflation or deflation.

Take the ideal situation where money rates might fluctuate considerably with much white noise but where this (and, more generally, money) does not get in the way of the market estimating efficiently the neutral rates of interest for medium and long maturities and of setting market rates at a level close to the respective neutral level. Then there would be significant upward and downward (positive or negative) shifts in the price level over the short- and medium-run, but no serious and prolonged monetary inflation or deflation.

Claim 8: EMU promotes regional and financial efficiency

The authors of the brief make no mention of Austrian School concepts (which descend from the monetary analysis of J. S. Mill). It is not surprising therefore that they make no connection between the credit bubble bursting process already evident in Europe from summer 2007 and earlier mistakes in euro-monetary policy. Nor do the authors identify the infernal combination of first, a speculative story about huge potential profits in the financial sector stemming from European integration and second, monetary disequilibrium as responsible for virulent asset price inflation. Instead they comment:

> By securing price stability, ECB policy contributed indirectly to many other advances in euro-area welfare.

> One example is the progress in capital markets and the financial system. Government bond markets appear to have been largely integrated at a very early stage in EMU. The rapid expansion of markets for corporate bonds and for many derivative instruments over the past decade partly reflected the stable euro-area economic environment.

> The breadth and depth of these markets facilitate the efficient allocation of savings in the region. The gradual evolution toward banking integration also contributes to regional efficiency.

It is not clear what regional efficiency is being referred to here – surely not the facilitation of lending from the savings surplus countries in Europe (principally Germany) towards the countries 'enjoying' high speculative temperatures in credit (including the government sector) and real estate markets (big examples include Spain and the UK). This transfer assumed such massive proportions due to irrational exuberance among financial institutions and their shareholders. Investors, under the influence of the asset price inflation virus, wore spectacles which filtered out credit dangers, not least in the inter-bank markets (see p. 105).

Claim 9: ECB deserves praise for its response to August 2007 quake!

The authors of the brief move on to discuss the issue of the ECB's role in financial stability and regulation and generally absolve it of responsibility for any serious misfortune so far. Indeed they even shower some praise on the ECB:

> In the area of liquidity provision as a lender of last resort, recent experience has highlighted important ECB successes. In August 2007, the ECB boosted liquidity supply early and aggressively to counter sharp increases in funding rates as banks turned cautious and alternative private sources of funding shut down. The ECB's Bagehot-style marginal lending facility (MLF, designed to cap overnight rates in normal times) can be viewed as an automatic mechanism for calming liquidity fears in a crisis. [...] It seems fair to conclude that the ECB's toolkit for liquidity supply has been crisis-tested and satisfies current 'best practice' standards among central banks.

Well, that is light-years away from the conclusion reached in our last chapter: that the ECB's application of the bogus separation principle (during 2007–8), meaning the injection of massive amounts of sterilized liquidity at subsidized rates while fostering simultaneously a rise in risk-free rates (rather than allowing a sharp fall), was utterly counterproductive, both from the viewpoint of monetary stability and financial system stabilization.

The alternative course would have been for the ECB to clear the way for an immediate fall of the risk-free rate to zero, which would have made possible a sharp widening of margins on profitable loan business (where margins are measured relative to the rate banks able to offer well-equity cushioned deposits would have paid on these) and inducing thereby an early re-capitalization of still solvent banks. In the same spirit, the involvement of the ECB in providing US dollar funding to European banks that found the supply of repo-financing largely from US money market funds suddenly drying up should have been on an emergency basis only.

These European banks should have been forced at the earliest date feasible to replace these funds by a stable source not dependent on irrational exuberance. US money market funds were not such a source because they turned on investors in these funds believing irrationally that they could never fall below $1 in the dollar, and on the fund managers themselves under-estimating the risk of repo-business with European banks. Forcing viable banks back into the markets beyond an immediate emergency period would have been close to the Bagehot principle. It was not the course which the ECB actually followed.

Claim 10: Passing the buck

One point which apologists for the ECB make in its defence against the charge of having promoted financial instability is that, due to no fault of its own, it lost the battle early in the decade for any strengthening of its supervisory authority.

Under the Eichel–Brown initiative of July 2002, EU governments and finance ministers, in view of their greater democratic accountability, were ultimately to be responsible for 'policing' financial institutions and financial markets. The Bundesbank in particular and also the ECB lost out at that time in the political competition as to who was to be responsible for the supposedly growing pan-European regulatory system. None of this means that the ECB or Bundesbank would have done a better job of regulation in so far as this is a valid discussion (invalid for those who consider that regulation is futile and harmful, with true financial discipline depending on competition, monetary stability, and transparency) but at least they have an excuse when it comes to the 'what went wrong with the regulators' issue!

And on the subject of excuses, the authors have a few of these up their sleeves! They quote for example Otmar Issing:

> What is unique for the ECB is the complex environment. [...] The ECB still is a young institution, and the euro area is very complex, not least due to the language and communication problem.

Few would argue with that assertion. But were these problems sufficiently highlighted by the advocates of EMU before its creation and did they exaggerate any offsetting benefits which have accrued?

The authors also raise the hypothesis (which could in part exonerate the ECB but not EMU) that the euro-area might be a sub-optimal currency area, complicating thereby the conducting of a one size fits all monetary policy:

> Risks remain because potential growth is low, labour markets are relatively rigid, and there is little scope for fiscal burden sharing. Moreover as Vice-president Papademos describes, some countries – including Greece, Italy and Portugal – exhibit divergent trends in the growth of unit labour costs that appear to diminish their competitiveness. [...] The ECB cannot alter its policy rate for the purpose of limiting economic divergence or to boost growth sustainably above potential.

The possibility – or indeed likelihood – that the euro-area is not an optimal currency area may indeed alleviate the blame for sub-optimal outcomes which should be borne by the ECB policymakers, but not by the creators of EMU. And there had been no shortage of warnings ahead of EMU that it might not be an optimal currency area. The authors do not pursue any line of defence against the charge of EMU being a non-optimal currency area.

Claim 11: Pride and satisfaction in hard effort

The brief concludes with a summary which is highly favourable towards the EMU and ECB:

> Our ECB interviewees rightly express pride and satisfaction in their accomplishment. Literally thousands of people worked diligently for years to make monetary union not only a reality, but a success. It is difficult to find major fault with the operational framework or the monetary policy decisions of the first decade of EMU.
>
> [...] The Maastricht Treaty ventured where no vessel had gone before, but it has worked well. That success presumably owes to the design and the crew, not to the lack of turbulence.

The readers of the previous chapters in this book know already the main planks of the counter-case to this glowing summary of the defence arguments.

An additional element in the counter-case has to be the sheer smugness of the leading officials in EMU, and their refusal to recognise (at least in anything public) the charges against them. That lack of self-criticism – or of real (as against staged) exposure to vibrant and powerful criticism from outside (some of which might filter emanate from a well-functioning liberal political system able to seek retribution for mistakes and meaningful remedies, including the occasional 'killing of the admiral to encourage the others') – has been a salient feature of the first decade and a half of EMU, especially as the flaws appeared crevasse-deep once the credit bubble burst.

ECB officials are not unique in smugness or in making serious errors of judgement (just take a look at the history of the Federal Reserve!). Much the same criticism can be justifiably levelled at other major central banks as regards the emergence of the financial crisis and their subsequent reactions. But as a new union with lofty ideals, could more not have been expected from Europe? There lies a main disappointment.

Towards buttressing the negative case against EMU as outlined in previous chapters and refuting the positive case put together in the Cecchetti–Schoenholz brief, we now turn to direct evidence of what the leading actors had to say. Let us start with President Jean-Claude Trichet.

Introduction to testimony of Jean-Claude Trichet

In an ECB tenth anniversary interview with *Börsen Zeitung* on 16 December 2008, President Trichet had the following favourable comments to make:

> As a symbol of European unity, the euro is already extremely successful. Since the outbreak of the financial crisis, the euro and the ECB have become, even more visibly, a central anchor for confidence. In this sense, I believe the emotional relationship of citizens to the euro has become stronger.

> [...] For me, the greatest success of the euro is that after having promised the citizens that the euro would be equal in terms of stability and the maintenance of value to the previously most solid currencies we have fulfilled this promise effectively.

Unfortunately the interviewer does not pick up any of the broad indictments against the ECB and EMU made here or elsewhere but does pluck up courage to ask:

Q: Knowing what we do now, was the interest rate increase in July this year (2008) a mistake? And why is it generally so difficult for central bankers to admit to mistakes?

A: Long-term inflation expectations threatened to become unanchored. In addition, wage and salary demands in some euro area countries caused us serious concern that there could be broad-based second-round effects. The interest rate decision enabled us to bring medium to long-term inflation expectations back under control in line with our definition of price stability. And this regained control of expectations was, by the way, the precondition which allowed us to cut rates strongly from October when the crisis worsened. Do not forget: our definition of price stability in the medium term is 'less than, but close to, 2%'. The interest rate increase in July must be related to the 'less than 2%' part. Our recent decrease of rates after the intensification of the crisis in September must be related to 'close to 2%'.

We can realize immediately that M. Trichet gave no answer to the second part of the question and the interviewer did not follow it up!

Let us consider the answer to the first part of what was in any case a tame question. Why ask about an almost meaningless 25 bp hike in rates when the big question should have been why the risk-free rate was then being pegged at 4.5% or higher, rather than zero?

The straight reply to the tame question would have been – yes, if we the ECB had made the correct diagnoses in spring and summer 2008 that the oil market bubble was a late symptom of the asset price inflation virus which had already moved on to asset price deflation phase (of which the credit market quakes of summer 2007 had been a first sign) and the euro-area was already in recession (from January 2008) with a significant risk ahead of financial panic, there could have been no question of a rate hike in July. And our concerns about wage pressures were misplaced, still influenced by events in a bygone age when labour markets had been extremely tight and anchors to low inflation expectations set adrift by monetary chaos well before any oil shock.

Instead M. Trichet provides justifications for the severe monetary tightness of spring and summer 2008 which could not convince even the most credulous! Who, other than a professor of philology, could really be interested in an exposition about the difference between an inflation rate less than 2% and a rate close to 2%? This is inflation-targeting gone mad, in the worst senses possible as ever imagined by Milton Friedman or the Austrian School! And yet ECB officials continued to repeat the mantra about a monetary pillar to its operating framework which distinguished the ECB from the inflation-targeting central banks.

The most outrageous claim of M. Trichet

Could anyone really believe a subsequent claim made by M. Trichet in Strasbourg on 13 January 2009 at a ceremony of the European Parliament to mark the tenth anniversary of the euro?

M. Trichet:

In recent months we have seen another benefit of the euro: the financial crisis is demonstrating that in turbulent financial waters it is better to be on a large, solid and steady ship rather than on a small vessel.

Would Europe have been able to act as swiftly, decisively and coherently if we did not have the single currency uniting us?

Would we have been able to protect many separate national currencies from the fallout of the financial crisis?

I believe that we can be proud of the reaction of the European authorities, parliaments, government and central banks, Together we have shown that Europe is capable of taking decisions, even in the most difficult circumstances!

It is difficult, in fact impossible, to make sense of this claim, except from the viewpoint of those players in the Greek, Portuguese, Spanish and Irish Ponzi schemes who succeeded in getting their funds out in full, courtesy of EU and ECB bail-outs, before the eventual wind-downs.

What was solid about the euro-ship as its members plunged into deep recession and its financial system froze in the aftermath of the Lehman bankruptcy shock? And without the shackles of EMU, some countries could have bailed out into smaller boats (cutting their interest rates and devaluing).

Instead they were all being driven into the storm's centre by ECB pilots, among whom the most powerful included a president renowned for inflexible toughness in France's long 'war for the hard franc', in the run-up to EMU and Bundesbankers (one ex-Bundesbanker) still convinced in early 2008 that Germany was in boom (a conviction based on the reality that indeed Germany's export bonanza was lagging the world business cycle). Even in summer 2008, these pilots were worried stiff about wage-led inflation.

As a matter of fact, a small non-EU non-euro European country was faring better (in terms of avoiding the severity of the downturn) than any euro-area member. Switzerland, whose central bank had to a moderate extent eased policy while the ECB and BoE were still allowing monetary conditions to tighten in 2008H1 and then in late 2008, had moved to a zero rate policy.

And to what swift decisive and coherent action could M. Trichet possibly be referring? The only candidate was the ECB action authorized from (but probably not initiated from – see p. 127) his holiday home in early August 2007 to lend unlimited collateralized amounts in the midst of the 'seizing up' of inter-bank markets. It has been argued here (see Chapter 5) that this was totally the wrong decision. And a similar point has been made in the US context by Taylor, 2009.

As for the national currencies to which the ECB would have been unable to offer protection, M. Trichet is most probably referring here to the counter-factual world of, say, Italy and Spain having their own currencies. If these had still existed and they had dropped sharply as the economic and financial climate worsened especially with respect to their own circumstances, then the devaluation would have given a fillip to their economic recovery prospects compared to the alternative prospect that now loomed of a Brüning-type policy dead end. That is to say cutting back spending within a recession so as to maintain solvency of the state and yet markets having no grounds to hope for economic renaissance.

M. Trichet's warnings and the warning that he ignored

Indeed in reviewing other evidence in the form of President Trichet's spoken comments, a 'patting on the back' or self-congratulatory aspect is often there. He told the Fifth ECB Central Banking Conference in mid-November 2008 that he was one of the policymakers to realize early that credit markets had warmed to a dangerous level. He dated his own warnings to 2006 when he was chairman of the Global Economy Meetings of Central Bank Governors:

> We knew that a storm was brewing but, admittedly, we did not know exactly where. Neither did we know what would trigger it, or when it would come.

This is an amazing statement.

If M. Trichet and his other central bank colleagues were so aware of the looming dangers why were there no contingency plans drafted to fit the different possible scenarios? Did these same ECB officials have absolutely no idea that monetary disequilibrium in the US and Europe was the ultimate cause of the storm or that the asset price inflation virus may already have reached a stage where monetary action could no longer safely attack it? (At an advanced stage the asset price inflation virus is likely already to be undergoing metamorphosis into asset price deflation and so monetary tightening might simply make the inevitable recession and bust even worse – see p. 9). And why did the ECB officials responsible for financial oversight make no effort to identify practices within the European banking field which might be the source of danger (for example, the off-balance-sheet vehicles used for getting round the BIS capital requirements, lack of prudence in the inter-bank markets as regards credit exposure, European banks' dependence on overnight funding in the dollar repo markets where the source was primarily US money market funds etc.)? Once identified, these practices should have been the subject of discussions, as initiated by the ECB within the constitutional remits of the Maastricht Treaty, with the relevant authorities in Brussels or with member governments.

Should there not have been more urgent consideration given to a more assertive monetary policy, putting a higher probability on evidence of rapid money and credit growth being symptomatic of serious monetary disequilibrium and less fixation on inflation-targeting (by any other name)? Perhaps, though, 2006 was already too late for such forcefulness. Asset price inflation might already have been pre-programmed to move on to the next phase of asset price deflation.

M. Trichet could not deny that he had been warned early on about the possible consequences of the US residential real estate market bubble. Back in November 2005 at his regular monthly press conference a reporter had posed the following question:

Q: May I put a question in French? I am from Canada. In the communiqué you said that you were looking at the situation and there's a lot of uncertainty at the moment. In this case, I would like to know whether you are worried about the real estate bubble in the US and whether you think that the situation could get even worse and if it were to get worse would you change your position?

Trichet: On this precise point I would only say that I signed the last statement of the G7. We had a consensus [...] that each continent and each major industrialised economy had its own homework to do. As far as Europe is concerned for us the homework is structural reforms. Structural reforms which we all think are absolutely essential. Looking at the US, it is quite clear that their main problem is the fact that savings in the US economy are far too low. So we agree as far as the diagnoses are concerned and we agree that these defects have to be corrected. We also agree that we have to correct them in the most resolute way possible. This is all what I would like to say on that point, but it is quite clear that there are defects that have to be rectified in all the major international economies.

Note that M. Trichet does not answer the question about real estate market bubble at all! And his comment about US citizens saving too little misses the main point that the huge size of the savings deficit was symptomatic of monetary disequilibrium. That is something legitimate for central bankers to focus on. Frugality, or lack of it, on the part of households and businesses can be taken care of by the invisible hands in well-functioning markets across the globe so long as there is monetary stability and unrestricted capital flows.

In sum, M. Trichet recited the well-rehearsed mantras about each country doing its homework, without any mention of the serious monetary errors which were in fact occurring in both Europe and the US and for which central banks were responsible. And instead he focussed on savings behaviour and structural reform – issues for which central banks are not responsible!

At the time of this question the ECB had just made its first tiny rate rise from the absurdly low level of 2%. The official rate (and related market rates) had been stuck there since 2003, in spite of accumulating possible symptoms of rising temperature in some European countries. A persistently weak US dollar against the euro (reflecting the Greenspan-Bernanke Federal Reserve's novel 'breathing in inflation') had torpedoed any moves within the policy-making council of the ECB to tighten monetary policies during 2004.

In fact in his pride about having spotted credit market heating at an early stage, M. Trichet told a specially convened meeting of the EU's economic and monetary commission on 11 September 2007 (where he was to explain the massive ECB lending operations undertaken in August 2007) that already in the first issue of the *ECB Financial Stability Review*, published in December 2004:

We had said that a high level of risk appetite was encouraging a search for yield amongst investors across a wide range of markets and asset classes.

Of course M. Trichet had not related 'the high level of risk appetite' and 'search for yield' to the monetary disequilibrium on both sides of the Atlantic, nor had he realized that these were classic symptoms of the asset price inflation virus. The rest of that 11 September 2007 address was the customary pat on the back for action taken – action that we have argued here was highly damaging both in terms of economic and financial outcome (see p. 76). Suffice it to say that in retrospect at least M. Trichet made the following self-damning comment with respect to ECB policymaking:

> We have considered that our monetary policy stance is still on the accommodative side.

That was just four months before the January 2008 onset of euro-area recession, in the wake of a giant quake in the credit markets amid all the signs of a credit bubble now bursting (except for the ECB's data on bank lending which continued to grow for some months as bank intermediation grew in partial offset to rapid shrinkage of the shadow banking system) and with money market rates up at 5%!

M. Trichet defends the indefensible separation principle

More of a similar misdiagnosis can be found in President Trichet's press conference of September 2007. In particular Trichet introduced to his listeners (and viewers) the erroneous separation principle – whereby the ECB had one set of policies for dealing with illiquidity in the money market and another for price level stability:

> Let us not confuse the appropriate functioning of the money market and the monetary policy stance. [...] It is very important to make a clear separation between these two factors. [...] In what is observed today, there are elements of correction that were diagnosed before the correction took place [I could find first pages of financial papers in which I had expressed that opinion] and, as is very often the case in such circumstances there are hectic episodes in this correction, there is a level of volatility that can be quite high and there is also a large deal of overshooting. Again, we have to play a very important role in the central bank constituency, in both having the preoccupation of the medium and long-term solid anchoring of inflation expectations, and having a good understanding of what the pertinent trends are in the medium and long term, of the global economy

and of each particular economy; and on the other hand having to care for the appropriate functioning of the money market.

A journalist did in fact take up the separation principle, albeit only in a fleeting way (this is no criticism of the journalist, given the time and other constraints):

Q: The ECB makes a clear-cut distinction between liquidity help for the money market and monetary policy in the medium term. Some economists argue that it is not really possible to make this distinction and that you have to use monetary policy, let's say the interest rate instrument, to rebuild confidence in the financial markets. What would you say to these people? What is your argument on that?

A: As I said, we have our responsibilities. If we were to tell the market that the short-term considerations are now such that we are hampering our medium-term responsibility, then we would not improve the situation, but make it worse. The dis-anchoring of inflation expectations would probably be the worst thing that we could do in the present circumstances.

There were two key issues not confronted by M. Trichet (or evidently by his fellow policymakers).

First, the bursting of the credit bubble had surely gone along with a substantial lowering of the risk-free interest rate in the euro-area which was consistent with overall equilibrium (even though it was possible that simultaneously the equilibrium cost of risky capital would have risen and it was a matter of debate how far the average interest rate across all risk-categories had fallen).

Second, the choice of the overnight money market and of one interest rate there as the appropriate operating target of monetary policy was particularly destabilizing. The heterogeneity of credit-risks between banks even with respect to overnight borrowing meant that there should be a spread of rates (if not artificially restricted) rather than by one rate applicable to all.

M. Trichet on the startling misdiagnosis of September 2007

In this September 2007 press conference, M. Trichet assured his audience that a sharp US slowdown (or recession) in consequence of the unfolding sub-prime mortgage crisis would not have big impact on the euro-area. In his initial briefing he stated that:

> Global economic activity is expected to remain robust, as the likely slowdown in the US is expected to be largely offset by the continued strong growth in emerging markets. This will continue to provide support to euro-area exports and investment. In addition, consumption growth in the euro-area should strengthen further over time, in line with developments in real disposable income, as employment conditions improve further.

It seemed like an occupational hazard for the ECB to expect on the eve of recession (whether in late 2000/early 2001 or late 2007) that the euro-area would be on the edge of the storm. Perhaps the hazard stretches back to the run-up to EMU when one main plank of the advocates (of EMU) was that, in consequence of monetary union, Europe would be more sheltered from US shock. Already there were grounds in summer 2007 for doubting this hypothesis given the revelation of the extent to which the European banks had become caught up in the global credit bubble including its key US component and given the extent to which the ECB had been imitating the Federal Reserve's policies of monetary instability.

Trichet's ignoring of US monetary danger

The fact that the ECB had turned off all alarm bells that might ring in response to growing US monetary instability had already become clear as far back as July 2004 in the course of a press conference given by M. Trichet. There was a revealing question-and-answer for those listening carefully:

Q: Mr. Trichet, does the move of the Federal Reserve yesterday [1 July 2004, the first rate rise – in effect by a trivial amount – since the 'breathing in inflation policy' had been adopted by the Greenspan/ Bernanke Fed] to raise interest rates influence or affect the ECB's decision in any way?

A: We all have responsibility, all over the world. Certainly across the Atlantic the Federal Reserve has a very important responsibility, and it is not my responsibility to elaborate on that. We have our own responsibility: the US is the US and the euro area is the euro area! We are in different universes with different fundamentals and different episodes in the business cycle. Furthermore, we are both responsible for price stability in these different universes. So we are not influenced in any way by what has been decided across the Atlantic or what has been decided across the Channel, or what has been decided elsewhere in the world. Because of our own analysis of the present situation in the euro area, we have not changed our monetary policy stance. Again, on the basis of European judgement and diagnosis, we have no bias and we remain vigilant.

Of course we must be careful about over-interpreting statements in question-and-answer sessions at press conferences.

Perhaps if M. Trichet had had time to reflect and edit he would not have agreed with everything he said on the spur of the moment! Even so one obvious critique of this interchange is that M. Trichet and his ECB colleagues were deluding themselves about their independence or the independence of the euro-area from strong US influence.

Yes, in principle, the ECB could have composed an entirely different framework of monetary policy from the US, but it chose not to do so, and in fact in spring 2003 had mimicked the strategy of seeking to prevent inflation from falling too low. So what could M. Trichet possibly mean by saying 'we are not influenced by decisions across the Atlantic'. This could be true only in the trivial sense of whether there would be a 25 bp rise in policy rates this month! Given the similarity of monetary framework on both sides of the Atlantic, and the considerable interdependence of credit market conditions, M. Trichet should have been taking more notice of US monetary actions or non-actions! The likelihood was that if one key segment of the credit market universe was overheating – in this case the US – something similar was happening in the European segment also!

The criticism follows from all of this that EMU had itself bred a complacency of insularity within the ECB, while in fact both the ECB itself and European financial markets had become more intertwined with US developments and fashions than in the pre-EMU decade. And one key factor which had increased the interdependence of US and European credit and monetary developments was the ECB's concern during 2004–5 about the strength of the euro against the dollar.

M. Trichet wears old hat of French currency diplomat

A rise of the euro towards 1.30 against the dollar triggered crisis activity at the top of the ECB, with M. Trichet, who had been appointed president in autumn 2003, revelling in his old role of G7 diplomat, this time seeking to negotiate a fall back of the euro and rise of the East Asian currencies – see p. 74. That alarmist response to the euro's climb against the dollar is perplexing from the perspective of early 2008 when the ECB seemed totally calm about the euro heading for 1.60 despite the euro-area economy already being in recession!

The alarm ringing out loud at the Eurotower in 2004, triggered by the rise of the euro against the dollar, neutralized any better inclinations policymakers there may have had towards charting a course independent from the Federal Reserve amid the evidence of credit and real estate market temperature rising.

M. Trichet had told a questioner at the February 2005 press conference that:

> In the euro-area – and it is the euro area as a whole that we have to look at – we have signs that credit dynamism might foster increases in the real estate sector. And this calls for vigilance.

There was, however, no rise in the key short-term money rate pegged by the ECB until near the end of the year – and then only by a trivial 25 bp.

At the December 2004 news conference just two months earlier, M. Trichet had told his audience that he considered recent rises of the euro as 'unwelcome' and 'brutal'.

The message – also confirmed in individual discussions by the author with ECB officials – was that the ECB intended to hold back from tightening monetary policy because of the strength of the euro. The rationalization was that the strong euro would mean first, lower than otherwise inflation and second, weaker than otherwise aggregate demand (taking account of pressure downwards on profits in some key industrial sectors, perhaps most of all in Germany). Both shifts should translate into a downward adjustment of so-called neutral and natural rate levels with respect to short and medium maturities for the euro-area as a whole.

The hazard in such a line of analysis was to exaggerate the significance of a likely transitory swing in exchange rates (euro up against the US dollar) on inflation expectations and equilibrium real interest rates in the euro area. The ECB in responding to the near-term good news on inflation by delaying rate rises could destroy the potential partial insulation created by monetary independence against the US monetary virus of asset price inflation spreading to Europe.

ECB officials – at least those who spoke about such matters on the record – just did not see it that way. They diagnosed the euro's rise and the dollar's weakness as symptomatic of 'global imbalances' which had to be corrected.

Testimony of Professor Jürgen Stark

Monetary historians could imagine that Bundesbank officials would be least sympathetic to the concern about global imbalances given the long tradition within that institution during its heydays (1960–86?) of emphasizing potential clashes between external and internal stability, and the importance of keeping the focus on the latter. And indeed the German successor in June 2006 to Otmar Issing on the ECB Board (with more restricted power in that President Trichet used the transition to divide the research and economics empire over which Issing had ruled into two), ex-Bundesbank Vice-Chairman Professor Jürgen Stark, put it like this in a speech on 10 December 2008:

> The mandate of the ECB is to maintain price stability over the medium term. The mandate must be adhered to both in normal times and in times of crisis. The monetary policy stance appropriate to fulfil the ECB's mandate depends exclusively on its assessment of the balance of risks to price stability and nothing else.

In so far as this oblique statement meant not being diverted by stabilizing the exchange rate at the cost of internal stability that was strictly according to long-established Bundesbank principle and practice.

The disturbing element was the implication that Professor Stark, even at this late date, was unready to countenance the possibility that the framework of inflation-targeting or quasi-inflation targeting as designed by the ECB (never adopted by the Bundesbank when sovereign) had been basically flawed, as the Austrian economists had long maintained, and as BIS Chief Economist Bill White had argued during the recent years of asset price inflation around the globe led by the US and Europe.

Instead Professor Stark came out with the same paper-thin mantra as President Trichet:

> We should not forget how Europe would look today without the euro. The euro-area countries would be significantly worse off. Multiple crises would arise simultaneously; currency crises would go hand in

hand with banking crises and real economy disruptions at country level, potentially ending up in political tensions between countries. [...] By eliminating the exchange rate channel, the euro has mitigated the risk of contagion stemming from national economic or financial crises. In this sense, the euro has been a very important stabilizing element in difficult times.

Saying something over and over again though is no proof!

As an ex-Bundesbanker, Professor Stark seemed to be surprisingly unaware of the counter-argument which could be put forward by the euro-sceptics, some of whom had occupied the highest positions of authority in the Old Bundesbank, about how the euro might well have made the crisis worse.

And Professor Stark was certainly not above repeating the mantra about global imbalances being a scourge in the international economic environment and how this had been an important factor in the generation of the US 'central component' of the global credit bubble. He had done so when commenting a month earlier on the role of global imbalances in causing the crisis (in the course of a speech 18 November 2008 to the 11th Euro finance week). His speech had started with an introductory quote from Goethe:

Error repeats itself endlessly in deeds. Therefore we must repeat the truth tirelessly in words.

To be fair, this quote seemed to be attached to the section of his speech on general macro-economic matters rather than to the recitation of the mantra about global imbalances. But in this section there is no mention of the truth that asset price inflation, like goods and services inflation, is everywhere and at every time a monetary phenomenon. On the basis of Goethe's quote that is what Professor Stark should have been repeating tirelessly.

Instead, in the speech, Professor Stark dwelt on the contribution of general macro-economic policy to the crisis in Europe, not just in the US, and ostensibly avoided pointing the finger at monetary policy:

Expansionary macroeconomic policies around the globe have contributed to the build-up of macroeconomic imbalances. These policies have facilitated the strong credit expansion, excessive house price increases and the build-up of large current account imbalances, in particular in the US but also in other regions including some euro-area countries.

Testimony of Christian Noyer

Banque de France Governor and ex-vice chair of the ECB, Christian Noyer, displayed no such inner pangs of conscience when he added his voice to the anniversary chorus of self-acclamation in a speech in early autumn 2008 (10 October) under the title *A Founder's Perspective on the Euro as a Global Currency* (before the Peterson Institute for International Economics in Washington). Here are snippets of his self-congratulatory remarks:

> Actually, one of the main gratifications of the job during the crisis has been the quality of our collective interaction and deliberation in the Governing Council, based on our willingness, in very challenging circumstances, to share judgements and exchange views in a spirit of friendship and mutual respect. [Author's comment: if so proud, why the obsessive secrecy which blocks all record of the discussions from ever seeing the light of day!] I am very proud to be part of such a group. [...] Overall, it is fair to say that the euro has passed the test and comes strengthened out of the current difficulties. The euro system will keep fulfilling its priority mandate of price stability while also contributing to the broader objective of financial stability. [...] So the eurozone has shown it is well equipped to live up to its responsibilities as a truly global player in the international monetary system of the 21st century.

Did ECB and Fed throw a monkey wrench?

Let us step back from these self-congratulatory exclamations to one of the biggest underlying issues in appraising central bank performance in the euro-area through the middle years of its first decade.

Was the global credit bubble which formed at this time stimulated in large part by policies of monetary disequilibrium in the US and Europe?

Or are the apologists for the US and European central banks correct in claiming that the fundamental source of disequilibrium lay outside the monetary arena and in fact stemmed from 'unsustainable global imbalances' (code for excess saving in East Asia and, in some accounts, under saving in the US)?

In assessing the role of the ECB in creating monetary disequilibrium and the contribution of that to growing the virus of asset price inflation which attacked various credit markets and real estate markets in Europe there is no realistic alternative to constructing a joint test for the ECB and Federal Reserve.

Did both central banks, together following similar policies, play a key role in the formation of a virulent asset price inflation virus? If yes, then we can consider the follow-up counter-factual question of whether the ECB, following a quite different policy stance from the Federal Reserve, could have limited severely the spread of the US asset price inflation virus to Europe.

Alan Greenspan denies Fed (or ECB) to blame

The most eloquent defence of the view that central banks do not, in consequence of their monetary stance, share responsibility for the global credit bubble comes from ex–Federal Reserve Chairman Alan Greenspan. That is surprising in one respect.

If Greenspan could bring himself to concede that central bank monetary error played a large role – that, to use J. S. Mill's metaphor, the central bankers threw a giant money wrench into the machinery of the economy (in modern metaphor, they corrupted the software of money which then spread a virus to all the software determining the key price signals to which the invisible hands of the capitalist economy respond) – then that would remove the floor from below those critics who argue that a more fundamental flaw of free market economics was to blame (such as essential inefficiencies in global capital markets or the impossibility of the market 'matching' high savings propensities in East Asia with investment opportunity in the wider world).

Yet to provide that rescue for liberalism such as would be consistent with the Ayn Rand idealism which he long ago espoused, Greenspan would have to admit his policy was at fault – or at very least that he had unwisely allowed his better judgement to be swayed in 2003 by the bad advice from Professor Ben Bernanke, then the new Governor just arrived from Princeton University. There is absolutely no evidence on public record that Greenspan has made such an admission even to himself, although his oblique criticisms of Professor Bernanke for persisting with QE policies for so long could suggest that he might question in retrospect whether he should have respected so highly the advice from that source when he was in charge.

Greenspan rejects the view that over-easy money policy was to blame by pointing to the fact that long-term interest rates remained at a modest level even once the Federal Reserve started to raise its key overnight rate from late/mid 2004 onwards. He attributes this lack of long-term rate response to the huge surplus of savings in East Asia. To quote from his *Wall Street Journal* article of 11 March 2009 ('The Fed Didn't Cause the Housing Bubble'):

There are at least two broad and competing explanations of the origins of the crisis. The first is that 'easy money' policies of the Federal Reserve produced the US housing bubble. The second, and far more credible, explanation agrees that it was indeed lower interest rates that spawned the speculative euphoria. However, the interest rate that mattered was not the federal-funds rate, but the rate on long-term, fixed-rate mortgages. Greenspan omits here the point that the share of floating rate mortgages rose sharply during this housing market boom. Between 2002 and 2005, home mortgage rates led US home price change by 11 months. This correlation between home prices and mortgage rates was highly significant and a far better indicator of rising home prices than the fed-funds rate. This should not come as a surprise. After all, the prices of long-lived assets have always been determined by discounting the flow of income by interest rates of the same maturities as the assets. No-one to my knowledge employs overnight interest rates to determine the capitalization rate of real estate.

The Federal Reserve became acutely aware of disconnect between monetary policy and mortgage rates when the latter failed to respond as expected to the Fed tightening in mid-2004. Moreover, the data show that home mortgage rates had become gradually decoupled from monetary policy even earlier – in the wake of the emergence around the turn of this century of a well arbitraged global market for long-term debt instruments. [...] Between 1971 and 2002 the fed funds rate and the mortgage rate moved in lockstep. The correlation between them was a tight 0.85. Between 2002 and 2005, however, the correlation diminished to insignificance.

The presumptive cause of the worldwide decline in long-term rates was the tectonic shift in the early 1990s by much of the developing world from heavy emphasis on central planning to increasingly dynamic, export-led market competition. The result was a surge in growth in China and a large number of other emerging market economies that led to an excess of global intended savings related to intended capital investment. That ex ante excess of savings propelled global long-term interest rates progressively lower between early 2000 and 2005. That decline in long-term interest rates across a wide spectrum of countries statistically explains and is the most likely major cause of real estate capitalization rates that declined and converged across the globe resulting in the global housing price bubble.

Before taking issue with this defence claim by Alan Greenspan, let's join it with the claims of his successor to the chair of the Federal Reserve.

Ben Bernanke adamant that central banks did not create bubble

Greenspan's successor at the top of the Federal Reserve, Professor Ben Bernanke, expanded on the same line of explanation, notably in a speech in spring 2009 (Morehouse College, Atlanta, Georgia). Modelling his enquiry on the 'four questions' of the Passover Haggadah, he asked the key opening question:

How did we get here? What caused our financial and economic system to break down to the extent it has?

Then simplicity gives way to complexity, which is always a dangerous sign! Bernanke continues:

The answer to this question is complex. Experts disagree on how much weight to give various explanations. In my view, we need to consider how global patterns of saving and investment have evolved over the past decade or more, and how those changes affected credit markets in the US and some other countries. [...] In the past 10 to 15 years, the US and some other industrial countries have been the recipients of a great deal of foreign saving. Much of this foreign saving came from fast-growing emerging market countries in Asia and other places where consumption has lagged behind rising incomes, as well as from oil exporting countries that could not profitably invest all their revenue at home. The net inflow of foreign saving to the US, which was about 1.5% of GDP in 1995 reached about 6% of national output in 2006, an amount equal to about $825bn in today's dollars. Saving inflows from abroad can be beneficial if the country that receives those inflows invests them well. Unfortunately that was not always the case in the United States and some other countries. Financial institutions reacted to the surplus of available funds by competing aggressively for borrowers and in the years leading up to the crisis credit to both households and businesses became relatively cheap and easy to obtain.

Refuting the evidence of Messrs Greenspan and Bernanke

Let us step back to Greenspan's alleged disconnect between long-term and short-term interest rates before returning on the further elaboration by Bernanke. A first general point is that the lack of close correlation between long-term and short-term rates in the years 2002–5 is not quite a conundrum.

Long-term rates already by late 2003 discounted some scepticism or even rejection of the deflation risk story put out by the IMF and the central bankers club. The discounting was evident in the steep yield curve in the T-bond market, illustrated by long-maturity yields being far above short. Long maturity yields had jumped through the second half of 2003 on growing evidence of a growth cycle upturn in the US economy and a fading of deflation concerns in the marketplace if not in the Federal Reserve. In any case, the historically unique policy of deliberately breathing inflation back into the US economy (especially in the context of such scepticism as to its appropriateness) was likely to bring some perturbations of the normal cyclical relationship between short- and long-term rates.

The fact that long-maturity yields did not climb further in 2004–5 as the Federal Reserve eventually proceeded with its long series of micro-adjustments upwards of the Federal Funds rate is consistent with the simple hypothesis that this policy had already been anticipated in the marketplace. In this episode the Federal Reserve had laid out more precisely its projected path over the short and medium term for its official short-term rate peg than at any previous time in its history. This was a first case of what central bankers later described as the tool of 'forward interest rate guidance' (launched first by Professor Bernanke in Summer 2011 and then copied by ECB President Draghi in Summer 2013). Previously the view had been dominant in the marketplace that money rates were to a considerable degree unpredictable, even by the central bankers. The rates were seen as dependent on supply and demand conditions in the money market such as to be consistent with a given stipulated path for high-powered money supply growth.

Moreover, central bank policy explanations can themselves influence the expectations formation process that determines near and even distant forward interest rates in the term structure of rates. The broadcasting of the 'Asian savings glut' and its hypothesized downward influence on equilibrium interest rates – emphasized by the central bankers (prominently Alan Greenspan, Ben Bernanke and Claude Trichet) in many of their speeches and commentaries – surely played some role in containing any rise of long-term rates as the economic expansion built up through 2004–5; even though the Asian savings glut hypothesis, as we shall see, was highly dubious.

The thrust of Federal Reserve action at this time (2003–5) in driving market rates (for medium and even long maturities) well below neutral level may have contributed towards a general lowering of risk premiums whether with respect to equity, credit, currency or term mismatch. The latter would mean that the gap between far out forward-forward rates in the US Treasury bond market and reasonable expectations of future interest rates at these distant points in time became abnormally low, so reinforcing the lack of steepness in the yield curve.

Finally, a speculative factor containing the rise of long-maturity US government bond yields, even as the temperature continued to rise in real estate and credit markets and the economy boomed, might have been a growing concern in some segments of market opinion that there would be an eventual serious recession and financial crisis when the virulent virus of asset price inflation stemming originally from Greenspan-Bernanke monetary disequilibrium would eventually evolve into its next stage of asset price deflation! If the long-maturity yields were compared with likely much lower rates of price level increase (or even decrease) into the post-bubble aftermath, they were already remarkably high in real terms, especially taking account of the likelihood that the neutral level of rates would be very low in the asset price deflation stage.

In sum, the lack of close correlation between long- and short-maturity interest rates as commented upon by Alan Greenspan (specifically the failure of long-term rates to rise substantially once he embarked on his program of gradual upward adjustment of short-term rates) does not prove that Federal Reserve actions had little or nothing to do with the low level of long-term interest rates during 2003–5. The statistical appearance of non-correlation between short-maturity and long-maturity rates for some extended period of time was fully consistent with Fed-created monetary chaos. Also implausible is the view that East Asian savings surpluses in any case could have shifted the global equilibrium level of interest rates (neutral or natural) down by a large margin.

Numerical proofs are full of holes here. The estimates put together by the balance of payments statisticians on the Asian surpluses relate to observed magnitudes and these might, in a situation of economic disequilibrium, be quite different from the underlying surpluses. And there are giant measurement problems even with respect to the estimation process.

In particular, it is quite possible that though China's recorded savings and current account surpluses at their peak were running at $400–500 billion p.a., the underlying surplus was less than half of this.

Over 50% of China's savings surplus was in its business sector, where largely state-controlled corporations were building up mountains of retained profits (with no distribution of dividends to shareholders) out of an export bonanza to the US fuelled by (among other things) excessive monetary ease there. Indeed there was some rationality to this behaviour. The Communist Party-appointed managers realized earlier than many US managers (in Detroit especially!) that the bonanza could not last, and that they should behave like the ant rather than the grasshopper. And into the subsequent recession, the ability of the ants to spend exerted a stabilizing influence on the global economy!

There is a purely statistical point to note in the downplaying of the mega-Chinese trade surplus in the mid-2000s. The officially recorded trade and savings surpluses of China were an overstatement of reality due to the widespread use of trade invoicing techniques (under-recording imports, over-recording exports) by Chinese corporations to circumvent restrictions on borrowing funds abroad (mainly in US dollars) so as to speculate on continued appreciation of the yuan.

So, as illustration, let us assume that no more than a $200 billion increase in the underlying Chinese savings and current account surplus took place between 2001 and 2005. Can we really believe that this would have put significant downward pressure on the global equilibrium level of interest rates, especially when we take account of opposing upward pressure from such factors as the Bush tax cuts of 2001 and subsequent loosening of the reins on US federal government spending (defence, health, education in particular) or of credit market innovations (not all of them bubble-like!) which allowed a wider span of households to tap the credit markets?

Moreover, the successful assault on the Asian Dollar Zone by an Unholy Alliance of Washington, Paris and Frankfurt in 2003 (Dubai Summit, see p. 113) would surely have as one consequence an emerging currency risk premium on the transfer of capital into the US from the former member countries of the Asian dollar bloc. This new risk premium should have gone along with an upward revision of the neutral/natural level of the US interest rates (and downward revision of the East Asian level).

In sum, central bank policies considered in their widest sense were very much part of the explanation as to why medium- and long-term rates were most likely well below equilibrium rates during 2003–6, both in the US and Europe. But that is not where the rebuttal of the central bank apologists ends. A key further part of the rebuttal is the denial of Greenspan's claim that long-term rates rather than money-market rates (with the latter most under the control of the central bank) or any other measure of monetary conditions were critical for the heating up of the credit and real estate markets. Greenspan based that claim on the observation that long-maturity mortgage rates are dominant in the US housing finance market.

In fact it was arguably the very low level of short-term rates and the expectation that central banks would indeed keep those down for an extended period (as reflected in short-/medium-maturity fixed rates) that spurred the perception among investors of famine conditions for safe income. Towards maintaining or sustaining overall income, they became willing to assume a greater degree of credit risk exposure in their portfolios and at a lowered level of risk premium. And by the same token they may have become irrationally exuberant about the potential for human talent (for example hedge fund managers) to bolster rates of return above the thin levels available in an otherwise efficient market.

With market rates of interest so far below the neutral or natural level and for such an extended period, the supply of apparently suitable assets (including human talent) to satisfy the income famine-induced demand became self-generating. The irrational exuberance that is generated under such a situation of monetary disequilibrium grew and grew.

Prices of risk-credit paper and real estate rose under the influence of interest rates across the maturity spectrum far below the path consistent with a benign return of the US economy to prosperity (in contrast to another boom-and-bust sequence) in the years following the 2001–2 recession). In turn many market participants, perhaps wearing rose-coloured spectacles, became convinced that those rises were due to some real factor (or 'speculative displacement', see Aliber and Kindleberger, 2005). For example, in the case of real estate, the dawning of universal home ownership or societal shifts powering demand for residential space – which in turn lead to expectations of further rises. A booming construction industry and finance industry, thriving on the capital market prices distorted in its favour by monetary disequilibrium, drew in (directly or indirectly) savings from around the globe which otherwise would have eventually pressed down the cost of capital (and critically the equity cost of capital) to other sectors of the US economy, raising the level of investment there. This is what the Austrian school economists describe as 'malinvestment' (see Lachman, 1997). It would have taken time for this channelling of global savings into alternative investment opportunities in the US to become fully operative. The process of creative destruction including the emergence of sound investment opportunity does not occur quickly. In the interim, the Asian savings surpluses would have been constrained well below their equilibrium level due to the slow pace at first of US economic recovery.

The credit assets manufactured in the US residential real estate market were largely swapped into floating rate form in which they were absorbed by the rapidly growing credit hedge funds (themselves highly geared) or by the off-balance-sheet vehicles of the banks (these in turn issued asset-backed paper). The depth of the market (for investors) for the mortgage credit bubble assets was hence a function of the investor demand for a higher yield on floating rate paper. This is a point which Greenspan's focus on the long-term mortgage rate pure and simple fails to pick up. The availability of mortgage finance at growing levels of risk was a function of below-equilibrium floating short-maturity rates, and the expectation that these floating rates would remain below neutral for a considerable time.

Implications of verdict on Federal Reserve for euro-trial

All of the above discussion can be cast also in terms of the euro-area. Below-equilibrium levels of interest rates in Europe in the context of growing income famine generated demand for and supply of a rapidly expanding array of credit paper.

In the European context, this included the new phenomenon of residential mortgage asset-backed paper, much of which was based on real estate in Spain and the UK where speculative temperatures were rising strongly under the influence of the asset price inflation virus. There was also the leveraged corporate loan market and high-risk European corporate bonds much of which were lapped up either by hedge funds or bank off-balance sheet vehicles. And there were the massive flows of capital from Northern European member countries (banks and non-bank investors) into the sovereign debts of the southern countries riding on the popular speculative hypothesis that EMU should mean a compression of yield spreads between government bond markets in say Germany, Spain, Italy and Greece.

Given the full scope of financial engineering that utilizes currency swap markets, supply and demand of high-risk debts (for example mortgage-backed paper or highly leveraged corporate paper) in Europe would have been bolstered to some extent by monetary disequilibrium confined just to the US. In fact, accompanying European monetary disequilibrium magnified the euro-area source supply of and global demand for euro-denominated credit paper while stimulating US source supply of and global demand for dollar credit paper.

The effect of monetary disequilibrium did not stop at the credit markets. In principle there are risk-arbitrage flows between the credit markets and equity markets. Risk premiums (estimated rationally rather than under influence of irrational exuberance) most probably fell generally. (There can be no precision when it comes to the measurement of risk premiums in the equity market as the multi-period expectations of return are unobservable. Moreover risk premiums are in the eye of the beholder, and in some market situations, especially related to 'speculative displacements', vision is highly heterogeneous.)

It is plausible that the biggest fall in credit and equity risk premiums (if estimated in a sober-rational fashion rather than by measuring the expectations of irrationally exuberant investors wearing rose-coloured spectacles under the influence of the asset price inflation virus) occurred with respect to the increasingly leveraged, especially taking account of 'off-balance-sheet expansion', banking sectors in Europe and the US. In principle and in practice, risk-arbitrage between credit markets and equity markets is quite inelastic at times and so the extent to which the equity and debt paper of the financial sector became over-priced might have been quite uneven. Such inelasticity would have been an important barrier to equalisation of risk-adjusted rates of return across asset categories (for example, corporate debt and equity) in the climate of the mid-2000s so soon after the bursting of the NASDAQ bubble and given the shift of many investors away from equity risk (at the margins of their portfolios).

Suppose in all of this, the ECB had stood out by not succumbing to deflation phobia and then to fear of the weak US dollar. Correspondingly it would not have engaged in the manipulation of market interest rates (especially for medium maturities) by holding money rates at exceptionally low levels and trumpeting its intentions to do so for a considerable period of time. How different would have been the rise of temperature in credit and real estate markets in Europe and around the world?

A first point to consider is the interdependency between European and US monetary policies. If the ECB had indeed resisted the siren-calls of the inflation breathers-in, then the US dollar might well have fallen more sharply in 2003–4 (most of all against the euro), in reaction to which even the Bernanke/Greenspan Fed would have had to accelerate their glacial pace of rate rises. And so the monetary disequilibrium in the US might well have been curtailed by exchange rate shock – a slump of the US dollar and knock-on implications for inflation expectations in the US triggering a course correction by the Federal Reserve.

Secondly, in the universe of floating rate assets across all currencies a substantial sector, that in euro-denomination, would have been generating a good income, relieving any potential income famine generally and making investors globally less ready to take on extra risk at below normal levels of expected return (risk premium). Even so, the euro would have been bidden up to such a high level that the real rate of return on euros from the viewpoint of investors whose shopping basket was concentrated on items outside the euro-area would have been partially eroded by the prospect of subsequent decline (once US rates rose back to neutral level). But similarly the real rate of return on dollars from the perspective of investors who intended to spend much of their wealth in non-dollar countries would have been boosted from ultra-feeble levels by the prospect of exchange rate gain once the ultra-easy US monetary policy came to an end.

The ECB could not single-handedly have totally relieved the famine of income from safe assets (which resulted from the Federal Reserve's breathing in inflation policy) but there would have been some partial offset for many international-minded investors. In effect some of the higher income in the euro-sector would have been funnelled into the dollar sector as seen by international investors there, not to US domestic investors.

Thirdly, in the euro-area there would have been less heating up of domestic asset markets. With the ECB steering rates at a faster pace towards neutral, the mortgage and real estate markets would have remained cooler throughout. And the banks in the once-high interest rate countries (Spain, Italy) for example would have enjoyed less of a sudden bonanza of profit and the speculative temperature in their equity market (for bank paper) would have risen by less. A lower level of asset price inflation fever would have meant bank management teams would have been less inclined to continue along aggressive expansion courses.

Nonetheless, European banks could not have escaped the influence of US monetary-led credit warming, even though that US warming would have been less than otherwise due to the knock-on effect of the exchange rate to US monetary policy. The speculative fever in the market for US banking shares would have had a contagious influence on the European banking industry.

Those European banks which had expanded their businesses into the US high-temperature credit markets might well have found their share prices outperforming those that had not joined the dance, especially if the implicit leverage was camouflaged from view. Those 'aggressive' European banks would have been thereby in a position to take over other European banks that had remained more conservative. And similarly European banks that sought to match the rapidly growing earnings of their US peers by gearing up in the overnight dollar repo markets (using the proceeds to lend into the emerging market economies or to buy US credit paper) or in the Swiss franc inter-bank markets for lending into Eastern Europe (or into the Spanish mortgage market) might have been rewarded accordingly.

There may still have been some degree of imprudent lending from banks in savings surplus areas via the new overnight inter-bank euro market into banks in savings deficit areas (within the euro-zone), without due concern for the total risk of the inter-bank exposures created. But looking at the total picture, the temperature rise in European credit markets would have been less under a distinct and harder European monetary policy, and the risks would have built up less, albeit that the overall performance of European banking shares would have been less gratifying than otherwise during the years 2003–2007H1.

Could there still have been a Panic of 2008 unleashed by the post-Lehman freeze-up which would have sent the euro-area into deep recession?

Panics are not pre-determined. They are a risk along the path of credit and asset market temperature decline from hot levels (otherwise described as the phase of asset price deflation). The risk would have been less if the temperature had reached less hot peaks, as would have been the case if the ECB had not mimicked Federal Reserve policies throughout the first decade of the twenty-first century.

The extent to which European banks were caught up in the panic (themselves coming under deep suspicion) would have been that much less, with calming implications within Europe and knock-on-effects to the rest of the world. European asset markets themselves would have been less vulnerable to the panic (if indeed starting from a less heated position). Beyond these measured counter-factual statements, the compass becomes totally unreliable!

Why does the ECB continue to escape indictment?

As we journey further into the second decade of the twenty-first century and the observed costs of the 2008 Global Panic accumulate, European central bankers have escaped virtually all reproach at the level of mainstream political debate. Indeed many US-centric economists, including those who have walked the corridors of power, remain blithely unaware of the European contribution to the monetary disequilibrium behind the global credit bubble and burst. Some are also unaware of the potential for US monetary disequilibrium to spread a virus of asset price inflation around the globe even where other central banks are trying to keep to the path of monetary stability.

As illustration, Professor Taylor in his attack on the Federal Reserve for its role in the credit bubble and burst makes no international connection with events in Europe (see Taylor, 2009). And San Francisco Fed President Janet Yellen, who was bold enough in a speech in March 2009 to express soft criticism of the role of the Federal Reserve in creating the credit bubble via ultra-easy monetary policy, qualified her remarks by an erroneous observation:

> Fed monetary policy may also have contributed to the US credit boom and the associated house price bubble by maintaining a highly accommodative stance from 2002 to 2004. [...] But it clearly was not the only factor, since such bubble appeared in many countries that did not have highly accommodative monetary policies.

But was Professor Yellen really unaware of the simultaneous disequilibrium nature of European monetary policy during those years or, for that matter, of the disequilibrium policy in Japan (where the Bank of Japan was keeping rates below equilibrium level and thereby contributing to the bubble in the yen carry trade – see p. 67)? And was she also unaware of the asymmetric power of the Federal Reserve to spread the virus of asset price inflation (see Chapter 1, p. 9)?

In the following chapter we look at the possible remedies which might well lead to a better monetary outcome in Europe, but these will remain only remedies in principle until there is a recasting of the political debate. And essential to a constructive political debate is historical analysis rather than mythology. That applies as much as to the recent past, especially the conduct of monetary policy during the Great Credit Bubble of 2003–7, – as to the more distant past, especially the Great Credit Bubble of the 1920s and its sequel in the Great Depression. The difference is that the mythology of the latest great bubble has not yet formed in any fullness. A big challenge for economic analysts with a global perspective is to prevent the negative role of EMU and the ECB being omitted from the emerging mainstream account.

7
From Fed Curse to Merkel–Draghi Coup

US monetary chaos has been both a hugely creative and a destructive force in the history of EMU.

If monetary stability had reigned throughout in the US there would have been no impetus to monetary union in Europe at least in its modern gargantuan form. Each country there might well have adhered individually to an international US dollar standard.

Perhaps under this standard France and Germany would have created the modern day equivalent of a Latin Monetary Union with their currencies convertible into each other at par. A hypothetic Franco–German monetary authority would have pursued a path for the growth of high-powered money (the monetary base) such as effectively to make sure that the virtually common currency (even though francs and marks continued to exist separately) remained within its permitted band of fluctuation versus the US dollar. Other smaller countries might have joined the Franco-German union. There would have been no independent European monetary policy or framework.

Instead the inflationary path taken by the Martin and Burns Federal Reserves fanned direct US monetary conflict with Germany where monetarist titans had assumed power in the Deutsche Bundesbank. Eventually Germany 'broke free' from the deeply flawed worldwide dollar standard often described as 'the Bretton Woods system', floating the Deutsche mark in May 1971. The calculation in Frankfurt and Bonn was that that the gains for the German economy from domestic monetary stability now possible would more than match the losses from exchange rate instability. Even so there was considerable concern about those possible losses.

Right from the start of the floating Deutsche mark, the German government pursued diplomacy aimed at reducing currency turbulence vis-à-vis regional trade partners. The ideas on the table, some of which were implemented, included various forms of short-run exchange rate stabilization between the Deutsche mark and other key European currencies. Such effort, though, remained limited in overall scope as neither Bonn nor Frankfurt was willing to sacrifice domestic monetary stability. That was a problem for exchange rate stabilization in Europe so long as France was pursuing highly unstable monetary policies as was the case through much of the first 15 years that followed the end of the Bretton Woods system in Summer 1971 (see Chapter 8).

Federal Reserve monetary disorder as catalyst to EMU creation

The Federal Reserve under Paul Volcker gave the process of monetary integration in Europe a whole new impetus when it suddenly took the US down the path of new monetary instability in the mid-1980s (see Brown, 2013). A few years earlier (1979–82) Volcker had administered a powerful disinflationary monetary policy bringing to an end the high-inflation era ushered in by Martin and Burns. But already in 1983 he had abandoned his brief monetarist experiment and then come under intense political pressure to ease policies through 1985–6 as the US economy slowed sharply.

The US traded goods industries (exporters and import-competing sectors) were howling about the strong dollar, falling export market shares and rising import shares. Key mid-term Congressional elections were approaching in November 1986 at which the Republicans risked losing control of the Senate (they did not control the House). In early 1985 President Reagan had appointed as Treasury Secretary James Baker who, like Nixon's Treasury Secretary also from Texas (John Connally), had strong views about unfair foreign competition stemming from 'currency manipulation'. Volcker was deeply concerned about the widening trade deficit seeing this as leading to an unsustainable build-up of foreign debts and undermining US prosperity.

Volcker, once the top international finance official (under Connally) in the Nixon Administration, had not changed his spots. Back then, in 1971–3 he had spent two years orchestrating a devaluation of the dollar based on a view that the US trade deficit had become unsustainably large due to foreign countries, especially Japan, undervaluing their currencies. He had failed to acknowledge that the real source of the problem then was US monetary disequilibrium. If there had been monetary stability, a trade deficit in itself was not a problem. Its appearance would suggest simply that in global economic equilibrium the investment opportunity in the US exceeded domestically generated savings. The same blindspot led Volcker to judge the US trade deficit in the mid-1980s as sinister and implicitly he was ready to induce monetary instability towards reducing its potential size.

The idea that the world economy including the US could be in equilibrium with a huge US trade deficit matched by persistently strong capital inflows reflecting global demand for a hard dollar and super-attractive US equities left Paul Volcker cold. Instead the Federal Reserve chairman was convinced that Washington must sometimes wield a big stick in the form of exchange rate policy so as to banish the spectre of 'unsustainably'. To this end he was implicitly ready (though he would never have expressed such an analysis even to himself in the most secret moment) to steer monetary conditions in an inflationary direction, either towards asset price inflation or goods inflation or both, so as to achieve the devaluation of the dollar that Washington had demanded in September 1985 at Plaza.

Accordingly, through late 1985, 1986 and early 1987 the dollar plummeted on world markets. The Japanese yen and Deutsche mark rose to the sky. And though France had now abandoned inflationary monetary policy and was pursuing a hard franc its government could not convince markets that the franc was as good as the mark. Eventually by spring 1987 Volcker had embarked on a change of course, responding in particular to clear evidence of US economic rebound from the long growth recession of the mid-1980s. In the Louvre Accord the US and its G-7 partners agreed that the US dollar should now be 'stabilized'.

Volcker's disequilibrium monetary policy through the mid-1980s in support of dollar devaluation created a new virus of asset price inflation that spread around the world attacking not just the US but also prominently Japan and Europe. The symptoms that emerged, as usual hard to diagnose until the disease was at an advanced stage, included a rising speculative temperature in equity and commercial real estate markets in the US and globally. Real estate bubbles in Tokyo, Scandinavia, Paris, London, New England, and beyond were all part of the same phenomenon. Adding to the difficulty of diagnosis, as always, was the rotational form of the virus attack, with the spikes in speculative temperature occurring in sequence rather than simultaneously, and with some late spikes occurring when the virus was already transitioning to its next phase (see Chapter 1, p. 9).

First came the global equity market crash of October 1987 (albeit that speculative fever was to reach a new pitch in Tokyo equities during the subsequent two years) and later the crash in real estate markets around the globe. Due to the monetary boom that accompanied political and monetary union between East and West Germany in 1990 Germany did not suffer immediately from the asset price deflations occurring in the world outside. But when that boom turned to bust (1991–2) many of the business and political elites in Germany had become convinced, especially in view of the damage to the German export sector inflicted by the Deutsche mark's heady climb, that a EMU might well have more benefits than costs (see James, 2012).

The Baker–Volcker currency war had not just driven the Deutsche mark up against the US dollar but also against the currencies of Germany's European partners, given that the Deutsche mark, as the world's number two reserve currency, had been in particular demand as a safe haven. In principle were the Deutsche mark to be sacrificed to European integration then German industry would be spared such intra-European exchange rate volatility in future episodes of US monetary instability and moreover there would be more scope for Europe to steer a monetary path distinct from the unstable US path. By contrast, in the present state of monetary disunion the Bundesbank could only go so far in steering such a path before having to bow to concerns about a crushingly strong Deutsche mark especially against its European neighbours.

In addition there were all the 'fortuitous developments' driving negotiations on monetary union forward, including a grand deal between Germany and France following the Fall of the Berlin Wall whereby the former was ready to concede monetary hegemony in exchange for the latter agreeing to the admission of East European countries into the EU. Moreover, Chancellor Kohl's growing political control of the Bundesbank following the resignation of Karl Otto Pöhl in May 1991 favoured the European monetary enterprise at this time.

Opinion among the German political and industrial elites swung a little away from EMU into the business cycle recovery of 1993. Indeed in an ERM crisis that erupted during spring that year Germany insisted on a substantial widening in the permitted band of intra-European exchange rates. But then the Clinton Administration and Greenspan Federal Reserve unknowingly came to the rescue of the EMU project by waging a new currency war from 1993 to 1995. The chief 'enemy' target was Japan but US monetary instability coincidentally put severe upward pressure also on the Deutsche mark.

A headlong march towards monetary union was not the only possible defence (highly hazardous!) against US monetary instability from a

German or wider European perspective. There were alternatives. There could have been an agreement between the large European countries to implement jointly designed frameworks of monetary stability (in sharp contrast to the lack of any such framework in the US) and to adhere to these strictly. But could investors trust France or Italy? If not, every episode of severe US monetary instability would mean wild swings in the Deutsche mark against its European partners.

In principle, the power of a EMU to resist waves of US-led asset price inflation could be much greater than the aggregated power of each large country acting separately. That would be the case were there uneven resolve or capability to sustain individual national defences in a Europe without an EMU. Yet in practice the ability of the monetary union to repel a US-source asset price inflation virus would turn crucially on the designers of EMU finding the path of monetary stability and safeguarding this in constitutional law. Europe did not follow that path – and so its monetary union failed to deliver the prosperity promised by the EMU's founders.

Amidst that failure, on the eve of the 14th anniversary of the euro's launch in autumn 2012, German Chancellor Merkel together with ECB President Draghi organized their coup against the very imperfect and flawed monetary constitution which formed part of the Maastricht Treaty. The coup did not usher in reform but empowered the ECB to provide monetary finance to stressed individual member governments through what was soon to be dubbed 'the outright monetary transactions programme'. Yes, there were some curbs on those new powers, but how effective these would be was very much open to question.

The curse on Europe of Fed-created asset price inflation

EMU may well have survived without crisis and without coup for another decade or more, even given all its flaws, if it had not been for the huge monetary instability generated by the Federal Reserve in the early- and mid-2000s. This new instability on the other side of the Atlantic played a crucial role in spreading a severe virus of asset price inflation around the world. This assumed a particularly vicious form in Europe not least because the ECB was itself copying US monetary policy in many respects and the monetary framework designed and subsequently tweaked by Professor Issing was essentially flawed (see pp. 42–3). France had achieved its goal of ending German monetary hegemony but at the cost of leaving Europe critically exposed to the Federal Reserve-created virus of asset price inflation.

The progress of this disease in Europe has already been charted in this book. By early 2010 the asset price deflation phase was featuring a full-blown sovereign debt crisis. Meanwhile the Bernanke Federal Reserve's pursuance of its Grand Monetary Experiment (launched with the explosion of QE1 time bombs in 2009) greatly impeded any possible cure to Europe's ills. Bernanke-ite currency warfare (in which the new weapon was the monetary terror created by massive expansion of base money) meant the euro remained firm against the US dollar despite the European sovereign debt crisis and related banking crisis. Offsetting in some degree that bad news for the German export sector was the boom in sales to several key emerging market economies (including the oil exporters) benefiting transitorily from a new infection of asset price inflation virus stemming from the Federal Reserve's QE1 and QE2 policies.

This was hardly a robust recipe for German or European prosperity, given the likelihood that the boom in the emerging markets (and China) would turn eventually to bust. That scenario was increasingly preoccupying financial markets by Summer 2013. The result in the US of the Fed's Grand Experiment – the slowest economic recovery ever from severe recession (explained in large part by fear of the market crash and recession which could precede, preempt, or follow an exit from unconventional policy) – was also unhelpful for European recovery.

ECB chief Claude Trichet and his successor Mario Draghi were not of the mindset to challenge the Federal Reserve or to design a powerful European alternative regime which would ultimately gain admiration and popularity as had been the case with the hard Deutsche mark of Emminger fame. Both men enjoyed a reputation for skills in international economic diplomacy. Dr. Draghi prior to his succession was renowned for always being on the telephone to US Treasury Secretary Geithner and he was of the same Economics School (MIT) as Professor Bernanke. Both European Central Bankers were comfortable in the global central bankers' club wherever it met, whether in Basel or Kansas. Yet how could they be so blind to the harmful influences on the world and on Europe in particular of US monetary policies?

Claude Trichet had applauded the Bush Administration's efforts, underpinned by the Federal Reserve, to blow up the Asian Dollar bloc in 2003–4 and subscribed to Washington's view that the Asian savings and current account surpluses were the source of a serious global imbalance problem. If the Asians would spend more and their currencies rise in value then the US mega current account deficit would shrink, meaning a stronger dollar globally and against the euro. Trichet and his ECB colleagues, including crucially Professor Issing, failed to see that the weak dollar and the large US current account deficits at that time were symptoms first and foremost of disequilibrium US monetary conditions – notably the Greenspan Fed's policy (based in part on key academic input from a newly appointed Governor, Ben Bernanke) of breathing inflation back into the US economy. These monetary conditions lay behind a growing credit and asset bubble in the US and in Europe.

Claude Trichet was not the only central bank chief in Europe unseeing of the intense monetary danger from outside or indeed inside. Bank of England chief, Professor King, just did not grasp in 2003–6 that growing monetary disequilibrium in the two chief reserve money areas – the US and the euro-zone – had created a powerful virus of asset price inflation which was attacking the UK economy, itself particularly vulnerable given the importance of its financial sector. He failed to diagnose the disequilibrium in the first place, let alone make the links to the situation in the UK. If Professor King had done so, his options for defence would have been more difficult to design and probably less effective than for a large monetary area such as the euro-zone but they were not insignificant.

Any independent tightening of monetary conditions in the UK would have caused a sharp appreciation of the British pound, particularly painful to some industrial sectors in this medium size open economy unless wages and prices there became unusually flexible (falling transitorily during the period of maximum appreciation). There is no evidence that Governor King or his political master gave serious consideration to such options. Nor did the Governor emerge as a lone voice at international meetings imploring the ECB and Fed to pursue stable monetary policies. Rather he sang along with the chorus of the central bankers' club praising the benefits of inflation-targeting and stirring phobia against deflation. These missed opportunities for lone and distinct monetary policy or diplomacy had seriously negative consequence for British economic prosperity. The consequences of the ECB not making the correct diagnosis were even more regrettable in the sense that the options for ECB action if the diagnosis had been made were less harsh than for the UK and more promising.

ECB diplomats prepare path for Draghi–Merkel coup

Central bankers rarely if ever reflect on their possible mistakes. And there is absolutely no evidence that Claude Trichet has ever done so, especially mistakes in the midst of his hectic timetable from 2010 onwards to 'save the euro'. He and Mario Draghi together in Autumn 2011 (when Trichet about to retire) played a large role together in negotiating with Fed Chairman Bernanke and US Treasury Secretary Geithner a massive dollar swap facility for the ECB. In effect the Federal Reserve stood ready to lend US dollars to the ECB against the security of euro deposits to be placed as collateral. This dollar swap in turn prepared the way for the about-to-be-launched long-term refinancing operation (LTRO) programme, under which the ECB stood ready to make long-term (one to three years) loans to weak banks against any virtually dud collateral (either in dollars or euros). The LTROs would provide immediate relief for French banks in particular, now in the eye of the storm. Also in the eye of the storm, but with less dollar loan exposure, were Spanish and Italian banks.

The LTRO program also played a key role in 'stabilizing' the Italian bond market and banking system in the wake of a severe market crisis, which had culminated in the stepping down (in Autumn 2011) of Italy's Prime Minister Silvio Berlusconi and his replacement by the top ex-eurocrat Mario Monti. Bernanke and Geithner saw it as absolute essential to avoiding a 2nd Lehman crisis that European weak sovereign and weak banks should be propped up, with hopefully Germany playing the role of key provider. Geithner pursued intense shuttle diplomacy between his friends in Paris and Frankfurt on the one hand and Chancellor Merkel on the other hand, towards achieving that aim.

Many calmer heads in the marketplace were not at all convinced that a 2nd Lehman crisis loomed. After all that panic had depended on huge new disturbing information about potential insolvency suddenly emerging, whilst now all the scenarios and their effects on European banks had been churned over for a long time. Moreover, the ECB and Federal Reserve had contributed to the Lehman crisis by holding money rates at high levels well beyond the first quakes of bubble-bursting in Summer 2007, in large part out of misplaced concern at then high oil prices (in fact a late symptom of the asset price inflation virus when this was already well advanced in transitioning to its next stage of asset price deflation). Now they were all virtually at zero. The calm heads in the marketplace, though, were not on the same wavelength as the US or European political and central bank elites.

Towards avoiding the feared 2nd Lehman crisis, which incidentally would sink the re-election prospects of their commander-in-chief, President Obama, Treasury Secretary Geithner and Federal Reserve Chair Bernanke were prepared to put US taxpayer funds on the line by way of swaps with the ECB even though under some scenarios the

ECB might itself become insolvent. As part of the deal Chancellor Merkel was persuaded to put at stake a much larger amount of German taxpayer funds, either directly via the new EU bail-out entities, the European Stability Mechanism (ESM) or European Financial Stability Facility (EFSF), or indirectly by standing (albeit to an unknown extent) behind the ECB's vast loan programs. The LTROs were highly dubious in terms of constitutionality – with critics arguing that the Maastricht Treaty specifically banned such bail-out operations. What followed was even more dubious, and to such a degree that we describe it here as a coup against the monetary constitution in the Treaty.

Professor Bernanke's QE infinity – the Trojan horse in EMU citadel

This coup played itself out in Summer and Autumn 2012 as the Spanish government debt market plunged and another crisis of survival erupted in EMU, this time with the centre of the storm in Spanish banking collapse. ECB Chief Mario Draghi, buttressed by the US Treasury Secretary, persuaded German Chancellor Merkel that the only way to avoid 'catastrophe' in Europe would be to 're-interpret' the Maastricht Treaty so as to allow direct monetary financing of weak sovereigns, albeit subject to certain conditions. Simultaneously Chairman Bernanke launched his QE-infinity policy setting no time or quantity limit to massive monetary base expansion.

Many commentators wrote that QE infinity was a highly political move aimed at revving up the US equity market and countering an apparent economic slowdown in the crucial months before the US Presidential and Congressional elections in November 2012. In fact revised economic data published in Summer 2013 showed that the US economy grew by almost 3% p.a. through the third quarter of 2012, hardly justifying Professor Bernanke's panic about the economy! The announcement of QE infinity also fitted with concern in the Obama Administration about the electoral consequences of a deepening crisis in EMU, given its potential to seriously harm the fragile US economic expansion and to immediately trigger a sharp fall in the US equity market. In the event, QE infinity had a catalytic effect in global markets. Yield hungry investors made even hungrier by the intensified income famine conditions of QE infinity were willing to view the Merkel–Draghi coup (doing whatever it takes) as a 'huge accomplishment' that banished 'tail risks' in Europe.

Carry traders worldwide sang the praises of Mario Draghi even as the Bundesbank voiced its alarm. Funds started to pour into the weak European sovereign debt markets which rose sharply amid much simultaneous froth in global high-yield credit markets and amid a powerful upswing in the US, German and Japanese equity markets. (In Japan the new story to chase around the same time was 'Abe economics'; in the German stock market the new story was the success of the Merkel–Draghi coup and the widely broadcast 're-bound' in Chinese economic growth – with China the key export growth market for Germany).

Yet this US 'help' in the form of QE-infinity for Europe was a Trojan horse. It meant that a dangerous situation for Europe would get worse over time but not immediately. Bernanke's grand monetary experiment was a drag on long-run US economic expansion. Every investor, business person and their dog knew that there was an exit problem which could mean at worst a severe business cycle downturn and equity market slump (see Chapter 1, p. 13). Washington would continue to depress the dollar via the Bernanke Federal Reserve's interest rate manipulation and monetary terror. Hence the Trojan horse would prevent the substantial fall in the euro that very plausibly was an essential accompaniment of the path back to European economic prosperity especially in the 'periphery zone' countries.

Further, US monetary instability – the core of the Trojan horse – limited the long-run potential rise in the US stock market and the extent of any US economic renaissance given widespread anxiety about the eventual 'exit problem' (how would the Federal Reserve one day return to conventional monetary policy; what would happen if there were an 'emperor's new clothes moment' before that return when the vaunted power of the Bernanke-ite QE machine to fix long-term interest rates would be exposed as empty?) and the related risks of recession and asset price inflation turning to asset price deflation. Yes, in Spring and December 2013 the main US equity indices were making new daily highs. But how much higher would they have been if the US had enjoyed monetary stability then and during the previous decade? Meanwhile the Bernanke Fed's QE policies (dating back to 2009) had sucked the German economy along the path of mal-investment in its key export sector, given the importance of demand there from a range of countries – oil and commodity exporting, emerging markets – which were temporarily 'enjoying' the warm phase of the of Fed-induced asset price inflation virus (one aspect of which had been high commodity prices).

Stable money in the US would have meant a fundamentally stronger US economy, an ultimately higher US stock market, bigger US current account deficit (higher volume of imports from the rest of the world including Europe), smaller emerging market deficits (the counterpart to less capital inflows), greater exports from Southern Europe, bigger investment into Southern Europe (attracted in part by cheaper euro), and more robust domestic demand growth in the core European countries (less fear of taxation increases to pay for bail outs to the weak European sovereigns). Yet ECB President Draghi and Chancellor Merkel never put forward those counterfactuals.

The infernal role of Chancellor Merkel

Instead, in the end Chancellor Merkel saw no alternative to supporting President Draghi's suggested coup against the Maastricht Treaty. Nor did the Bundesbank take up those points although it spelt out forcefully the nature of the coup and wrote a testimony for a case before the German Constitutional Court as to why this should be deemed illegal. Ideally the Bundesbank should have joined in an incessant campaign against US monetary disorder and to thwart the ECB from copying this in any serious respect.

An incessant campaign may well not have persuaded Chancellor Merkel or ECB President Draghi that their coup had been a mistake. And of course in public both insisted there had been no coup. President Draghi presented his plan for outright monetary transactions (OMT) (described below, see p. 223) as a means of mending a 'broken money transmission mechanism' within EMU and for combating market 'irrationality' in the form of putting a significant probability on some weak countries exiting (EMU). According to the eurocrats and ECB officials this could and would never occur. For Chancellor Merkel, the coup of Summer 2012 came after two and half years of *realpolitik* through which she had eventually always backed the ECB President (first Claude Trichet then Mario Draghi) in essentially providing transfers to the weak EMU sovereigns and their banking systems through the ECB's back door, hopefully out of the sight of most German voters.

The extent to which German taxpayers were committed anyhow to propping up the ECB in real terms was in doubt. One day in the distant future Germany could leave EMU and the real value of the ECB's euro-denominated liabilities, including notes in circulation, would collapse along with the euro against the resurrected Deutsche mark. What happened to the ECB's dollar liabilities under such circumstances, including swap lines with the Federal Reserve, would be decided upon in international negotiations over the insolvency of the old ECB and its possible restructuring into a new ECB (without Germany). Or alternatively a collapse in the real value of the ECB's euro liabilities could take place via high inflation with Germany still inside EMU. For President Draghi, there was no alternative to 'saving the euro' whatever that would take and it was not for him to detail who would be the givers and takers. Indeed cynics would say that he and Chancellor Merkel had a joint interest in blurring the detail, each for their own political ends.

Mario Draghi did not argue in public for a Bernanke-ite type Grand Experiment with the aim of 'stimulating recovery from the Great Recession' and Chancellor Merkel would not have supported a coup for that purpose. Their joint interest in ECB balance sheet expansion was primarily to prevent an EMU implosion rather than to experiment with new forms of monetary stimulus although there is no reason to doubt Draghi's positive sentiment towards the US monetary experiment in the privacy of the elite central bankers club meetings. Draghi told a subsequent press conference that he was no fan of helicopter money. Chancellor Merkel remained opposed in public to anything smacking of money printing. Even so, in summer 2013 Draghi announced that the ECB would follow the Federal Reserve's novel policy step (first taken in Summer 2011) of 'forward rate commitment'.

According to this the central bank stipulates a fixed path (usually flat) for short-term rates stretching forward for say the next 18 months and it may encourage expectations about the path beyond that. The intention of the officials is to thereby manipulate longer-term interest rates. (In a regime such as monetary base control where short-term rates float freely and are unpredictable then long-term rates would be free of manipulation and could reflect the market's best collective estimate of the relevant neutral level). In so far as markets suspect that officials could be bluffing then the manipulation becomes less effective. And indeed if long-term fixed-rate bond markets plunged suddenly, reflecting a strong view about future inflation danger, then the central bank manipulators might be constrained to adjust upwards their path for short-term rates, never mind their commitments, so as to rein in those expectations and prop up confidence in financial markets.

ECB vs Federal Reserve 'money printing' – the differences

To appreciate the differences between ECB balance sheet expansion as driven forward by the Merkel–Draghi coup and Federal Reserve balance sheet expansion implemented as part of Bernanke's Grand Experiment let's review the three key elements of the latter.

First there was Professor Bernanke's (and subsequently Professor Yellen's) promise to keep short-term rates at near zero for an abnormally long period of time. That promise was strengthened by the removal of monetary base from the pivot of the monetary system. (In the classical system, monetary base pays no interest and it accounts for a substantial share of total money supply. Hence by steering the monetary base along a steady low-growth path, leaving interest rates to be determined in the market, the monetary authority can efficiently aim for monetary stability. Such market-determined money rates could not stay pinned at zero as under the Bernanke Grand Experiment). In 2013 a new dimension was added to the promise in the form of threshold levels of unemployment (well below the present) that would have to be reached before money rates could rise at all.

Second there is the huge bond purchase operation where the Fed issues special bills (overnight reserves) to the banks at above market rates (0.25% p.a. versus 0), collecting the proceeds to fund its mega purchases of primarily long-maturity government or quasi government debt. The ostensible aim here is to lower the term risk premium. There is also an element of 'the emperor's new clothes' fable. Fed officials did not protest that markets (especially the carry-traders) 'had it wrong' when they chased the hypothesis that the QE-infinity programme could fix prices of long-maturity bonds at prices far above those consistent with normal forces of gravity (concerns about inflation and the path of neutral interest rates over the long-run), implying negative term risk premiums if calculated on the basis of normal sober expectations. Eventually in spring and summer 2013 investors en masse came to realize that this was an empty hypothesis, perhaps shocked by the albeit transitory doubling of yields in long-maturity Japanese government bond markets over a few days despite the just- elected administration under Prime Minister Abe (including its newly appointed Bank of Japan Governor) having built and operated an even more impressive bond market manipulation machine than that of the Bernanke Fed.

Third, there is monetary terror. The dislocation of the monetary pivot and lack of tried tools for piloting money once the economy recovers strongly means there is a serious danger of inflation leaping in the future. Moreover, the US government, addicted to virtually zero-rate floating rate finance of its mega deficits, might well put pressure on the Federal Reserve to slow any eventual rise in the short-term rates which it controls, adding to the likelihood of severe inflation. This danger stimulates the search for real yields (especially on risky assets), which should, according the advocates of QE, bolster economic activity.

The balance sheet expansion at the ECB did not occur primarily for the purpose of monetary stimulus. Nonetheless the ECB did adopt in some respects the three elements of the Bernanke Grand Experiment. The ECB has had no qualms about 'managing' expectations regarding the path of short-term official interest rates over considerable periods ahead. The willingness to make bold rate projections increased under Draghi and was far away from the Bundesbank monetarist order of the 1970s and 80s when there was no such managing at all. Even so, the ECB stopped well short of the Bernanke-ite manipulation.

When Mario Draghi eventually adopted 'forward commitments' (as above) these were limited to 18 months and were stipulated in somewhat vague terms. The ECB did not embark on any buying of long-maturity core European government bond markets (for example German, French or Dutch) with the intention of reducing term risk premiums. Its outright intervention in bonds occurred within the scope of broadly unsuccessful attempts to stabilize the price of weak sovereign long-maturity debt (limiting the increase in credit spreads vis-a-vis benchmark German government bonds). There has been the contingent bond-buying programme (designed for short-maturity bonds up to around three years maturity) called the 'outright monetary transactions' (OMT) conditional on the borrowing country signing up to an EU/IMF administered austerity deal. In the first year following the launch of OMT its strong influence was produced by speculation on its possible implementation rather than on its actually taking effect. This OMT programme is a key component of the Merkel–Draghi coup.

Much of the ECB's manipulation of credit spreads has occurred directly in the bank funding markets rather than in the bond markets. We can trace the start of this manipulation to the Trichet-led massive intervention of summer 2007 when the ECB expanded its balance sheet (long maturity fixed-rate tenders) to effect below market-rate lending to stressed banks in the midst of the first quakes as the global credit bubble started to burst. The operations were expanded during the autumn 2008 global panic. At this stage the 'liquidity difficulties' of European banks could be seen as stemming in large part from simultaneous credit market quakes in the US.

The difficulties took a decided European turn as the Greek debt crisis erupted in early 2010 and a new element became the bending of the ECB rules on collateral as these fell below investment grade. The crisis spread to other periphery zone government bond markets and banks heavily involved there. ECB 'secured' lending at cheap rates (no risk premium) to the weak banks largely in the periphery zone countries boomed. Then there was the announcement of the Draghi LTROs of autumn 2011 – a precursor to the Merkel–Draghi coup almost a year later – in the midst of the threatened collapse of leading French banks and a panic in the Italian government bond market.

It is an open question whether these interventions were successful in manipulating down the market cost of funds to the weak banks primarily in the periphery zone. There was no market. Without ECB funding many of the banks in question could not have kept their doors open – unless their sovereign government had exited EMU and printed a new national money so as to mount a bail-out operation (in effect levying inflation tax on their citizens including in particular bank depositors); or alternatively there was the theoretical possibility that the insolvent banks in the periphery could be made solvent by 'bail-ins' – the imposing of windfall tax on the depositors (equivalently converting a share of deposits into bank capital) – without an exit from EMU. In neither case could the ECB jump-start a market in bank funding.

The ECB, unlike the Fed, did not intentionally seek to create long-run inflation terror so as to 'stimulate' the economy. But even without the intention, its massive balance sheet expansion was in a real sense more terror inspiring than that of the Bernanke Federal Reserve. In the case of the latter, were the political pendulum to swing back to laissez faire and classical liberalism, then a new monetary regime could be installed in which the monetary base would again become the pivot of the monetary system. The vast holdings of government and quasi-government bonds could be disposed of or frozen as the counterpart to higher reserve requirements.

In the case of Europe unless a miracle occurs it is hard to see how the ECB could dispose of its portfolio of bad loans made to weak banks in the periphery and of weak sovereign bonds. There is no political pendulum visible in Europe that could swing such as to install a new monetary regime. And even if a miracle was to occur and a European consensus on monetary reform came into being, there would still be the huge issue of how to share around between member countries the losses in the ECB balance sheet. Putting the possibility of miracle to one side, as the neutral level of interest rates eventually rises, the ECB would find itself under pressure not to raise the rate it paid on reserves as this would mean increasing loss on its loan operations with the zombie banks (who could not pay more than zero) as the interest it paid (on reserves) under the present regime increased in step. The overhang of vast excess reserves under those circumstances would fuel an inflationary process.

Yes, in the short run the ECB could attempt to prevent unleashing inflation by issuing non-monetary paper to the stronger banks and even paying an above-market rate of interest on this. But ultimately the markets would question ECB solvency in real terms meaning a plunge of the euro and an ultimate emergence of inflationary symptoms. And before that point, Berlin might call a pre-emptive halt to the ECB's paper issuance, threatening to withdraw from EMU unless there were burden sharing among all to make good the black holes in the ECB balance sheet. Yet such burden- sharing might be impossible to achieve given the weak public finances and virtual banking system insolvency in some member countries. The only way in which this burden-sharing could be implemented would be EMU break-up and the extinct European money collapsing in value.

In principle one way in which to implement burden sharing could be for the ECB to hike reserve requirements and put in place a new monetary framework with non-interest bearing reserves at its pivot. And so there would be an implicit tax on bank deposits in euros and the total tax take would increase in line with the level of interest rates. But such a scheme would be hard to implement. A level of reserve requirements that would absorb all present excess reserves held by the relatively strong banks in the strong sovereigns would be far above anything feasible in the weak periphery. In principle, reserve requirements could be set at differential rates across the monetary union (highest in the strong countries, lowest in the weak); in practice that would be a non-starter.

Economists can signal the dangers ahead from an unsustainable monetary path. They cannot predict the timing of the feared crisis, in this case inflationary. And they should not rule out the possibility of an emerging economic miracle that puts the feared crisis to rest. They can also help pierce the fog of political pretence and shed light on the essential policy choices that are available even if the politicians would not or could not spell them out. In the case of EMU there have been two broad possible choices for Berlin in responding to the insolvency of banks and sovereigns weaker member countries.

Two choices for Berlin in confronting EMU insolvency

First, Berlin could refuse to commit resources and instead insist that the weak sovereigns look after their own weak banks and weak finances. They could do that in principle while staying in monetary union by some combination of writing down government and bank liabilities (including bank deposits), lowering the path of government spending (so as to impress investors about progress in the road back to solvency and to banish the spectre of enterprise-killing rises in taxation) and undertaking economic reform (so as to stimulate economic renaissance).

All of this could mean great pain to wide sections of society. It is far from certain in view of the inherent dynamic instability that the weak sovereigns on their own could discover a path which would avoid their being forced through the EMU exit doors.

Second, Berlin could agree to commit resources towards reducing the pain in the weak sovereigns and also hopefully making it more likely that they could indeed remain in EMU. Committing resources is full of dangers. The commitment might encourage governments in the weak countries to kick the can down the road and avoid painful cut-backs and reform which otherwise they might have implemented. An EMU exit or break-up might still be the eventual destination. This becomes even more likely if German taxpayers become greatly concerned about the growing burdens that they may have to bear. A direct influence of that concern would be less prosperity in Germany as fears of future crisis and higher taxation weighed on present willingness to take economic risks. And indeed less prosperity in Germany would weigh on the chances of economic renaissance in the weak member countries.

Chancellor Merkel lacked the idealism or courage to follow the first policy choice. But she also hesitated to make a broad open commitment to the second policy choice, hoping instead to hide what options were taken as much as possible from the German voting public, at least until the general elections of September 2013. ECB President Draghi was skilled at playing on Chancellor Merkel's fundamental ambiguity for the sake of the historical mission of saving EMU and his own institution. Federal Reserve Chairman Bernanke, President Obama and his economic lieutenants pressed Berlin into becoming increasingly committed to the second choice raising the spectre of a second Lehman crisis and global recession if Chancellor Merkel continued to hesitate.

Yes, a great German statesman respectful of a classical liberal order would have said No to President Obama and No to ECB President Draghi, instead forging a strong alliance with the Bundesbank President who she would have supported in repelling those forces that would crush the Maastricht Union and replace it with a transfer union. That statesperson was not Chancellor Merkel. And as historical misfortune would have it, the consummate Italian diplomat and ex-investment banker then at the head of the ECB, Mario Draghi, was able to take full advantage of her weakness. Together they launched the coup against the Treaty which in the long run most likely would bury EMU and European economic prosperity.

8
EMU Is Dead: Long Live EMU!

When the first edition of this book was published in early 2010 it was still far from evident that a jury made up of citizens from across the euro-zone, appropriately chosen so as to be representative of diversity would sustain any of the indictments against EMU and the ECB. And a final catch-all indictment in the form 'it would have been better if EMU had never existed' stood hardly any chance of being upheld. Now, four years and two editions on, there is a much greater likelihood that a jury would deliver a guilty verdict, though much would still depend on the power of advocacy used by both sides. There are many floating half-credible hypotheses and prejudices out there which the defence attorneys for EMU and the ECB could bring before the jury.

As illustration, in Germany the view circulates (and is promoted by officials in the government of Chancellor Merkel) that if it had not been for the euro, industrial activity would have been crippled by a super-strong Deutsche mark. Instead, under the cover of the euro, German industry gained huge competitive advantages. The flimsiness of this viewpoint derives from its refusal to acknowledge the world of the counterfactual. Why would the Deutsche mark have been so strong in the context of lively currency competition in Europe where each country, or at least many countries, sought successfully to build and maintain highly attractive monetary brands? Then global investors would have been keen to diversify their portfolios into the French franc and Dutch guilder while also retaining some interest in the high cou-pon alternative monies outside the core (for example, Spanish pesetas and Italian liras).

If German citizens had been spared the eventual massive tax bur-den of bailing out insolvent sovereigns (and their banking systems) in EMU, as the disease of asset price inflation progressed to the phase of steep decline in speculative temperature and financial bust, and if their savings had flowed to a much greater extent into rationally designed portfolios of foreign equities rather than heading, under the influence of speculative fever, into Europe's 'hot spots' (for example Spanish mortgages or periphery zone government bonds), they could have become the most prosperous of any large country on Earth. Only fleeting and phantom prosperity can be obtained by digging holes in the ground (in this case German exports facilitated by dud loans within the EU).

Citizens in the periphery zone countries now suffering under EU-IMF drawn-up austerity programmes (for example, Spain, Portugal, Greece and Ireland) would be in many cases resistant to defence advocacy. But there could be exceptions (and one or more of these exceptions might find their way into the hypothetical jury!). Indeed in 2014 some citizens of those countries could still look back and reflect that they had done very well out of EMU, taking account of the highly prosperous early years. These fortunates would include investors who had got into and out of the bubble real estate markets with good timing and had benefited from the lavish EU bail-outs to extract their gains from local banks which otherwise would have gone bust and in euros (rather than the drachmas or pesetas which would have been resurrected by now without the ECB's life-support). Workers who had enjoyed boom-time income without suffering subsequent economic distress and beneficiaries of public services that were swollen by bubble tax revenues and hot flows of capital into the respective government bond markets would also be among the fortunate. And even the unfortunates could be swayed by non-economic advocacy particularly relevant to the periphery zone countries given their history. This would include EMU as a vital step in the long-run European integration process culminating in political union and how this would be a bulwark against fascism and war. Advocates of this view did not have a sure case especially as neo-fascist or near-fascist political groups started to gain support across the periphery and even inside the core of EMU.

Plausibly French citizens in the jury could be most swayed by the defence case for EMU and the ECB, if indeed the attorneys for the defence had a chance to speak to the jurors from France directly without risking the downside of annoying the non-French. Yes, French taxpayers will surely be picking up large bills for their share of the various bail-outs related to the credit bubble-bursting process in EMU. But the wider objectives of French foreign policy – and these resonate with some voters in France – have been at least superficially furthered in ways that few could have imagined at EMU's start (at the end of 1998).

Back then it seemed that the ECB, in Frankfurt, would be a Germanic ordo-liberal (outside politics) institution run as a re-incarnation of the Bundesbank. Yes, there was soon to be a French president of the ECB (as agreed in a spring 1998 deal between President Chirac and Chancellor Kohl), but the passport office to which he reported would surely have little relevance to any policy outcome.

The reality, though, is that Claude Trichet during his eight-year tenure (starting in autumn 2003) harnessed the ECB and EMU to French objectives. We have already seen in this volume how the ECB joined with the Bush Administration in ending the Asian dollar bloc in Asia even at the cost of seriously strengthening the virus of asset price inflation then attacking the US and European economies (see p. 71). Towards the end of his tenure, Trichet over-rode Bundesbank opposition in his desperate manoeuvres to mobilize the ECB towards providing massive funds to the periphery EMU zone and especially Greece albeit the eventual continuation of this strategy turned on Chancellor Merkel losing the diplomatic game with President Sarkozy. Claude Trichet's successor, Mario Draghi, has followed an effective diplomatic path towards reining back the influence of the Bundesbank albeit that this has involved forging close alliances with Washington and Berlin.

The strong influence of Paris on the evolution of EMU and the conduct of the ECB did not start, of course, with Claude Trichet. Noteworthy in the earlier years was the role of Paris in ushering Greece (a long-time especially close ally and armaments client of France) into EMU. In spring 2000 the French Board Member (and vice-president) in the ECB, Christian Noyer, presented a convergence report (at a specially convened press conference and to the EU Parliament) that put no obstacle in the way of Greek entry. True the report was bland. But according to the Treaty of Maastricht the ECB could have drafted a strongly negative convergence report. This history is consistent with the hypothesis that Paris was intent on its Hellenic ally (a few years later to be invited into the Francophone Union) coming into monetary union at an early date even if that meant some statistical sleight of hand. And Bundesbankers or others within the ECB Council who might have had their doubts chose to do the bidding of their respective foreign ministries who had entered into various trade-offs with Paris over Greece (for example, Germany would obtain further expansion of the EU into central and Eastern Europe).

French power within EMU has not ended with the retirement of Trichet. His successor, Mario Draghi, a consummate financial diplomat, dedicated to the status quo (a monetary Metternich) was supported by Paris throughout the drawn-out selection process, while President Sarkozy made no secret of his opposition to Bundesbank Chief Axel Weber, who eventually bowed out of the succession. Professor Weber voiced concern in particular about the transformation of the ECB into Europe's Bad Bank and the difficulties that he could have in announcing consensus decisions regarding Bad Bank expansion or indeed monetary policy when he might very likely find himself in a minority of dissidents. The Bad Bank expansion had occurred largely in pursuance of France's ambition, as implemented by Trichet, to hold the present broad EMU together, rather than beating a strategic retreat to a group of core countries in which Germany would be the hegemon.

It is not self-evident how many French jurors in a hypothetical trial of the euro would be swayed sufficiently by proof of gains for the aims of French foreign policy as drawn up by the policy elite to dissent from an unfavourable verdict. Election results in France and political polling there tell us that many French citizens resent their political elite and the costly projects (including Greek membership of EMU) to which they become committed whether in the European or global stage. It is implausible that in 2014 a unified French bloc of jurors together with 'politically correct' (distrustful of any motion which might smack of nationalism) jurors from other countries would be successful in preventing a negative verdict emerging on EMU. The reality, though, is that this verdict would not lead on to a set of remedies handed out by the presiding judge. Only public opinion, as filtered through the political process, together with the responsiveness to public opinion of the most powerful political actors, can determine the shape and form of remedies, if any, against EMU and the ECB.

Of course there will be no trial! No European institution exists which would set up a 'Truth Commission' to get to the bottom of how European monetary integration was so badly conceived and then mismanaged. It is also implausible that the German Parliament would set up a Truth Commission to find out how past and present German statesmen and stateswomen failed to put effective obstacles in the way of France moulding EMU in ways which violated fundamental principles that the Kohl government had assured Germans were inviolable. The implausible German Commission would also investigate how Professor Issing, as German monetary guardian at the ECB, totally failed to institute a monetary framework sufficiently resilient to prevent the descent of EMU into a giant credit bubble and burst, which in turn was to have such dire consequences for German taxpayers as the largest contributor to rescue missions largely driven by the French government and its close ally, Trichet, at the head of the ECB.

There will be no panel in Brussels or Frankfurt seeking answers to a list of questions including how the writers of the Maastricht Treaty failed to set up a constitution of monetary stability and instead handed over absolute power to central bankers who in turn instituted monetary authoritarianism; how the Maastricht Treaty failed to put any effective brake on the ECB's capacity to spawn within its balance sheet Europe's Bad Bank and thereby effectively becoming an agent of a European Transfer Union; how the Maastricht Treaty, by failing to provide for a full legal path and process whereby any member could exit EMU, increased greatly the dangers of monetary union transforming itself into a fiscal union; and how beyond those flaws in the Maastricht Treaty ECB policymakers made a series of such bad decisions.

Bold remedy: Paris and Berlin launch a new monetary union (EMU-2)

The boldest remedy for all the revealed flaws of EMU is to end the present union and start all over again. No group of European central bankers or finance ministers, however, acting together would ever come up with such a programme. And even if they were collectively leaning in that direction, it would be impossible to prevent leaks of information about proposals setting off a tidal wave of speculative capital which would roll through financial markets.

The most plausible scenario under which the boldest remedy could emerge would be one laden with crisis. In this scenario massive capital flight might be taking place out of weak member states (included in capital flight would be residents there making withdrawals of cash, reckoning that euro banknotes were safer than deposits in the local banks in that the latter would be devalued sharply if an exit from EMU were to occur) bringing an explosion in the ECB's Bad Bank operations and threatening to culminate in an almighty financial crisis involving waves of defaults by governments and banks throughout the euro-zone. Default here would mean most likely, a forced exit from EMU for the countries suffering a haemorrhage of funds (especially out of their banking systems) and re-incarnation of sovereign currencies in these countries at a steeply devalued rate.

Under these circumstances the future of EMU – in fact the question of whether there is to be a continuing union at all – would be up to the leaders of France and Germany to determine. If they took no action, by contagion capital flight might spread like fire. After the first one or two member countries had been forced to exit from the EMU (given that the ECB were unable to make an unlimited expansion of its Bad Bank operations and that a new intergovernmental bail-out did not become available), a torrent of capital flight from the next weakest countries could form, with investors trying to save their funds from devaluation or default in the probably short time before the gates slammed shut – what Kindleberger and Aliber describes as 'Torschlusspanik' (see Kindleberger, 1973).

This would be the 'De Gaulle–Adenauer moment' (the term is taken from the historic signing by those two statesmen of the Franco-German friendship treaty – see p. 23). The President of France and Chancellor of Germany would meet in secret at an undisclosed military airbase and draw up an emergency strategy for the 'survival' of monetary union. Some European federalists might argue that the only survival strategy should be a joint guarantee of all weak member government debts by the strong and the instituting of political union. As a matter of practical and legal fact the Franco-German summit would be powerless to produce such an outcome. The French president would be there only because he or she had concluded that the grand vision so long entertained by the Paris elite of a wide EMU with German hegemony totally destroyed was no longer sustainable. The German chancellor would be there out of a conviction that France, though economically feeble in comparison to Germany, still had a pivotal role in European integration and was an effective partner in this enterprise. The aim of the summit would be to save monetary union in Europe but not EMU as constructed by the Treaty of Maastricht with all its design flaws. And monetary union in Europe would not mean a union of 15 or more countries as in the present EMU. The essential core of monetary union in Europe is just France and Germany.

Indeed under the circumstances described the flawed union of the Maastricht Treaty would be non-salvageable. Survival of monetary union in Europe would depend on the French and German leaders realizing that fact (the realization would be particularly painful and difficult for the French leaders, but the alternative would be the total liquidation of the euro project so prized by the Paris elite over many decades) and moving promptly forward. They (the French leaders under duress!) would start by formally agreeing that the main flaws of EMU as constructed at Maastricht (let's call this EMU-1) are first, the lack of any constitution for monetary stability based on strict application of monetary rules; second, the virtually unrestricted scope for the ECB to turn itself into a Bad Bank by making huge back door loans to weak sovereigns and banks; and third, the absence of any legal provision and protocol for member countries to exit EMU. The leaders would then agree on a contingency plan whereby France and Germany would leave EMU-1 and form a new monetary union EMU-2. This new union would be constructed without the identified flaws. And the intention would be to send out invitations to all members of EMU-1 to join the new union, EMU-2.

A new monetary union cannot be constructed in one summit meeting. An emergency structure, though, for managing an immediate makeshift union between France and Germany and possibly those few countries that signed up for immediate membership could be put in place. A Monetary Council would be formed from the participating countries (at the start plausibly just France and Germany). France and Germany would technically leave EMU-1 by declaring that euro deposits (reserves) held by French and German central banks (and thereby indirectly in the euro-clearing system) could be used for clearing payments only within or between France and Germany but not outside. There would be a commitment to negotiate a full and comprehensive monetary treaty for the new union, albeit with no going back on the summit agreement to correct the three mentioned flaws of EMU-1. And the members of the new union (EMU-2) would have to agree with the ex-members of the now defunct EMU-1 who did not accept the invitation to join EMU-2 (their non-acceptance could be due to EMU-2, without a Bad Bank, being unable to offer them life support without which they could not survive inside) how to divide up the negative wealth of the ECB once it were liquidated (its liabilities would far exceed the market value of its assets including the now devalued or defaulted loans to the periphery-zone countries and holdings of periphery-zone government debt).

Hence the French central bank would continue to clear euro payments with the German central bank but not outside. Instructions in accordance with this would be sent to the Target System (which clears interbank funds) operated within the ECB. During an interim period, banks in France and Germany might have to suspend or impose limits on 1:1 conversion of euro banknotes into bank deposits, as otherwise they would be faced with a flood of banknotes from all the old union coming into accounts on speculation that the currency (say the 'francmark') of EMU-2 would float to a much higher value than 1:1 against the new sovereign currencies of previous member countries which were not strong enough financially to join the new union. The old euro banknotes (as had circulated in EMU-1) might well sell at a discount to (less than full principal equivalent of) deposits in the EMU-2 member countries and also at a discount to the new banknotes in EMU-2 when eventually printed.

From the date on which emergency decrees set up the new Franco-German monetary union (EMU-2), the ECB would cease to have any monetary policy-making function with respect to the new union, though the new monetary council might on application make use of the ECB's money market operational capabilities as far as required and under strict instruction. There would be the big issue to consider of currency losses (or gains) which banks in France and Germany would make as a result of loans and deposits to ex-member countries who did not choose to join the new union being now denominated in old euros or new national currencies, which would presumably be at a steep discount to the new French–German euro. Some type of bank compensation fund might well have to be set up (backed by French and German taxpayers) to facilitate re-capitalization for those banks most seriously impaired.

It is possible that all present member countries of EMU-1 except for the weakest at the periphery would reply positively to the French–German invitation to join EMU-2, in which case immediate potential losses on translation would be much smaller than if EMU had totally disintegrated. The in-between countries (not as financially weak as those at the periphery of the old euro-area but not as strong as those at the core) would face a difficult decision as to whether to accept the invitation to join EMU-2. Their governments would realize that a period of distrust in the marketplace about whether their banks could remain afloat without European Bad Bank support and without access to money printing facilities or EU bail-out funds would go along with interest rates inside their country being much higher than in the core of EMU-2. That could impose heavy economic costs (which would have to be weighed against the alternative option of not joining EMU-2 and re-incarnating sovereign money). Perhaps in view of the close economic and financial links between Germany and Italy, Berlin would enter into a bilateral deal with Rome involving direct German support to promptly re-capitalize the Italian banking system and so reduce the extent of interest rate premium there.

Some financially strong small members of EMU-1 might decide that rather than accepting an invitation to join EMU-2 they would rather have a national sovereign money, but peg this within narrow bands against the francmark (or whatever the currency of EMU-2 would be called). One advantage of staying outside on this basis would be to retain some scope for independent fluctuation of short-term interest rates within the limits consistent with the national currency not straying outside its bands. This scope could be helpful in terms of reducing the severity of a business-cycle fluctuation that was specific to that economy. More important though than such an at best modest plus (so long as bands of permitted fluctuation are narrow) would be the greater ease of a unilateral separation from EMU if only tied to it by a fixed exchange rate system.

EMU-2 closer to Latin Monetary Union than to EMU-1

The monetary union drafted in the 'De Gaulle–Adenauer moment' would be much closer to the grandparent than the grandchild from the perspective of European monetary evolution. The grandparent here is LMU, the grandchild EMU-1. LMU for most of its life (1865–1927) operated under the gold standard (with some relics subsisting from the bimetallic gold/silver standard). There was no committee of central bankers in LMU making monetary policy. Rather the growth of the monetary base, whether considered for each member country separately or in aggregate for the union as a whole, was determined by automatic mechanisms. These mechanisms set the global production of gold and silver and also how monetary stocks of these precious metals were distributed among countries. The fact that gold (and silver) coins – all of standard size and content across the union – from any member's mint could be exchanged freely at par meant that the scope for exchange rate fluctuations between member currencies in the exchange markets was considerably smaller than for gold standard currencies outside the union. But national monies were retained and any member country could exit LMU at any time.

EMU-2 would not be created under gold standard conditions. It would resemble, though, the gold monetary system in certain respects.

A monetary authority separate from government (but tightly subject to constitutional rules as explained here) would strictly limit the growth of high-powered money supply (monetary base) for the union as a whole, setting this according to a formula which would be consistent with price level stability over the very long run (while leaving considerable scope for price level fluctuations over the short and medium run). The simplest formula would be an annual rate of expansion (of monetary base) of $x\%$ p.a., where $x\%$ is the long-run estimated trend growth in demand for high-powered money in real terms. Sometimes there would have to be overruns or undershoots of the formula (say, $x\%$ p.a. expansion of the monetary base) but this would be according to a set of principles which mimicked the gold standard system. For example, a big dip in prices of goods and services on average below a long-run flat path would bring some overshoot of $x\%$, as indeed occurred when a fall in mining costs relative to a fixed nominal gold price brought an increase in production. Or a sudden surge in demand for monetary base as might happen during a financial crisis would be met by a temporary increase in supply.

High reserve requirements would be restored on the deposit liabilities of EMU-2 member banks – meaning a return to the high reserves that were typical during the gold standard era (or during the high-tide of monetarism under the Old Bundesbank and Old Swiss National Bank). High reserves are essential to monetary base having a stable and powerful position at the pivot of the monetary system (see Brown, 2013). It is also essential that interest is not paid on reserves (or on excess reserves). Then demand for these is likely to be elastic with respect to money-market rates, meaning that a fixed quantity rule for monetary base expansion would not produce wild money rate fluctuations. (And in any case long-term capital market rates would be largely unmoved by these). As this volume has highlighted already (see Chapter 3), the abandonment of high reserve requirements and of the zero interest paid on reserves as applied by the 'old Bundesbank' was a big flaw in the design of EMU-1.

Interest rates in the money markets would be set by demand and supply in the market for reserves (rather than by central bank rate-pegging operations) and other market interest rates would be totally free of the arm-twisting (concerning future rate pegging operations and more general considerations) that has typified EMU and indeed virtually all monetary systems around the modern world. Rates that are determined freely in the capital markets and that are not distorted by central banks trumpeting the likely path of their future money-rate pegging operations should come closer to the neutral level on average over time than is the case for those rates arrived at by arm-twisting. In consequence there would be less danger of severe strains of monetary virus emerging, whether in the form of goods inflation or asset price inflation. In particular, potential speculative temperature fluctuations in asset markets should be smaller.

National monetary denominations would be restored within EMU-2 (these were abolished after the first two years of EMU-1) as indeed they were maintained in the LMU. These denominations would be standardized – specifically 1 French euro, 1 German euro, 1 Dutch euro – capable of being converted at 1:1 into each other. Banks in member countries of EMU-2 would clear balances between themselves in whatever member currency on a 1:1 basis (meaning that debts in, say, French euros would be cleared against credits of the same amount in German euros). And throughout EMU-2 banknotes in each national variety of euro would be exchangeable and acceptable (in retail payments) on a 1:1 basis although there would be no legal regulation to this effect. Inside each member country, governments would give preference to their own money in terms of requiring payment in this particular euro denomination. Similarly wages, rents, and other contractual payments would generally be settled in the national denomination of euro (in France, French euros; in Germany, German euros).

The provision as regards 1:1 clearing of payments throughout the EMU-2 area regardless of particular national denomination would mean that there would be no spot exchange market for the respective national currencies (unlike under LMU, where tiny fluctuations of spot rates within highly confined gold import and export points were possible – albeit that the rates remained very close as costs for transporting gold between the member countries were tiny relative to value). There could be forward markets in the national currencies. These would function essentially as insurance markets – quoting premiums to cover loss by a particular date due to any suspension of the 1:1 relationship between two given member currencies. Such forward or insurance markets would in normal circumstances be fairly narrow, if they existed at all, as the fixed costs of using them would far outweigh the minute risk of an exit taking place. Once, though, any tiny but significant risk of exit for any one member emerges, a discount on the suspect currency would form in the forward market, which optimistically, though not necessarily, would spring to life. Correspondingly interest rates on the suspect currency would rise to a premium above those in the safe areas of the monetary union defined by no significant risk of an exit.

A monetary union in the style of LMU as described above is a rigorous regime, and more so than LMU was historically. There is no scope, however small, for the spot exchange rate between component currencies to take some of the strain of distrust in the continuation of membership for a particular country. Where the spot rate can fall slightly to the bottom of its band of permitted fluctuation or of possible fluctuation as set by the gold export and import points, then the emergence of distrust does not necessarily trigger immediate crisis. Investors who are not absolutely confident in the continuing membership of a given currency can trade off the possible exchange rate gain which they would make by holding the currency if such fears dissipated as against the possible loss should the fears intensify. There is no such trade-off in the case of monetary union in the style of LMU, as described here for EMU-2, as the member currencies are fully convertible into each other on a 1:1 basis. Hence all suspicion becomes expressed in the current level of interest rate so that holders can see sufficient income advantage (with no possible supplement from exchange rate gain within the possible margins of fluctuation) to offset the risk of loss.

As soon as any significant risk of exit from monetary union emerged, banks in particular would swing into action in managing their possible risk exposure. They would not leave big mismatches between their liabilities and assets in the given member currency, but seek to cover these either by adjusting denomination of particular sections of their balance sheet or taking out insurance in the forward market (if these do indeed spring into activity). Interest rates could jump to fantastically high levels in the money markets and short maturity debt markets denominated in the suspect member currency if the risk of exit rose to even a modest level from zero. The toll of such interest severity on the economy of the suspect member country (greater for smaller member countries than for larger) may become so great as to produce a self-fulfilling prophecy. Alternatively the potential toll might be a tremendously strong lever on the government of the suspect member effecting emergency measures capable of restoring confidence.

There would be no intergovernmental bail-outs or Bad Bank operations by a ECB to sustain membership of any country. Indeed the EMI piloting the monetary base (as defined in aggregate for all member countries of EMU) according to the set of constitutional rules discussed above would have no authority to lend to banking institutions beyond absolutely normal limits of everyday type operations which would be set in tight rigorous fashion. The institute would not have any authority to buy government paper either in new issue or secondary markets except as strictly set out towards achieving its overall target for monetary base growth.

A new European monetary treaty

Unlike the Treaty of Maastricht, the new treaty would not leave it up to the central bankers to design the key elements of the monetary union. And the central bankers would have much less overall power. Indeed, there should not be a ECB at all. Instead, an EMI would be in charge of controlling the growth of monetary base for the union as a whole. The stipulated aim of the EMI would be monetary stability and long-run price level stability. This would be defined as the situation where first, monetary conditions do not become a persistent and serious source of economic disequilibrium and second, the price level is stable when considered over the very long run.

The first part of that aim would correspond to J. S. Mill's warning that 'most of the time the machinery of money is unimportant, but when it gets out of control, it becomes the monkey wrench in all the other machinery of the economy'. In modern idiom this first aim would be to prevent the corruption of the software of money such as could spread a serious virus (whether goods and services inflation or asset price inflation) to all the other software determining the market prices that incentivize the invisible hands of the capitalist economy (see Chapter 1, p. 4). The Treaty would set rules so as to prevent the software of money from becoming corrupted, at least in a big way. Such corruption would occur if the EMI tried to drive market interest rates across short, medium, and even long maturities, far away from the respective neutral level (for each maturity), and with much greater persistence than could occur if market forces were free to operate without interference. This last term, 'without interference', means nonetheless within an overall framework of monetary stability. Monetary base would be at the pivot of the monetary system and the EMI would set the growth rate of monetary base according to constitutional rules.

Where the monetary authority by its actions (either inadvertently or deliberately) pulls market rates seriously away from neutral persistently in the same direction over time potentially it feeds the two viruses which attack the economic system. The symptoms of these viruses may take some considerable time to appear and to be recognizable with a high degree of confidence by even the most trained observers. The first virus, asset price inflation, manifests itself as a rise of speculative temperature across a continuously shifting spectrum of asset and credit markets, where heat is measured by the extent of irrational exuberance. The second virus is goods and services price inflation, where the focus is on evidence of underlying monetary inflation, rather than price fluctuations which occur over time related to such factors as productivity swings, terms of trade changes, cyclical swings and which are consistent with no monetary disturbance.

Monetary stability as defined above and to be the first aim of the EMI as specified in the Treaty and long-run price level stability, the second aim, are not in continuous harmony with each other. There are periods of friction between the two as indeed was the case under the gold standard. In particular, fulfilling the first aim (money not becoming the monkey wrench in the machinery of the economy – or equivalently its software not becoming corrupted) could mean that the price level strayed far from its long-run average level with no prospect of return. This would occur if there was a multi-year surge in productivity growth, followed by no period of sub-normal productivity growth. Under such circumstances the pursuance of price level stability in the very long run could mean injecting a shot of extra monetary base growth, albeit done repeatedly by small amounts over a lengthy period, which could cause at least a small monkey wrench to get into the machinery of the economy so producing a moderate rise in asset and credit market speculative temperatures.

Managing the possible friction between the aims of monetary stability and long-run price level stability would not be left to the discretionary judgement of officials. The monetary constitution would lay down strict guides and rules to be followed in any injection process specifying, for example, how much the pace of monetary base growth should be boosted above the normal x% p.a. in relation to any persistent deviation of the price level from its long-run flat path.

The new Treaty would stipulate a monetary framework such that the aim of monetary stability and long-run price level stability would be pursued efficiently and with least risk possible of derailment by human error. The framework would be monetary base control, with high reserve requirements and no interest paid on reserves, an x% p.a. expansion rate, subject to various overrides, as described in the previous section. Any change in reserve requirements could take place only after an exhaustive process of justification and subject to a super-majority vote (67%) in every national parliament. This fence around high reserve requirements has been proved necessary by the failure of the first monetarist revolution that occurred in Germany and Switzerland in the early 1970s, where monetarism retained power for a decade or more. Ultimately banking lobbies in each country were able to whittle down the level of reserve requirements, so reducing the pivotal role of the monetary base and tarnishing the reputation of monetarism for stability.

What would be the enforcement mechanism for making sure that the EMI followed the monetary framework as set out? In that there is no political union, the EMI board would be answerable to either a council of ministers from the member countries or to the European courts or to national parliaments severally. Ministers or parliaments would not have the power to override the monetary framework or constitution except under highly restrictive conditions (super-majorities in every national parliament and subject to challenge by referendum and in the courts). Parliaments could demand full access to the decision-making records (which must be comprehensive) of the EMI and require full explanations for actions, such as extent of overrides on the basis of various rules, and in the ultimate press for a revision or alteration of these if against the rules. Perhaps the construction of EMU-2 would include an independent panel of expert auditors that could judge on such matters, having received complaints from any national parliament. And the panel's decisions could be challenged in court.

Enforcement could also take place via private parties challenging the EMI's actions, whether through domestic political processes or directly in the European courts. And all of this would occur in the context of virtually complete freedom of information. Anyone could demand detailed transcripts of all meetings within the EMI leading up to any decision as regards the setting of monetary base expansion or any other monetary policy matter. Note though that the EMI would not play any direct role in the setting of money interest rates – these would be wholly market determined.

The treaty setting up EMU-2 would include clauses to guard against a resurgent cult of the maestro central banker who could thwart the operation of monetary rules within a constitution designed to secure the aim of monetary and long-run price level stability. After all, in the world of the gold standard, no one outside the money markets even knew the name of the central bank governor, and in the case of the Bank of England (pre-1914) the governor served a two-year term with no possible extension. In similar fashion, officials appointed to the EMI would serve only fixed three- or four-year terms with no renewal possible. The head of the EMI would serve a two-year non-renewable term. Perhaps there could be some system of rotation based partly on nationality to determine the head at any time.

As outlined in the previous section, there would be clauses dealing with how any individual member nation could pull out of the monetary union, and its construction would be in a form so as to facilitate this. And so we have seen how national monetary denominations and banknotes would be maintained, even though these would all exchange against each other on a 1:1 basis. Among other matters the given clauses would stipulate procedures for the exiting government to provide compensation for losses within the interbank clearing system at the time of exit and also for how the EMI should adjust its target path for monetary base to take account of the shrinking of monetary union.

And there would be tightly scripted clauses to prevent the EMI turning itself into the European Bad Bank as the ill-fated ECB did. Indeed there would be a positive prohibition against the EMI acting as lender of last resort. In any period of great financial tension where governments became convinced of the case for making highly speculative 'solvency loans' to stricken financial institutions, then it would be for their national agencies to lend, not for the EMI to act. If these agencies could not raise capital due to widespread investor scepticism about solvency of the financially weak government taking on such obligations, then a flight of funds might develop forcing the given government to pull out of EMU. Collateralized lending against government securities by the EMI would be limited to no more than what would be required to match the growth in monetary base as determined in accordance with the formula as detailed above (see p. 235). Government bonds held or lent against by the EMI would be strictly weighted by the relative economic size of each member country.

Total EMU dissolution and a return to free floating

Suppose there were no 'Adenauer–de Gaulle' moment in which the leaders of France and Germany, in the midst of an almighty flight of capital out of periphery zone countries, assured the future of monetary union in Europe at least between their two countries by bringing an end to the old flawed union and launching a new one in its place. It would be a pre-condition of this moment that the present-day French leader could wear the Algerian cap of de Gaulle, explaining to his fellow citizens why the one-time grand aim of 'Europe in France', which had driven the euro project to date, was no longer attainable and why a more prosaic aim was now 'on the table'. Both the German and the French head of state would have to convince each of their respective publics about why partnership between the two countries remained an essential condition of peace and prosperity. Cynics understandably doubt the willingness or ability of Chancellor Merkel and President Hollande to act in this way. Instead EMU blows apart.

First, the periphery zone countries would call banking holidays, as their insolvent banks could not pay the fleeing depositors without massive new loans from Europe's Bad Bank (the ECB) – and these would not be available, let us assume, beyond 'a certain point'. At the end of the banking holiday deposits and loans would have been redenominated according to the emergency decrees passed by the departing member government, while for an interim period (until new banknotes could be printed) euro banknotes would float freely against the new domestic euros.

Second, as the waves of capital outflow engulfed the middle-tier member countries (measured by financial strength), they also could be forced to exit EMU – although there could be a long interim during which deposit interest rates and bond yields in the middle-tier towered well above those in the core, meaning that hot money could be drawn in to replace the fleeing capital. Beyond that interim, and with only an inner core still left in EMU, a wave of capital flight out of France could sink the remaining union of core countries.

Let's leave to one side the gigantean process (in which there would be many losers and many gainers) of restoring financial order after the massive disruption of these successive waves of capital flight. What would be the shape of the new monetary universe that might evolve in Europe from the ruins of the old?

At one extreme, every country, small or large, that had been a member of the now defunct monetary union, could institute a regime of monetary base control founded on the same principles as already described above for EMU-2ß. Each independent national monetary institute would set a target for monetary-base growth consistent with price level stability over the very long run. Each country would draw up a constitutionally enshrined set of rules that tightly constrained the actions of the national monetary institute (overrides of the $x\%$ expansion rule only allowed according to certain fixed criteria and challengeable by both parliaments and the courts; high reserve requirements proof against whittling down by banking industry lobbies). All the currencies would be freely floating against each other. Interest rates in money markets also would be freely floating throughout, so no rate pegging by central banks meaning that market rates elsewhere especially in the capital markets would be free of official suasion.

In practice and principle it is dubious whether the periphery zone countries which dropped out of EMU first in a crisis of insolvency, then succumbing to high inflation, could join anywhere near the start in the suggested world of freely-floating European currencies each with their monetary base control. High inflation would be part of the bankruptcy proceeding in those periphery zone countries – in effect levying a windfall inflation tax on bank depositors and holders of government bonds. Only after some considerable period of time would the road to monetary purity become at all open to them.

The currencies of those European countries in the MBC and freely floating universe would be far less volatile against each other than has been typical for the experience of the main traded currencies (say, the yen versus the US dollar versus the euro or previously the Deutsche mark) over recent decades. Much of that volatility has derived from divergent monetary paths (central banks in their interest rate pegging programmes sending their economies along different trajectories of monetary instability meaning that the viruses of goods inflation and asset price inflation evolve indistinct fashion). Moreover, a high degree of real economic interdependence between the European countries means that the real sources of potential intra-European exchange rate fluctuation (for example divergent business cycles, shifts in comparative advantage) should be fairly modest.

In no way should this European MBC and freely floating universe be presented as a first best system. The issue is whether it is a superior second best to others feasibly on offer, including EMU-1, EMU-2, or EMU-x.

One drawback of the European MBC and freely floating universe is the unstable relationship between demand for reserves, even with high reserve requirements and no payment of interest on reserves and real incomes, even over the long run in the very small and open economies. Households and businesses in these small economies are likely to hold diversified monetary portfolios; the shifts between the domestic and foreign monies may be considerable and yet not in accordance with any prediction, whether by rule of thumb or modelling process. Moreover, even where MBC were administered strictly in a given small country, this could be affected in a very bad way by monetary disequilibrium generated in the large country next door (or further afield). As illustration, if the German money machine got out of control, then symptoms of goods and services inflation or of asset price inflation could appear in Luxembourg or Holland, notwithstanding strict MBC in these latter two countries. And on the global scene, the US money machine getting out of control becomes a potential engine of asset price inflation or goods and services inflation elsewhere (see Chapter 1, p. 9). Yes, incipient inflation in the small country appearing via traded goods prices could be reined in by local currency appreciation under the situation of strict MPC control. But local currency appreciation does not in itself prevent a tide of global irrational exuberance coming ashore in the small country and fuelling asset price inflation there in some markets.

These troublesome monetary overspills from large neighbours may be deliberate or accidental in nature. Perhaps the European big neighbours would indeed run MBC control with the best of intentions aiming for monetary stability. But the monetary controllers might make mistakes. They might not apply the various overrides in a timely or efficient manner to the core rule of $x\%$ p.a. expansion in their monetary base. (These overrides would take account of evidence about shifts in the trend demand for monetary base in real terms, or a significant deviation of the present price level from the long-run norm, and other factors see p. 235). And so an episode of monetary instability in the large neighbour throws a monkey wrench into the rest of the European economy as well as in the large country itself. If there is not complete trust, then the small neighbours might suspect that the accident was not an accident and that in fact the neighbour was following a policy of clandestine currency warfare. Sometimes these fears would be justified.

There can never be complete trust between European countries each running their independent MBC systems, even if there are high standards of transparency and other important piecemeal confidence-building measures. And there is the problem already referred to of instability in demand for monetary base in the small countries. Lack of trust and the problem of small countries might stir at least some European governments to contemplate alternative monetary arrangements. These could include a limited monetary union between France and Germany with other countries pegging their exchange rates tightly to the Franco-German currency (the francmark). The small country under this arrangement has a greater ability to exit than under a grand monetary union where divorce has a higher cost. And the potential influence sacrificed by the small country on the common MBC authority when it decides to operate as a monetary satellite of a large country rather than joining in monetary union might be trivial.

Ideally monetary trust could be built within Europe by absolute transparency. If all decision-making by each national MBC authority (monetary institute) were wholly transparent with observers present from any country, this would help build trust. But there would still be the question of competence. If the monetary authority in say a small or medium-size European country (or the respective government) becomes fearful that the MBC authority in the biggest regional economy might be steering a disequilibrium path is there scope for any re-assuring dialogue on the subject to take place openly and with any result? That question should be asked in full recognition of the fact that the small country even in EMU would have little direct power over the actions of the EMI or ECB. Arguably, in fact, the small country which pegs its currency to a much larger country's currency has a bigger influence on the monetary outcome in the large country than if in monetary union or if treading the independent path of MBC. This would be the case if the authorities in the large country were concerned about the adverse effect on its national money 'brand' were a small country to break the link to it out of dissatisfaction with its MBC piloting skills.

In a Europe without any monetary union most likely some smaller countries would indeed opt to peg their exchange rates to the currencies of a larger country. A pre-condition for that to happen is that one or more large countries are trusted to pursue monetary stability. There would be a choice – most likely whether to peg to a larger European currency – the French franc or the Deutsche mark (both re-incarnated) – or to the US dollar. That choice would be the basis of monetary competition – in which the hypothetical MBC authorities of the larger European countries would be aware that sloppy performance could mean a dwindling of their wider monetary zones of influence.

If indeed the total breakdown of monetary union in Europe led on to a system of floating currencies and MBC piloting under strict constitutional rules – albeit with some variations allowing for smaller currencies to be pegged to larger ones – and all within the context of full transparency and trust-building such that currency warfare in any form were impossible, that would be a big achievement to celebrate. Yes, it would be a pity that France and Germany had not managed to build EMU-2 as outlined at the start of this chapter. But the political liberal (in the classical sense) would find much to cheer in contrast to his or her despair at the monetary authoritarianism and instability that prevailed under EMU-1. After the era of mal-investment and squander that occurred under monetary union as constituted by the Maastricht Treaty a real likelihood of economic renaissance and growing prosperity would open up for all its one-time members.

However, there are also ugly possible aftermaths to the breakdown of monetary union in Europe, although not necessarily uglier in a total sense than EMU-1. In particular one or more of the large countries might come under nationalist inflation-targeting regimes overseen by officials steeped in Bernanke-ism with its deeply disturbing features of deflation phobia and legitimization of currency warfare. Even in Germany, with Switzerland the joint cradle of the first monetarist revolution, it is far from certain that there would be a return to monetarism in any form. The modern Bundesbanker regards pure monetarism (built by putting monetary base firmly at the pivot of the monetary system) as impractical and in any case disputes that the old school Bundesbankers ever practised monetarism except in a highly diluted form. Nowhere in Europe, unlike in the US, are there powerful political forces that could potentially lead to the success of a second monetarist revolution (which, unlike the first revolution, would derive wisdom also from Austrian School teachings). If political forces in the US against Bernanke-ism prove too feeble to triumph, Europe would be vulnerable to the disruptions of US currency warfare irrespective of whether its monetary order was EMU-2 or MBC with freely floating exchange rates.

Twin menaces – US currency war and French monetary nationalism

We saw in Chapter 7 how US monetary instability including lurches into currency warfare from the 1960s onward has played a crucial role in determining Europe's monetary destiny. Another key factor has been France's pursuit of monetary nationalism – broadly defined so as to include episodes when this showed up as aggressive currency devaluation (as occurred intermittently in the decades before EMU) or alternatively as the pursuit of 'France in Europe' meaning 'Europe in France'. In speculating about the future contours of the European monetary map, predictions about those two factors – US monetary instability and French monetary nationalism – should be uppermost.

Historically the advocates of European monetary integration (and some of those advocates were French monetary nationalists!) made much of US monetary shock. They cited extreme US monetary turbulence as having caused great harm in Europe. First the monetary instability generated by the Martin Federal Reserve in the 1960s meant that the European countries, then effectively on a dollar standard, imported inflation. German resistance to imported inflation led to the Deutsche mark ultimately breaking free of the dollar in a process of revaluations and 'temporary' floats in the late 1960s. The arrival of Arthur Burns at the Federal Reserve in early 1970 brought the greatest US monetary disturbance yet (in the post-war world) culminating in the Deutsche mark's float of spring 1971 – the precursor to the breakdown of the Bretton Woods system. Paris, in particular, bemoaned the lack of common European response to US monetary turbulence and the related breakdown of fixed exchange rates in Europe. (When all countries in Europe were on the dollar standard, as was the case through the mid-1960s, then intra-European exchange rates were fixed within narrow bands of permitted fluctuation.)

Through the 1970s, France at first engaged in a period of beggar-your-neighbour devaluation, allowing its currency to plunge versus the Deutsche mark during the 1974–5 Great Recession and its immediate aftermath. Then as France, unlike Germany, became immersed in a Great Inflation, there was a change in the pendulum of monetary thinking among the French political elite. France had to get a grip on the inflation problem or the franc would become one of Europe's second-tier currencies (together with the British pound and Italian lira), while Germany would be in a strengthened position of monetary hegemony on the Continent. The French president, Valéry Giscard d'Estaing, engaged in intensive rounds of diplomacy with German Chancellor Schmidt towards launching a process of European monetary integration. This diplomacy was backed by a disinflationary shift in French monetary policy The diplomacy culminated in the EMS, launched in 1978, which Chancellor Schmidt defended in private session to the reluctant Bundesbankers by stressing Germany's special obligations to Europe in view of its Nazi past.

Barely three years after EMS was launched, French monetary and currency policy mutated from 'France in Europe and Europe in France' back to aggressive devaluation of the franc. The Mitterrand Administration, coming into power in spring 1981, effected a series of franc devaluations so as to gain the necessary 'monetary freedom' to pursue its socialist agenda. As economic and social utopia failed to arrive, but high inflation returned, popular support for the Mitterrand Administration plunged. President Mitterrand and his advisers hit on the strategy of embracing 'Europe' as the grand aim to revive electoral fortunes. And a whole string of historical coincidences culminating in the fall of the Berlin Wall – together with a remarkable close relationship forged with German Chancellor Kohl – allowed this to move forward with remarkable speed.

During the series of negotiations leading up to EMU, the French advocates argued adamantly that continuing US monetary turbulence made the present Deutshe mark-based monetary order (the EMS) unsatisfactory. In particular, as tidal flows of money crossed the Atlantic in either direction, powered by US monetary disequilibrium, the Deutsche mark was driven up or down against other European currencies, including in particular the French franc. And so US monetary turbulence produced strains inside the fixed exchange rate bloc centred on the Deutsche mark. This complaint also struck a chord with much business and political opinion in the Federal Republic, given that German industry had to make painful adjustment to sometimes significant rises of its currency against those of neighbouring European currencies.

The complaint was always short on substance. If the French franc were to become as attractive as the Deutsche mark to international investors, why would the tide of money flows from the US dollar concentrate any more on one currency than the other? The exchange rate between those two leading European currencies would be largely unaffected. But the French political elite never had an interest in promoting the franc as hard money to rival the Deutsche mark. Perhaps the elite just regarded this as mission impossible given German industrial might. Rather Paris had its sights on overturning German monetary hegemony by driving forward to EMU and it was hard to distinguish its promotion of 'Europe' from that of France.

In the years running up to the launch of the euro, there was significant tension between France and Germany about the form of the union to be constructed. Paris favoured a union that would extend also to 'economic governance'. Bonn, and later Berlin, was adamant that there would be no 'economic government' and that there should be no potential burden sharing. Fatally, however, the German negotiators never realized that the only real defence against monetary union turning into fiscal or transfer union was to have a clearly defined possible exit route for individual delinquent members together with effective obstacles to the ECB bailing out governments and banks via its back door. If a member country lost the confidence of investors then it would be driven out of the union by massive capital flight and no one would come to its rescue.

It is dubious that there was ever any realization in Berlin of the extent to which a French head of the ECB could turn EMU into an instrument of French policy and with what serious results for all. M. Trichet had not even fully taken the President's Chair in autumn 2003 when he used the Dubai G7 summit to join with the Bush Administration in demanding a break-up of the Asian dollar bloc. It had long been an aim of Paris to see a diminution in the dollar's global role with this being taken over in part by the euro. In the two years that followed the Dubai summit, Trichet used his skills as an economic diplomat to promote the mantra that the main problem in the world economy was 'global imbalances', meaning that the US had to take steps to reduce its current account deficits and Asia to reduce its surpluses. But in carping about the lack of savings in the US and the responsibility of this for the mega US current account deficit, Trichet ignored totally the true threat to the global economy – a powerful virus of asset price inflation with its origin in the monetary disequilibrium created by the Greenspan/Bernanke Federal Reserve; and the ECB, suffering from the same deflation phobia and following the same disequilibrium policies as the Fed, was empowering the forces of contagion to Europe and elsewhere!

In consequence of his flawed diagnosis of global ills based on long-time hang-ups of the French political elite, Trichet failed to see that EMU was failing in one of its main objectives – to insulate Europe against US monetary shock. In fact the ECB ended up creating a monetary shock as large as, if not larger than, that emitted by the Greenpan/Bernanke Federal Reserve during the years 2003–6. Of course Trichet and the French political elite would never admit that. The closest to a confession about the ECB's key role (alongside the Federal Reserve) in generating the global credit bubble and bust came from the Bundesbank President, Professor Axel Weber. But one of the bizarre twists of EMU history was that he found himself let down by the German government, with Chancellor Merkel making one concession after another to Paris as the bust phase which followed the bubble intensified.

The decisive date in Chancellor Merkel's yielding to French demands (as fully supported by Trichet at the ECB) was May 2010 when Bundesbank President Weber buckled at Trichet's proposal for a further big expansion of the ECB's Bad Bank role – specifically in the direction of unlimited further lending to Greek banks against the collateral of Greek government debt (even though this was now rated as junk by the credit agencies) and of purchases in the secondary market of weak member sovereign debt (especially Greece). In the EU summit of May 2010, though, Chancellor Merkel effectively repudiated the Bundesbank President's position by agreeing with French President Sarkozy to a vast bail-out for Greece (a long-time close ally and armaments client of France) and for a new European institution, the EFSF, to be set up, which would borrow in global capital markets with the benefit of guarantees provided by the financially strong members and would take part in agreed lending programmes to the weak. No limit was imposed on the Bad Bank operations of the ECB.

Paris viewed the EFSF (and its successor the ESM) as an embryo European Monetary Fund that from its start has been a key institution in the transformation of EMU into a transfer and fiscal union. In an EU summit a little over a year later (July 2011), just three months before Trichet's scheduled retirement, Paris achieved substantial further progress in its ambition to turn EMU into a deeper union spanning 'economic governance'. The role of the EFSF was to be now expanded into providing credit lines to the governments of member countries under 'payments pressures' and whose banks required re-capitalization (Greek banks were potentially at the front of the queue given their large holdings of Greek government bonds and the looming default on these).

Trichet throughout the second phase of the Greek crisis (as in the first) remained adamantly against a resolution in the form of no further bail-out – meaning most plausibly an exit of Greece from EMU. In this he was entirely in line with the French government. And in fact the view from Berlin, at least from the office of the chancellor,– was not so different. Despite his unhappiness in early 2010 at the direction in which Trichet was taking the ECB (and which may have been one factor culminating in the German professor's resignation from the post of Bundesbank president early in 2011) Professor Weber never advocated exits from EMU. Indeed he spoke of a 'Marshall Plan' for Greece. And so there remains some essential ambiguity about his position.

From the standpoint of spring 2014 it remains unclear how far EMU has journeyed into being a transfer and fiscal union with area-wide economic governance. Much will depend on whether Berlin agrees to further increases in the resources of the ESM including its possible leveraging-up and how far it retards more generally the growth of that institution. Also the attitude of Berlin to further Bad Bank expansion at the ECB, including implementation of the OMT program (see Chapter 7) will be crucial. The clash between French monetary nationalism on the one hand and the German traditionalist vision of monetary union without economic governance and transfer union seems set to continue, albeit that at the time of writing Paris has won several (but by no means all) showdowns. A much bigger showdown, though, may yet lie ahead. Also likely to continue is a failure of EMU to provide any defence against US monetary instability.

It is always difficult to write history while it is writing itself. But in the new episode of US monetary instability which started with the Bernanke-ite QE-2 inflation time-bombing campaign of Autumn 2010 and then moved on to 'multi-year forward guidance of short-term interest rates' in Summer 2011 and then QE-infinity in Summer 2012, it seems that yet again EMU as an institution has failed to provide any insulation against US shock. Instead, the ECB, doubtless influenced by the sharp devaluation pressure on the dollar (induced by the QE-campaigns), took the route of zero interest rate policy and aggressive monetary base expansion (albeit that an important driving force behind ECB officials was the desire that EMU should survive, whatever the cost in terms of non-orthodoxy).

In Summer 2013 ECB President Draghi explicitly imported Bernanke-ite 'multi-year forward guidance' into the ECB's policy-making apparatus. This time the intention was to prevent medium- or long-term risk-free rates in euros (again measured in German government bond market) from rising in line with an upward trend in the US (sparked by speculation that the Federal Reserve would soon start tapering the extent of its QE interventions). If successful then the euro could fall relative to the dollar, which the ECB might view as a much-needed stimulus to the euro-area outside Germany.

In sum, the most recent past appears to demonstrate that EMU as constituted by the Treaty of Maastricht has failed to cope with two big challenges – US monetary instability and French monetary nationalism. EMU has provided less insulation both within Europe and globally against US monetary instability than did the Old World (pre-EMU) with a monetarist Bundesbank running a Deutsche mark-bloc. And that Old World had more defences against French monetary nationalism than the Maastricht monetary union, though both in the end succumbed. French monetary nationalism defeated the old Bundesbank order. It also seems to have won several battles along the way (while also losing some) to mould the Maastricht monetary union according to its vision and to turn it into a transfer union. But victory for French monetary nationalism is far from assured. The monetary menu now hanging on the wall for those European citizens interested to look – for they may well not have a chance to choose from the alternatives there – include the following possible futures.

First, EMU, as constructed at Maastricht, evolves into a full transfer union in which the French elite's vision is triumphant. The ECB continues to operate the present monetary framework – remarkably similar in many respects to the Bernanke-ite system (characterized by deflation phobia, inflation targeting, bond market manipulation) except in the crucial respect of no QE in the form of quantity targets for purchases of core government bonds and no waging of currency war. Germany would not countenance that. But everything else is there (deflation phobia, inflation targeting, rate manipulation and so on). In this first menu item, US and European monetary instability will continue to reach high crescendos mostly at the same time and inter-reacting to magnify the harmful effects both domestically and in the outside world.

Second, EMU-1 collapses, to be replaced by EMU-2. This new monetary union is founded on 'second generation monetarism' (featuring well-constructed defences founded in constitutional law against the central bank deliberately or inadvertently breeding, the asset price inflation virus) and on no bail-outs. The realization of EMU-2 does not have to mean the death of French monetary nationalism but an important metamorphosis would have taken place. It would not now be France in Europe and Europe in France but a dual French–German monetary order in Europe. US monetary instability, even in its present virulent Bernanke-ite forms, would most likely continue to co-exist with EMU-2, meaning sometimes violent fluctuations in the euro–dollar exchange rate. But EMU-2 would create a bulwark against US monetary instability being imported into Europe where it would become a secondary source (alongside the primary US source) of instability in the global economy. Eventually Bernanke-ism might fall and a second monetarist revolution, much better grounded than the first fleeting US revolutionary experience under Paul Volcker, would triumph in the US. Then Europe would no longer suffer the violent exchange rate fluctuations and the world generally would enjoy a degree of monetary stability unseen since gold standard days.

Third, EMU-1 collapses, and there is no EMU-2. But all previous member countries of EMU agree on a new form of monetary cooperation. In this they all introduce monetary base control regimes designed to achieve monetary stability, and exchange rates are freely floating with the possibility of some small countries deciding to become monetary satellites of a larger country. By construction, French monetary nationalism dies under this menu item. Yes, US monetary instability might continue even including the Bernanke-ite aspect of currency warfare. But as each of the European monies would be highly attractive to international investors there would be no reason to assume that waves of capital flows in or out of the dollar would cause turbulence in intra-European exchange rates. And each independent monetary authority in allowing their currency to float up freely in response to US inflationary monetary shocks would be confident that other monetary authorities (in neighbouring European countries) would be acting similarly. Again, as for the second item in the monetary menu, this third item would be much more enjoyable if the second monetarist revolution took place and triumphed in the US.

Fourth, EMU-1 breaks down, there is no EMU-2, and French monetary nationalism undergoes metamorphosis into its previous form of currency belligerence (beggar-your-neighbour devaluation). One or more countries might adopt monetarism (monetary base control with a freely floating exchange rate). But with France ready to launch currency warfare especially during a period of economic weakness, and French monetary and currency policy subservient to wider national interests as perceived by the Paris policy elite, other countries, even Germany, could decide that the adoption of monetary base control and a freely floating exchange rate would just leave them defenceless against French attack. If against this background a second monetarist revolution triumphs in the US, then life for the monetarist economies in Europe would become less harsh, although they would still have to deal with intermittent French monetary shock.

Isolated, the French elite can only be a monetary nuisance. France does not have the power on its own to set a big monetary monkey wrench in the machinery of the global economy. But Europe in France does have such power. And it is not just the monkey wrench which is troubling. It is also the use by Paris of EMU power to pursue its agenda of a special relationship with Beijing so as to promote multi-polarism and combat US monetary hegemony. The deals have been increasingly blatant. Beijing supports increased resources for the IMF and its use to shore up EMU. It also endorses members of the French elite for the top job at the IMF in exchange for Paris using its best endeavours to thwart any aggressive stance by Washington in a campaign to force Beijing to sharply revalue its currency against the US dollar.

So far, under EMU, successive US Administrations have acted apparently without seeing how monetary nationalism as pursued by the French policy elite has undermined progress in the biggest economic conflict area globally – trade and currency relationships between China and the rest of the world. The French political elite, like the neo-mercantalists in Washington, have had no interest in pressuring Beijing to adopt a fully convertible currency regime. Some conservative economists suggest that full convertibility would be effective in reducing the power of the communist party to dominate the Chinese economy and so strengthen the forces promoting political and economic freedom. But this has not been of interest to the French political elite, which values its alliance with the present Chinese elite. And the neo-mercantalists in Washington fear that currency convertibility would in fact lead to a weaker yuan and larger trade surplus for China as the counterpart to huge capital exports. Hence although the US mercantalists might complain about the French lack of zest in pursuing the goal of yuan appreciation, they would not wish a shift of emphasis at the IMF or in the G20 to the virtues of currency convertibility.

In practice, the greatest contribution by the US to the building of monetary stability in Europe would come from a repudiation of Bernanke-ism. In Europe the exit routes from monetary failure all pass through a junction where the Paris political elite suffers terminal setback to its ambitions for "Europe in France". There is also another key junction along the exit routes where both French and German public opinions come to realize the full extent to which needless and avoidable monetary instability, where this is interpreted to include the virus of asset price inflation, has been generated by EMU in its Maastricht form and this is to blame for erosion in their living standards. Hopefully this volume will help navigate the way towards those junctions on the exit routes from European monetary failure – as well as revealing some tantalising glimpses of possible end destinations.

Bibliography

Aliber, R. Z. 'Client letter', 29 April 2009.

Aliber, R. Z. and Kindleberger, C. P. *Manias, Panics, and Crashes*, Palgrave Macmillan, 2005.

Baba, McCauley, R. and Ramaswamy, S.'US dollar money market funds and non-US banks', *BIS Quarterly*, March 2009.

Bank for International Settlements. Annual Report, June 2008.

Bini-Smaghi, Lorenzo. 'Conventional and unconventional monetary policy', Keynote Lecture at the Center for Monetary and Banking Studies, Geneva, 28 April 2009.

Blamen, Robert. 'Bernanke-ism: Fraud or menace', Paper Delivered at Burton S. Blumert Conference on Gold, Freedom & Peace, LawRockwell.com.

Broaddus, J. Alfred and Goodfriend, Marvin. 'Sustaining price level stability', *Federal Reserve Board of Richmond Economic Quarterly*, 90 (3), Summer 2004.

Brown, Brendan. *Monetary Chaos in Europe*, Routledge, 1986.

———. *The Yo-Yo Yen*, Palgrave Macmillan, 2002.

———. *The Euro on Trial*, Palgrave Macmillan, 2004.

———. *Bubbles in Credit and Currency*, Palgrave Macmillan, 2008.

———. 'The case for negative interest rates', *Financial Times*, 20 November 2008.

———. 'This is not a tale of two depressions', *Financial Times*, 18 June 2009.

———. *The Global Curse of the Federal Reserve*, Palgrave Macmillan, 2013.

Brown, William Adams. 'The international gold standard reinterpreted 1914–31', New York, National Bureau of Economic Research, 1940.

Bruner, Robert and Carr Sean, D. *The Panic of 1907: Lessons Learned from the Market's Perfect Storm*, Wiley, 2007.

Brunnermeier, Markus K. 'Deciphering the 2007–8 liquidity and credit crunch', *Journal of Economic Perspectives*, 23 (1), pp. 77–100, Winter 2009.

Buiter, Willem, H. 'Overcoming the zero bound on nominal interest rates with negative interest on currency: Gesell's solution', *The Economic Journal*, 113 (490), pp. 723–46, 2003.

Butler, Eamonn. *Adam Smith – A Primer*, IEA, 2007.

Cecchetti, Stephen G. and Schoenholtz, Kermit. 'How central bankers see it: The first decade of ECB policy and beyond', NBER Working Paper 14489, November 2008.

Dimand, Roger and Geanakoplos, John. *Celebrating Irving Fisher: The Legacy of a Great Economist*, Blackwell, 2005.

Eggertson, Gauti. 'How to fight deflation in a liquidity trap: Committing to be irresponsible', IMF, 1 March 2003.

Eggertsson, Gauti and Woodford, Michael. 'The zero bound on interest rates and optimal monetary policy', Princeton University Working Paper, 26 June 2003.

Eichengreen, Barry. *The Gold Standard in Theory and History*, Routledge, 1997.

———. 'Viewpoint: Stress test for the Euro', *Finance and Development*, June 2009.

Friedman, Milton. *Essays in Positive Economics*, University of Chicago, 1966.

——. *The Optimum Quantity of Money*, Aldine Transaction, 2006.

Friedman, M. and Schwartz, A. *A Monetary History of the United States*, Princeton University, 1963.

Galati, Gabriele and Tsatsaroris, Kostas. 'The impact of the Euro on Europe's financial markets', BIS Working Paper, No. 100, July 2001.

Gerrats, Pera M. 'ECB credibility and transparency', ECB Economic Papers 330, June 2008.

Gesell, Silvio. *The Natural Economic Order*, Peter Owen, 1958.

Hayek, Freidrich A. *Denationalization of Money: The Argument Refined*, The Ludwig von Mises Institute, 2009.

——. *New Studies in Philosophy, Politics, Economics, History of Ideas*, Routledge, 1978.

Hayek, Freidrich A. and Salerno, Joseph T. *Prices and Production and Other Works on Money, the Business Cycle and the Gold Standard*, The Ludwig von Mises Institute, 2008.

Hetzel, R. L. 'Monetary policy in the 2008–9 recession', *Economic Quarterly*, 95 (2), pp. 201–33, 2009.

Hirsh, Michael. 'Channeling Milton Friedman', *Newsweek*, 17 July 2009.

Hördahl, Peter and King, Michael. 'Developments in repo markets during the financial turmoil', *BIS Quarterly*, December 2008.

Issing, Otmar. *The Birth of the Euro*, Cambridge University Press, 2008.

Issing, O., Gaspar, V., Angeloni, I. and Tristani, O. *Monetary Policy in the Euro-Area*, Cambridge University Press, 2001.

James, Harold. 'Making the European monetary union' Bank for International Settlements, Basel, 2012.

Jordan, Thomas. 'Central banks in action; financial market turbulences and policy measures', Speech to the 36th General Assembly, Association of Foreign Banks in Switzerland, Geneva, 6 June 2008.

Kindleberger, C. *The World in Depression*, University of California Press, 1973.

Lachman, Ludwig, *Capital, Expectations, and the Market Process*, Institute for Humane Studies, Menlo Park, CA, 1977.

Leaman, Jeremy. *The Bundesbank Myth*, Palgrave Macmillan, 2001.

Lowenstein, Roger. 'The education of Ben Bernanke', *New York Times (Sunday Magazine)*, 20 January 2008.

Mankiw, Gregory. 'It may be time for the Fed to go negative', *New York Times*, 18 April 2009.

Marsh, David. *The Euro: The Politics of the New Global Currency*, Yale University Press, 2009.

McGuire, Patrick and von Goetz, Peter. 'US dollar shortage in global banking', *BIS Quarterly*, March 2009.

Meltzer, Alan. *A History of the Federal Reserve, 1913–51*, University of Chicago Press, 2004.

Pollock, Alex. 'Towards creating a systemic risk adviser', *American Banker*, 17 July 2009.

Rogoff, Kenneth. 'Risk of deflation', *Nihon Keizai Shimbun*, 17 July 2003.

Rothbard, Murray N. *America's Great Depression*, The Ludwig von Mises Institute, 1972.

Schwartz, Anna. 'Man without a plan', *Wall Street Journal*, 26 July 2009.

Stark, Juergen. 'Economic prospects and the role of monetary policy in the current situation', Speech to the Deutsche-Luxemburgische Wirtschaftskonferenz Luxembourg, 9 March 2009.

Streit, Manfred D. and Wohlgemuth, Michael. 'The market economy and the state: hayekian and ordo-liber conceptions', Max-Planck-Institut zur Ergorschung and Wirtschaftsystemen, Diskussionsbeitrag, 06–97.

Taylor, John. *Getting Off Track: How Government Actions and Interventions Caused, Prolonged, and Worsened the Financial Crisis*, Hoover Press, 2009.

Vanberg, Vicktor J. 'The Freiburg school: Walter Eucken and Ordoliberalism', Freiburg Discussion Papers on Constitutional Economics, 04/11.

Volcker, Paul. 'Winning over the Americans', in 'Schmidt and the World, Tribute to Helmut Schmidt', 13th Annual Conference of the German–British Forum in Hamburg, October 2008.

Von Mises, Ludwig. *The Theory of Money and Credit*, The Ludwig von Mises Institute, 1971.

———. *Human Action: A Treatise on Economics*, The Ludwig von Mises Institute, 2003.

White, William. 'The coming transformation of continental European banking', BIS Working Paper, No. 54, 1998.

Yellen, Janet, speech, 'The uncertain economic outlook and the policy responses' 25 March 2009, presentation to the Forecasters' Club of New York.

Index

Printed and bound in the United States of America